UNDERSTANDING MENTORING

UNDERSTANDING MENTORING

Reflective strategies for
school-based teacher preparation

Peter Tomlinson

Open University Press
Buckingham · Philadelphia

Open University Press
Celtic Court
22 Ballmoor
Buckingham
MK18 1XW

and
1900 Frost Road, Suite 101
Bristol, PA 19007, USA

First Published 1995

A catalogue record of this book is available from the British Library

ISBN 0 335 19306 4 (pbk)

Library of Congress Cataloging-in-Publication Data
Tomlinson, Peter.
    Understanding mentoring: reflective strategies for school-based
teacher preparation / Peter Tomlinson.
        p.   cm.
    Includes bibliographical references (p.   ) and indexes.
    ISBN 0-335-19306-4
    1. Mentors in education—Great Britain.   2. Teachers—Training of—
Great Britain.   I. Title.
LB1731.T597   1994
370.71—dc20   94-27609
                                                                   CIP

Typeset by Graphicraft Typesetters Ltd, Hong Kong
Printed in Great Britain by Biddles Ltd, Guildford and King's Lynn

Contents

Preface and acknowledgements

It is surely no exaggeration to say that in the UK we stand at another significant watershed in the history of teacher preparation, which is also being reflected in a number of other countries. Doubtless for a multiplicity of often competing motives, the move is towards school-based courses and the involvement of teachers in the preparation of entrants to their own profession. I believe this has great positive potential. Yet as David Hartley (1993) has pointed out, these changes come in a postmodern era of epistemological and political confusion, whose new age threatens to be a very dark one. What school-based teacher preparation gains by way of relevance, it may lose by way of unreflective narrowness, not to mention lack of effectiveness even at the instrumental level of teaching, since for teaching to be effective, it must at least be intelligently skilful.

The perspectives and assumptions of teacher educators have not received the scrutiny accorded to those of schoolteachers over the last couple of decades. Yet what work there has been perhaps suggests that teacher education has been characterized by no greater level of reflectiveness than that found amongst teachers. On this view, not only do we now have something of a new beginning from which to encourage critical thinking about teacher education; the technicist pressures not least from government make it vital to assist this.

In saying this I am attempting neither to hark back to any supposed certainties of the bygone modern age, nor to compensate for any presumed ignorance on behalf of anyone. For this writer there never were any such certainties anyway. But there were and I think are perspectives, whose focuses and range of convenience, in George Kelly's terms (1955), make them highly relevant to teaching and teacher preparation and whose evidential grounding make them worthy of consideration within the cycle of teacher-educators' experience and learning. This seems to me to be the case particularly in so far as such perspectives and their constituent constructs may assist articulation and reflection upon already possessed craft wisdom.

My attempt here is therefore to offer a practical examination of quite concrete aspects and possibilities in school-based teacher preparation in the light of a range of mainly psychological perspectives, many of which have paradoxically still not penetrated much into the world of education. This book began life as part of a Partnership Foundation Programme (PFP) for participants in the Leeds University Secondary School Partnership PGCE scheme which was rather hastily compiled and offered during 1993.

I therefore wish to thank various people associated with the scheme. These include school and university colleagues who gave me their reactions to the materials, but in particular the members of the PFP core planning team: Dave Carter, Gary Chambers, John Monaghan, Michael Rayner, Geoff Welford, and especially Maura Healy, who chaired the group and provided very welcome support and perspective from which I learned much. Most of all, however, I thank my partner Janet Hodgson, who not only put up with the inevitable disruption of personal life brought about by these endeavours, but also read the manuscript, often at awkward times, and rescued it, as she has me, from a number of shortcomings.

List of figures and tables

Figures

List of further detail sections

School-based teacher education: opportunity and challenge

Starting points

In a number of countries at present initial teacher preparation is undergoing an important transition from settings and systems dominated by separate, often higher education institutions (HEIs), to being situated much more in schools themselves. In Britain, at the time of writing, the government is requiring school-based initial teacher training (ITT) courses within school–HEI partnerships in England and Wales and going beyond this to experiment with wholly school-centred arrangements. As usual, the Scots are taking a more thoughtful, experimental approach, Northern Ireland likewise, in a similar direction.

As with any major development in something as large and complex as an educational system, the current moves are recognized as posing both opportunities and challenges. Perhaps most significant is the widespread view that as a practical activity, teaching needs to be learned through engagement in the practice of teaching. There is evidence that this is the majority opinion of today's teachers, which they typically relate to their own university and college-based courses: 'you only really learned anything once you got into teaching practice'. Existing teachers are therefore tending to see school-based ITT courses as an opportunity to make teacher preparation more relevant and effective, and most teacher educators seem to concur with this. Teachers are also welcoming this development as a recognition of their professional competence and status.

On the other hand, apart from the crucial issue of adequate resourcing, there is also evidence of a range of concerns and uncertainties. Those in higher education institutions remember their own lack of formal preparation for the transition from teacher to teacher-educator and worry that their own early mistakes will now be replicated on a massive scale in the more powerful setting of the school. They also fear that teacher preparation may swing too much from a professional education model to a craft apprenticeship training, which merely inculcates currently dominant ideas of 'good practice'. Also, teachers rightly sense that they have rich resources of experience to pass on and assume that their own training could be improved, but their uncertainties and apprehension tend to grow as they contemplate how exactly all this is to be achieved.

What little evidence we have so far from school-based ITT arrangements such as Articled and Licensed Teacher schemes and the beginnings of the new school–HEI partnerships appears to confirm these suspicions. Student-teachers are welcoming the idea of getting into the action early on and like being treated as some sort of 'proper' teacher, rather than just as a student. On the other hand, some already complain that when they do receive help and advice, they are offered little justification and there are even some who are asking for 'more theory'. Again, once teachers get into such schemes they often report considerable rejuvenation through having to discuss issues which 'got them into teaching in the first place', but which they've hardly had time to think about since. Yet, in the face of the new demands, the apprehension and defensiveness of some teachers threatens to exclude them from such benefits.

As I see things, therefore, it isn't overstating matters to say that we stand at a momentous point in the history of teacher education. We have a radical shift of setting towards school and classroom and a whole new force of teachers is beginning a more active involvement in the process. This does offer the opportunity for a quantum increase in the power and effectiveness of ITT, but as the above indications suggest, the change of setting is in itself by no means sufficient to guarantee the realization of that opportunity.

After all, we're not talking here about some sort of change in production-line machinery that has a willy-nilly effect on output. Success and quality in teacher preparation are much more a matter of what the human participants bring by way of perspective and strategy, both as individuals and by way of organizational arrangements (though not forgetting resources). Moreover, the new teacher–mentors will want an active involvement in shaping new arrangements; the present changes are occurring at a point when our cultural expectations take for granted a good deal more consultation and democratic participation than was the norm when the traditional HEI-dominated model of ITT was generated.

The situation is in many respects new and different, so that the more we can draw upon or develop explicit insights through joint experience and reflection, the better we're likely to succeed. The alternative would be just hoping to 'muddle through'. Apart from being no way to conduct professional activity (and without claiming that we can have a total understanding of *every* aspect), this also runs the danger of simply transferring the old assumptions to the new situation. This not only when they might not be appropriate to the new setting, but when their basic flaws were probably what led to our dissatisfaction with the traditional model anyway!

What sort of book?

Purpose

My purpose in this book is therefore to promote awareness and critical understanding of practical ways of mentoring, by which I generally mean: assisting student-teachers in learning to teach in school-based settings. The basic tenet is that whilst there may be some quite powerful types of procedure which any school-based ITT course is likely to include, there can be no specific recipes that should be adopted in all cases. Rather, as mentors we need *both* to be aware of specific training strategies *and* to understand their pros and cons.

I should perhaps add that by *critical* understanding I don't intend to signal anything particularly negative, just that any ideas we contemplate using in practice ought not to be taken simply on trust, from whatever 'authority'. We should assess them, open-mindedly but carefully, for their degree of:

1 *coherence:* how far do they make sense in themselves, hang together consistently?
2 *relevance:* how closely do they relate to our concerns and to which aspects?
3 *well-groundedness:* how well are they supported by appropriate evidence?

When we assess possibilities in these respects we're probably unlikely to find that we can arrive at any all-or-none decision, rather that we have more or less indication that the idea in question may be worth trying out (eventually the best test on all three counts).

This sort of critical understanding means in the first place that we shall have a basis for deciding which things to do in which settings. When we go about implementing what we've chosen, we should therefore be more successful, because we know what we're doing. It also means that we're able to offer reasons and justification, for example to other teachers and mentors, to school management and governors and, not least, to our student-teacher 'mentees'. And, finally, by having a relatively clear idea of why and what we're about, we actually make it easier to review our ways of working and to develop improvements.

Assumptions

It may help at this point to indicate briefly my working assumptions. Please note that here I am only indicating them, not yet trying to justify them. That will involve much of the remainder of the book.

To start with the positive: I take the view that learning to teach does require thoughtful involvement in practical action within real school contexts and that teaching is of such complexity and subtlety that 'one never stops learning'. By the same token, those who have any degree of teaching experience have considerable resources from which to help novice teachers get the most out of the important early parts of their learning careers. It is also the case that especially over the last couple of decades, educational and related research has yielded many more relevant insights and perspectives than hitherto on teaching, learning and their development. These perspectives, together with what we have been gleaning directly in recent school-based training schemes, offer a basis for assisting effective use of our resources in such arrangements.

However, I also view the situation as involving some negative features which are ignored at our peril. One is that in our culture we seem to have inherited some unfortunate assumptions about skilful activities (like teaching), expressed in our ways of talking and thinking, which actually get in the way of applying insights to the improvement of action. We need in fact to reconsider how we see relationships between thinking and doing, or I think it likely that we shall perpetuate some of the less desirable features of traditional ITT. As mentioned, some useful perspectives are now available in this respect and I should like to bring them to the attention of anyone concerned with school-based ITT. However, I am also aware that England has been particularly noted for its resistance to systematic thinking about teaching and learning (Simon 1988). I also know that when as students many of today's teachers opened their minds to what they hoped would be relevant educational 'theory', they were very disappointed by what they received.

If this is a valid picture, then it has potential implications for the sort of approach a book such as this should take. As I see it, these include the importance of making the nature of that approach quite explicit, as I'm now doing. Others are that a book such as this must place a premium on practical relevance, but that any ideas and perspectives offered must also be explained and justified as far as space will allow. These features will therefore be reflected in the approach I propose to take.

Approach and outline of the book

This book is intended to have practical relevance, which means getting to grips sooner or later with specific strategies, tactics and procedures for aspects of mentoring. However, even from the viewpoint of practicality, it cannot simply restrict itself to the details of action recipes, because situations and students vary too much for there to be any universally valid procedures. What we do in practice needs adapting to circumstances and this requires an understanding of the relevant influences within situations. This is the reason behind the saying 'there's nothing so practical as a good theory'; a good theory is one that alerts us to consideration of what is important in reality. Given the sometimes magical expectations of student-teachers, it's perhaps worth reminding ourselves that a book is in a real sense, 'all theory'. That is, however direct and practically oriented, a book is only a symbolic medium, it isn't part of the practical action. It can only contain messages, which it's up to the reader to act upon or not. I shall therefore go into details of concrete strategies and will offer tactical tips at various points. But I will also be offering reasons and rationales and will hope to provoke you into critically appraising such ideas as well as bringing them to bear on your own assumptions.

My general strategy will be first to get clear about the basic features of what is being considered, then to seek a coherent understanding of what it tends to involve. Thus we first ask what we actually mean by, what are the essential functions of, say, coaching (or any other aspect related to mentoring, such as learning, teaching, managing, motivating, or whatever). Then we seek an understanding of 'how it works', using whatever ideas seem relevant and well-grounded. On that basis we're then in a position to consider particular strategies and practical procedures, how they relate to the overall purpose in question and to other strategies, what factors tend to influence their success, how they are adaptable in practice.

A two-level approach

Although I am taking the view that we need to consider both the what *and* the why in mentoring, it's clear that there is some tension between staying close to practical issues and pursuing a fuller understanding of them. In this book I am therefore offering two levels of approach, in which the general text will deal relatively directly with aspects and issues in mentoring, whilst further detail and particular perspectives will be introduced in clearly marked 'further detail' sections (FDS). These may on occasion be quite lengthy, since a major purpose of the book is to bring relevant ideas to the attention of the teacher education world.

Thus the main intent is to offer quite a wide range of perspectives to inform the considerable complexities of mentoring, but the two-level approach will hopefully assist readers who have limited time or inclination to consider practical possibilities in prioritizing their reading effectively. So the general text will contain only the basics of what is developed in the further detail sections and almost all referencing to books and articles will be left to such sections. This will tend to be the pattern within each of the book's chapters, but I should point out that it is in some respects replicated across the book as a whole, with some chapters being more practically focused and others more concerned with underlying perspectives and general ideas.

Outline of the book

A glance at the contents pages will show how the topics unfold. Following the present introduction, the second chapter attempts some ground-clearing and basic foundation work by reviewing what is actually involved in teaching and considering what we know about the nature of skilful capabilities like teaching. This is designed to yield basic ideas and vocabulary, enabling a closer consideration of two sides of the mentoring function in the two subsequent chapters. Of these, Chapter 3 will consider the coaching function, dealing with what is involved in assisting skill development and Chapter 4 will look at the interpersonal or counselling side of this which impacts on the motivation and feeling side of student-teachers' learning.

Chapters 5 and 6 consider what it is that mentoring is trying to promote through all this, namely the nature of classroom strategies for the management of learning. An assumption in this book is that teachers do typically have rich resources and insight from their own experience regarding this, but often at a largely intuitive level. Analysing basic functions and typical strategies for managing behaviour and promoting learning is therefore intended to offer a framework and vocabulary which teacher mentors may use to develop and communicate their contribution. The seventh chapter will then extend these ideas to the specifics of teaching competence profiles and their use in student-teacher assessment and development.

The last two chapters will deal with more detailed applications of the previous material. Chapter 8 will offer specific coaching tactics for use in the various student-teacher learning activities and Chapter 9 considers what might go into student experience programmes and aspects of roles and organizational issues in school-based ITT.

The index can also be used as a glossary reference and there is an appendix dealing briefly with specialized recent approaches to the development of teaching skill, namely the use of audio and video recording and radio-assisted practice.

Ways of using the book

From what I've said so far, you'll realize that the fullest way of using this book would be as a whole, proceeding through in sequence and considering all levels. The more obvious forms of selective use would include a 'practical details' approach restricting itself to the main text of Chapters 8 and 9. I should point out that I have tried particularly to relate underlying perspectives to practical implications, so that if you take this route, you may find yourself wanting to go back to other preparatory chapters in order to make fuller sense of what is offered. On the other hand, someone wanting to reflect on mentoring and pursue issues further, perhaps in connection with a formal course, may find Chapters 2 to 7 and their further detail materials of particular interest. Further reading will be suggested at the end of chapters.

A note on terminology

The terms 'mentor' and 'mentoring' are currently being used with a variety of connected meanings, so I should make clear once more that here I am using them in a relatively general way. By *mentoring* I broadly mean assisting student-teachers to learn how to teach in school-based settings and thus a *mentor* is anyone involved more or less directly with the student for that purpose. So various functions and personnel may be involved in mentoring, as will be discussed in later chapters, though in secondary schools especially, at the centre of things will be teachers of students' specialist subjects. Such expressions as *teacher-mentor* and *subject-teacher-mentor* may thus be used on occasion to indicate more specific mentoring personnel and the issue of role specification will be considered explicitly in Chapter 9.

Correspondingly, *student-teachers* will mainly be referred to as such, but also as *student interns, interns* and occasionally as *mentees*. Similarly, it seems easier and clearer to stick to traditional terminology and refer to those who are taught by teachers and student-teachers generally as *pupils*, though sometimes *school pupils* or *school students* may be used.

As regards gender reference in general statements, I have sought to use 'they' where possible and otherwise to follow a random pattern of gender/pronoun use and strict alphabetical ordering where relevant.

Further reading

An excellent collection of papers on mentoring and the present context is provided by *Mentoring: Perspectives on School-Based Teacher Education*, edited by Donald McIntyre, Hazel Hagger and Margaret Wilkin (see references at the end of the book for details). A journal called *Mentoring* was founded in 1993 to provide a forum for issues and ideas of relevance to school-based teacher preparation.

Learning teaching: a framework for understanding mentoring

In the previous chapter I indicated that my general strategy in dealing with aspects of mentoring would be first to stand back and get clear about the basics, then to understand how they work and see what we can do by way of influencing the process. This suggests that if we really want to get clear about teacher preparation, we should start by considering the nature of teaching itself, since that's what the preparation is for.

An obvious suggestion, perhaps, but one that can seem very unnatural, particularly to the main participants in school-based teacher preparation. Students have had many years as 'recipients' of teaching, but haven't had to think beyond appearances and sometimes don't think they need to: 'just tell me what works'. For experienced teachers, much of teaching has become intuitive and second nature. Perhaps for different reasons, then, the idea of teaching tends to appear simple and unproblematic to both groups. Worse still, the education world continues to be littered with disputes dominated by oversimplified polarizations. Even more difficult, the same terms get used in alternative ways; we all bring our own ways of using words and the possibilities of serious cross-purpose are legion. In spite of this, in fact to a considerable extent *because* of it, it's worth beginning the way we should go on, by establishing clear meanings as far as possible, starting here with the essentials of what we mean by teaching.

Teaching and teacher preparation: what are we talking about?

Teaching: essentials of the concept

If you do ask people precisely what they mean by *teaching*, then in my experience you're likely to get a considerable variety of answers. This isn't surprising, because long-established words in any language tend to be used with a range of meanings, usually connected. The question is whether some of these meanings are more basic and important than others. For instance, in responding to your question some people may name particular *forms* of teaching, like telling people things, or showing them, answering questions, setting up group work and so forth. But the more important issue here is why all these notions count as teaching; is there a basic idea implicit in all these versions of teaching? In other words, what do we mean when we say that we're hoping to help students become good at teaching?

Teaching

Educational philosophers specializing in this sort of analysis suggest that there is indeed a core meaning implicit within these ways of talking, namely that basically *teaching is activity designed to promote learning*. Like most human actions, teaching is defined by reference to its purpose and that is learning. An activity isn't a case of teaching just because it's done in a classroom or by a teacher – it's whether or not the action is in the service of learning, directly or indirectly, and in a classroom or not. In turn, then, we need to be clear about what we mean by 'learning'.

Learning

Similarly, the word *learning* can be used with many meanings, but arguably basic to them and to what teaching means is the following core meaning: *learning is the acquisition of capacities or tendencies through action or experience*. The capacities typically involved in formal education include concepts, knowledge/understanding and skills. The tendencies (more controversially) may include attitudes, values, ways of behaving. So teaching is activity that teachers (whether 'official' or informal) do to promote action and experience whereby learners are likely to make such gains. This is indeed putting it in basic, general terms and saying what teaching *always* is. But, of course, teaching can and should take particular forms and styles according to other elements in the interaction.

Some implications of the interactive nature of teaching

When we probe further into this basic conception of teaching (as in Further detail section 2.1) we find that implied within it are the elements of teacher, learner, intended learning outcome, learning/teaching process, context and resources. But of course these aren't just separate bits which teaching always possesses, they interact with and influence each other. Teaching is a

Further detail section 2.1
Teaching as a purposeful interaction to promote learning

Philosophers of education such as Hirst (1971, 1974) and Fenstermacher (1986) offer an analysis according to which teaching is essentially an attempt to promote learning. Teaching is thus defined with reference to learning, it's always intended to promote it, though it doesn't always succeed. Learning is the more basic concept, defined in its own terms. You can have a gain in a capability (learning) without this being due to teaching.

Further examination reveals that any act of teaching actually includes a number of elements:

* a *teacher*: a person who is attempting to promote learning by
* a *learner* or *learners,*
* a set of *intended learning outcomes*: what the teacher is teaching and the learners (hopefully) learning, e.g. concepts, understanding, skill
* a *learning/teaching process* of activity whereby the learners are likely to acquire the intended capabilities, i.e. how the learning is achieved
* a *context*, including *resources*, which may offer as well as limit possibilities for learning and its promotion

These elements interact and influence each other: teaching is a social interaction within a setting and is driven by a purpose: learning. This interactive nature of teaching can be portrayed visually as in Figure 2.1. This is a somewhat crude diagram in that for instance the lines of influence ought arguably to be shown making other connections besides those indicated and we might also show that there can be varying types of learning/teaching process. Even so, it may help remind us that all the elements in a teaching interaction are important and must be thought of in relation to each other.

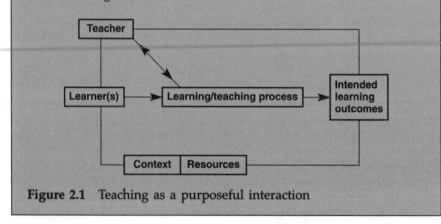

Figure 2.1   Teaching as a purposeful interaction

purposeful form of social interaction, in which teachers relate with learners, so as to get them to do what will tend to achieve the intended learning gains.

Stated so baldly, this probably sounds obvious, if elaborate. Yet it has so often been forgotten in educational debates and by educational bandwagon riders. It therefore bears emphasizing that when we're thinking about teaching, for example, when planning a piece of teaching or arguing the merits of a particular teaching approach, we do need to remember *all* of these aspects and the differences any one of them or their interplay may make. Teaching has to address its aims (subject/topic/product) *and* the actual learning process *and* the nature of the learners, not forgetting the context and resources. So, for instance, a particular teaching approach may be better for some types of learner in some subject topics, but less useful for other learners or topics. Thus this *interactive* view of teaching shows up traditional polarizations into 'subject-centred', 'student-centred' and so on, for the oversimplifications they really are.

It should also be made clear that this interactive view of teaching does *not* imply any sort of mechanistic, one-way arrangement in which teachers put passive pupils 'through their paces' to produce inevitable learning outcomes. If anything it implies the opposite; it highlights the presence of pupils, for instance, and the possibility that whilst pupil learning may be the teacher's goal, the pupils may have their own intents and motives (which may or may not include learning or the activities needed for it!) so that the interaction may be pulled in various directions. On this view, then, proficient teaching is likely to require considerable flexibility of insight and strategy, as well as the practical capacity to apply them.

Teacher preparation: educating, training or what?

If this is what teaching entails, the immediate question arises as to whether systematic preparation is possible or useful for teaching and, if so, what form it should take. Traditional responses to this have tended to be rather polarized. The predominant approach in the post-war UK saw it as the need for *teacher education*, stressing the role of understanding and intelligent awareness, and at least implying that the copying or inculcation of specific teaching procedures cannot suffice, given the varying contexts teachers will need to deal with. An alternative, recently resurrected tradition talks about *teacher training*, emphasizing that teacher preparation should be if anything geared towards practical teaching capability and perhaps going as far as to contend that 'teaching is a skill that can be trained'.

How we respond to this issue will depend on the ways we conceive of teaching, skill, education and training. However, the polarization between the traditional approaches is in my view most unhelpful and is based on assumptions we have good reason to revise. These are central ideas in relation to the preparation of teachers, but they're particularly difficult to get to grips with, partly because people do use the terms in somewhat different ways and partly because this has become so habitual that these ideas often operate all the more powerfully at the level of implicit assumption. Nevertheless, both in traditional debates and in some modern versions of 'educator-speak', some of these assumptions appear rather questionable when brought under the focus of critical examination.

Thought versus action?
At the back of much of what we hear in this domain there seems to lie a view which sees thinking as radically different and separate from action (this two-way split has led to it being called a *dualist* view). Thinking and understanding are mental matters, this view says, they take place in the mind. The mind is radically different from the body, dealing in thoughts, feelings and other mental abstractions. These contents of the mind may be influenced by a process known as teaching or, more generally, educating (traditionally taken to mean putting things into people's minds by telling or showing them).

On the other hand, according to this dualist approach, action and skill have little to do with understanding because they're about *doing* and doing is different from thinking, it's 'brute action'. In turn, skill – the capacity to do particular things – tends to be seen in a rigid sort of way: being skilled is seen as being able to do the procedures which guarantee success at the activity in question. The process by which skill is acquired is called training, with this perspective seeing training as essentially a matter of showing and telling the trainee 'the right way to do it', which s/he then learns by repetition. Awareness and understanding have little to do with it. This approach to action and skill was formalized within a school of psychological thinking which flourished from the middle part of the century under the title of 'behaviourism'. It was so called because it accepted the dualist split between thought and behaviour, rejected the importance of the former and tried to focus exclusively on the latter.

A dilemma
Without implying that even this dualist view gets things totally wrong, it does nevertheless tend to present us with a dilemma. To the extent that we think of teaching as intelligent activity needing to be based on insight and judgement, the dualist view pushes us to emphasize teacher preparation as a form of *education* involving knowledge, critical awareness of alternatives, discussion and so forth. But this may then sound one-sidedly intellectual. From our own experience, if nothing else, we may wonder how far it's likely to affect what student-teachers actually become able to *do*.

On the other hand, to the extent that we emphasize the practical skill aspect, the dualist view pushes us to the alternative pole of practical action and makes us think in terms of teacher *training*. In its more extreme versions, this might be conceived of as experts and authority figures inculcating the thoughtless 'good practice' of 'correct' procedures into novices by demonstration and drill. But this sort of 'mindless action' idea then conflicts with our awareness that teaching actions need to be intelligently adapted to pupils and circumstances. We probably doubt whether intelligent action can just be inculcated by demonstration and repetition, even if there were experts who held the secrets of good practice! This reaction can even extend into another, particularly pessimistic (and I think very British) assumption: that if you can't train effective teaching in this simple way, because teaching isn't a 'sure-fire' skill anyway, then you can't do *anything* to help student-teachers become capable teachers (at worst this becomes an 'inborn talent' assumption or at best, the 'teaching is caught, not taught' line).

An alternative perspective on teacher preparation
If I'm right in this analysis and if the idea of effective school-based teacher preparation is to have any plausibility, we seem to be in need of a different perspective on the nature and acquisition of teaching capability. In my experience, teachers often sense anyway that there's more to teacher preparation than either of these traditional extremes allows; much of what they themselves have done by way of formal or informal supervision of student-teachers wouldn't be seen by them either as 'pure education' or as 'pure training'. However, in our conscious thinking, we still tend to lack a systematic perspective which would get us away from the traditional polarizations and out of dilemmas of thought versus action, theory versus practice, whilst retaining appropriate aspects of both.

But are there any grounds for such an alternative view? I think there are. Although they have only comparatively recently made their presence felt in educational circles, there exists a range of ideas and research findings which combine to support a more adequate conception of the nature of skill in general and of teaching capability in particular. These resources do not in my view solve all the issues, but that is neither a realistic hope nor our requirement. They do however enable us to go considerably beyond one-sided past perspectives, whether in relation to schoolteaching itself or mentoring assistance for student-teachers. The present shift to school-based arrangements therefore seems an obvious moment to bring these resources to the attention of the widening range of participants now getting involved in teacher preparation, so that they can at least judge these ideas for their coherence, relevance and practical validity. That is a major purpose of this book.

I am saying, then, that we have a need and an opportunity to rethink our assumptions and approaches concerning teacher preparation. But I should also offer the realistic warning that 'changing one's mind', whether individually or collectively, is not something that occurs easily, if only because well-learned assumptions continue to live underground in our thinking, especially whilst we're in the process of mastering new perspectives. Let's anyway start to look at these.

Learning teaching

Teaching as a complex, open skill

Teaching can be skilful
Skill has been summed up as *relatively consistent ability to achieve goals in contexts through economic action* (for more on this see Further detail section 2.2). Teaching is an activity with a goal. As we just saw, the goal of teaching activity is in itself pretty complicated, being the acquisition of capabilities (in themselves typically complex and varied) by what is usually a relatively large number of pupils at a time. Teaching is an ability; it can be done with varying levels of effectiveness, economy and consistency. Some teachers are consistently outstanding at it, others less so, though these degrees of capability may be limited, for example to certain age-ranges, classes and/or topics, or combinations of these. In these basic respects, then, teaching may be considered a skill.

But it's an open, complex form of skill
The demands of teaching are *complex*, it involves a lot going on at once and much of this is relatively unpredictable or *open*, yet requiring immediate coping. Like many such capabilities, these features make teaching 'messy', which is one reason why it's difficult for the novice to see *how* the effective teacher is actually doing it. They're probably doing it differently from many other teachers; complex activities like teaching and learning typically allow many ways. However they are doing it, they're almost certainly doing a lot of things at once, and typically they'll be doing them in a fluent and more or less intuitive way which even they may find difficult to describe consciously (try describing in words, for example, how you recognize that look on a pupil's face which says they don't really understand but don't want to ask).

Yet often even outstanding performers find themselves having to think on their feet, as they encounter a particular variant of problem they've never quite met before. Doubtless, their possession of an intuitive repertoire of strategies for reading, judging and acting on the situation helps them react smoothly. It minimizes the demands for ongoing problem solving. But teaching, like any open, complex skill, also typically involves explicit knowledge and understanding, used in decision making and problem solving during the action.

Further detail section 2.2
Views of skilled capability

The traditional dualist view of skill as 'brute' action may have had venerable beginnings (at least as far back as medieval philosophy), but it has been heavily criticized by thinkers across the ages and particularly by twentieth century philosophers such as Gilbert Ryle (1949) and Donald Schön (1983, 1987). Although the same view can be seen in the behaviourist psychology which still underpins many approaches to training, modern psychology has studied skilled expertise from a variety of angles and revealed a more complex and messy picture of human capabilities, which complements the contributions of Ryle and Schön.

Far from being thoughtless brute reaction, skill means having *knowhow* (Ryle), ability to achieve particular types of purpose through actions based on effective reading of relevant contexts. The involvement of *purpose* means the involvement of *values* (goals) and *motivation* in skill as well as *insights* into how goals may be achieved. Skills vary considerably, for instance in the content of what's involved (e.g. driving cars, reading) as also in general features like the *simplicity/complexity* of their constituent purposes and actions or, importantly, in their *openness/closedness*; closed skills involve relatively more predictable and regular context demands, open ones less so (Poulton 1957). Nevertheless, even closed skills require know-how.

The know-how of skill is *strategic*; the skilled person has a repertoire of ways of reading situations and acting within them, typically with a degree of anticipation and not just reaction. Well-developed skill (American writers like to call this *expertise*), is typically fluent, economical and takes relatively little effort. In open-complex skills this economy tends to include possession of multi-purpose strategies which fulfil a number of functions at the same time or the same function in different ways.

The knowledge underlying skilled action seems to come in a number of forms, including two major ones. Ryle distinguished between *knowing-how* and *knowing-that*. He and others have stressed the importance in skilled action of knowing-how, which they see as 'craft' or 'procedural' knowledge which is deployed tacitly and automatically. This automatization is more likely the more embedded a subskill is within the action (e.g. grasping a door handle as part of going out to go home). Schön calls this 'knowledge-in-action' or 'theory-in-action'.

By contrast, Ryle saw knowing-that as a more conscious type of awareness which can be expressly articulated, which is why it is also referred to by cognitive psychology as 'declarative' knowledge and by Schön as 'espoused theory'. Whereas Ryle's tradition tended to emphasize intuitive know-how, Schön and more recent psychology (e.g. Reason 1990; Eraut 1992) point out that skill or professional knowledge actually involves a mixture of both types. The more complex and open the skill (like teaching), the more it tends to require factual awareness and understanding, as well as explicit problem-solving (Schön's *reflection-in-action*), using *heuristic* strategies, which are likely but not guaranteed to succeed. This is in contrast to closed skills, which can utilize fixed 'sure-fire' procedures or *algorithms*, which become habitual and tacit more easily.

These characteristics apply to a wide range of skills, from those of physical movement through to social interaction and intellectual analysis. Skills typically have a degree of generality, but this is limited, sometimes surprisingly so; the skill of doing something sometimes appears to be very different from the skill of analysing and communicating about it, and vice versa, an effect partly due to the automatizing of subskills with practice. So two of the *paradoxes of skill* are 1) as intuition (potentially habit) takes over with increasing experience, so we lose conscious awareness and control as we improve, 2) teachers of a skill surely need to know how to do it to share it, but experienced practitioners thereby tend to have difficulty in articulating just how they do do it!

It appears that most aspects of most skills are learned, even if people do have varying aptitudes, whether from experience or heredity. The learning may not be entirely conscious, however, and for this and other reasons the *teachability* of any given skill is by no means guaranteed, particularly to the extent that it's a complex and open skill.

So our views on teacher preparation may need some qualifying
At this point, then, it seems pretty safe to say that *if* we were taking skill to mean a rigid set of behaviours which somehow get it right and training to mean inculcating such practices by drill, then we ought to say no, teaching isn't a skill in that sense and no, as such it can't simply be 'learned through the right training'.

However, we may accept as more adequate modern ideas on the nature of skilled expertise (see Further detail section 2.2) which characterize it as capability employing considerable knowledge, often intuitively, and including not only 'closed', definable procedures, but also 'open' strategic capabilities for dealing with 'messy' and somewhat unpredictable contexts. In that case, teaching does appear to qualify as a particularly complex, open sort of skill and the next thing to ask would be what it takes to become

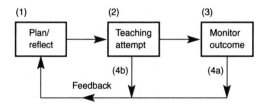

Figure 2.2 The teaching cycle

skilful at such activities. We start to do this in the following section, as a basis for going on to examine ways in which mentors may assist student interns' acquisition of teaching capability.

Acquiring teaching capability through the (teaching) skill cycle

There is a good deal of research evidence to confirm the view that sooner or later the acquisition of practical capabilities like teaching requires learning by doing. That is, what's involved in doing planful action tends also to be what is required for learning it (see Further detail section 2.3 for more on this) and this applies equally to the learning of teaching capability. But what is actually involved in this 'doing'?

Learning functions within the teaching skill cycle
This 'learning by doing' doesn't just mean separate or random acts. Any action requires some idea of what to actually do. In turn, this needs application in actual attempts and adjustment on the basis of how things went, usually over quite a few experiences. This learning is sometimes portrayed simply as a continuous teaching cycle of *plan–teach–reflect*, but in Figure 2.2 the idea of an outcome plus some extra arrow pathways have been retained and these are dealt with below.

It's also important to point out that this reflective cycle can apply to many different 'chunks' of teaching – from the lesson 'outward' to larger units like the topic or the week or term's work. Or going within the lesson, it can apply to smaller-grained segments, such as the opening part and particular transitions, or even down to particular exchanges with particular pupils and to even finer grains, as will be illustrated in Chapter 8. Going round the teaching cycle of Figure 2.2 then:

- Box 1 *Plan/reflect* represents the fact that anyone about to engage in teaching activity has to have some idea of what they're doing. The *plan* is their representation of the *what* (intended outcomes) and the *how* (the means or strategy). In an interactive activity such as teaching, this know-how includes insights and ideas about how to adapt one's action flexibly to unfolding events and reactions, and such adaptive strategies turn out to be very subtle and complicated. Such plans may be deployed at varying levels of awareness, with novices tending to have to work things out consciously and experienced skilled teachers, as I've said, often able to do so largely intuitively (and like many experts, perhaps getting so intuitive they find it difficult to articulate what they are in fact doing).

As noted, a plan depends on what level of action is involved. It may be as complex as a set of arrangements for a lesson, with various specific teaching strategies and tactics contained within it or it may relate to one of these subactions. Such is the embedded nature of most human skills, including teaching, that to understand them we usually need to constantly switch consideration between different-grained views.

- Box 2 denotes the actual *teaching attempt* in the classroom, lab, gym, etc. This isn't separate from the plan, it embodies and expresses the plan in action. From our own experience and as confirmed by research on skill, however, we know that our consciously held plan may not always be the plan that's actually guiding our action, particularly in the intuitively done subskills. In Schön's terms, that is, our 'espoused theory' may not be the same as our theory-in-action.

- Box 3 indicates the *monitoring of the outcome* of the particular segment of teaching/learning interaction in question. It seems only logical, but there is anyway considerable research evidence that systematic effectiveness in skill requires an awareness of how things have gone in relation to original purpose. This is no less true of the purposeful activity of teaching; to get better at it, we need to know 'whether it's working/how we're doing'.

- Lines 4a and 4b: This knowledge of effects requires relating back to our strategy/plan as *feedback* so that what happened is compared with what was intended, as a basis for adjustment of plan or action strategy. Line 4a refers to feedback about the actual outcome of the action, which is compared with the desired goal. Line 4b represents our ability to focus more closely on the action-attempt: were/are we anyway doing it like we intended? For student-teachers, such adaptive improvements may have become intuitively 'natural' in simple physical activities like writing or steering a car or in well established social practices, but in the complex subtleties of teaching, especially in the early stages, they probably require varying degrees of explicit thinking and problem solving and are likely to demand experimentation in their own right.

- This is why, returning full circle to box 1 we find the word *reflect*. In our culture we're used to the idea of standing back and thinking about things, but as Chris Argyris and Donald Schön (1974) are now noted for claiming, complex professional learning requires us to think and reflect in the midst of the action (their idea of 'reflection-in-action'), as well as some time after it ('reflection-on-action'), a view that is consistent with skill psychology emphases on the need for ready access to feedback.

Motives and values
It's the learner, in this case the learning teacher, who must achieve the above functions within the teaching cycle if they're going to increase their teaching capabilities. The sorts of learning function just referred to – systematic planning and reflection, actual engagement in the action, invention and risk-taking in new directions – pose a series of demands on the student's motivation and values; *they* have to try things out, become aware of outcomes and errors, have the courage to try again. This central involvement of motives and feelings has been a central emphasis in the *experiential learning* movement and constitutes an important extra dimension to traditional skill studies (see Further detail section 2.3). In traditional terms, teacher preparation is also to be seen as initiating student teachers into a profession and into its values as a profession; indeed, educationalists such as John Elliott (1991) contend that Schön intends 'reflection' to refer not only to the strategic solution of classroom problems (the means: 'how am I doing?'), but also to basic considerations of aims (the ends: 'what should I be aiming at anyway?').

Phases in the acquisition of teaching skill
The study of teachers' own experience (consult your own on this) of the acquisition of teaching capability tends to indicate its 'messiness', but also to reflect the sequence of overlapping phases generally found during skill acquisition (see Further detail section 2.3).

- In the early *cognitive* phase, the problems tend to be a matter of getting clear on what to do. Perhaps because they have a simplistic view of teaching, perhaps equally because of their anxieties about survival (and more often because of both), student-teachers at this stage can crave simple, universal procedures which 'get it right'. Even if this solution were possible, this would still be a frustrating time, because it's typically impossible anyway to keep all the necessary factors consciously in mind.
- As they get into actual teaching attempts, novice teachers take on the further challenge not only of finding out what counts and what works, but of getting it more and more 'together'. This is typical of the *associative* phase of skill acquisition.
- With further reflective experience of teaching attempts, students gradually find things becoming easier and more intuitive. Much of the improvement in this *autonomous* or *intuitive phase* will take the form of more efficient and ready execution of all aspects of classroom subskills, including not only actions and interventions, but also reading and awareness of the classroom setting. This can be a benign circle, in that it allows more time to think and reflect, and thus to pick up more and more useful strategies, so becoming still more economical and efficient in their teaching and in their further learning. Such learning can go on for a lifetime,

though, as we all know, there is nevertheless always the temptation to be satisfied as soon as things feel noticeably easier or better.

Mentoring: active assistance for student teacher learning

The very complex forms of skill characteristic of human beings (such as speaking, writing, social interaction, deployment of formal understanding) cannot be learned in isolation, but require assistance. That assistance is often informal, but it is active. It is of course the learner who learns and there is evidence that in order to get anywhere they need to go repeatedly through something like the skill or experiential cycle functions described above and in Further detail section 2.3. Even then, there is no guarantee that skill development to any particular level will necessarily occur. In most skills they can probably only (or at least only *effectively*) get anywhere with active assistance in these various skill cycle functions. To anticipate the next chapter, then, the implication is that the basic functions in mentoring are to actively assist student teachers with:

* *acquisition of awareness and strategies* relevant to teaching;
* *engagement in teaching activity* which deploys such strategies and awareness;
* *monitoring* of these teaching *activities and their effects*;
* *adapting* strategy and awareness in the light of *reflection* on such feedback.

In all this, the mentor will need to act and communicate so as to

* *motivate* the student-teacher and *harness their personal strengths* through appropriate interpersonal strategies and awareness.

At this point it's worth referring back to the question that featured as an earlier subheading, as to whether teacher preparation and development should be seen as a form of education or training or what. I have presented a view of teaching as a form of complex, open skill that is knowledge-based and with the know-how deployed at varying levels of awareness. This implies, as many teachers have long concluded for themselves, that initial and further development of professional teaching capability cannot simply be a matter of education for contemplative, 'theoretical' awareness, but neither can it just be focused on thoughtless behaviour, since skill always involves knowledge and 'theory', even if built intuitively into the action. We therefore need an integrated combination of traditional aspects from both 'education' and 'training', but these terms tend to call up the old dualist division. I therefore prefer expressions like *teacher preparation* and *teacher development* which can more easily be taken to signify such an integration.

Mentoring: all of the above applies

It's perhaps worth pointing out that these various aspects of skill, skill acquisition and its assistance actually apply at all levels of learning and

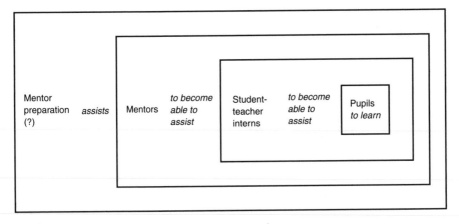

Figure 2.3 'Russian doll' view of embedded aspects in mentoring

teaching, whether it's pupil learning being assisted by teachers and student-teachers, student-teacher acquisition of teaching being assisted by teacher-mentors and tutors, or any of us gaining capability at mentoring. As has been pointed out by others (e.g. Stones 1984) the situation in which teacher-mentors now find themselves embedded is rather like a multi-shelled Russian doll which extends from the preparation of mentors in towards the core of school pupil learning. The diagram portraying this (Figure 2.3) may also help correct the old saying 'if you can't do it, teach it; and if you can't teach it, teach others to teach it'. Namely, the further back one goes from the pupil level, the more one needs to take into account, so it's likely to get *more* difficult, not less. A mentor has to understand not just how adult student-teachers may learn to teach particular subject knowledge and skills, so as to assist them effectively, but this also requires an understanding of what the student-teachers are trying to do, that is, how teaching works. This in turn requires not only understanding how the relevant pupils may learn it, but also the nature of the basic capabilities, the subject skills and knowledge involved. On such an extensive basis a mentor may intelligently engage in the complex business of assisting the student-teacher to assist the pupils to learn.

However, at all levels, from the school pupils at the centre of it all, out to the teacher-mentors, are learners faced with the need to acquire capabilities. Although such skills don't always have simple, universal procedures, especially when we're talking about the teaching and mentoring levels, we'll see that these do admit a variety of useful strategies. As already indicated, their mastery requires active thought, experiment and practice.

It's not only pupils who need active assistance to learn from teachers or student-teachers who need active assistance from mentors. Teacher-mentors can by the same argument profit from systematic assistance and support

Further detail section 2.3
The skill cycle: functions and phases

Given the various features inherent in skill (see FDS 2.2), it's perhaps not surprising that skill acquisition involves a number of interrelated functions and aspects. Various types of modern research support the idea of a cyclical process as basic both to performance and learning of skill: the one presented below comes from cognitive psychology research and previously systems theory. It is deliberately abstract, so that it can pinpoint needed functions in skill performance and acquisition across a wide variety of types and content.

Starting at the left of Figure 2.4, the learner/performer has some representation of a *goal* or purpose, a state of affairs they wish to bring about, whether a concrete physical state like a tied shoelace, a mental state like knowing the right answer, or whatever. A *comparison* of perceptions with goal concept either confirms hopes ('hooray!') – leading (line 1) to selection of another goal (or enjoyment of this one for the moment) – or indicates absence of desired state ('Ugh!') – leading (line 2: 'what are we going to do about it?') to the selection of *strategies* for action to achieve the goal, given the context in question.

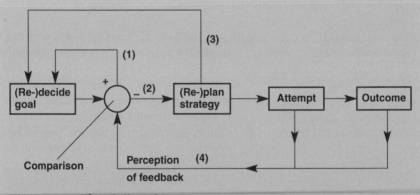

Figure 2.4   The skill cycle

Planning the action may involve drawing out well-established routines from our repertoire of 'action programs' on the basis of knowledge of the context and its elements, or it may require some degree of invention and problem-solving, in which case new subgoals and substrategies may be called into play (line 3). Our action strategies and linked awareness may be stored in various forms (verbal, visual, etc.) and are deployed at varying levels of awareness – the more embedded the detail, the more likely unconscious.

Sooner or later, one of the alternative available strategies needs to be translated into an actual *attempt* producing some sort of *outcome*, which may be within any time-scale from immediate to much longer, depending on the unit of action involved. It is then important for the learner/performer to *feed back* information about the actual outcome and the nature of the action attempt (line 4) into a comparison with the intended goal conception, so as to adjust the further action planning where necessary. This sort of readjustment may be needed all the time just to keep the action going in continuous skills such as driving and teaching, but acquisition or improvement of any skill generally requires repeated planful attempts with feedback, or as it has also been termed, *reflective experimental practice*.

So skill learning generally requires 'learning by doing', but this includes the above sorts of specific functions. It requires the learner to arrive at action plans which specify what to do and when; these therefore include knowledge: awareness and recognition of relevant events as well as action instructions. Sooner or later it also requires active attempts to do the action, with feedback and awareness informing revision of strategy. The everyday phrase 'trial and error' captures something of this, but does tend to leave out the strategic nature and makes things sound too random (though random events can yield learning).

In the last decade or so, Chris Argyris and Donald Schön (1974; Schön 1983, 1987) have become famous for arguing that effective learning of real life professional competences by doctors, teachers, etc. requires not just 'reflection-on-action', after the event and possibly in abstract terms, but also 'reflection-in-action', that is, mini thought-experiments within the ongoing flow of events. These views very much complement the above skill cycle ideas from psychology. They are corroborated by long-standing experimental confirmations of the importance of an awareness of how things went (in formal terms, feedback) being related back to one's strategies. Once a skill gets well established, as in carrying a cup of tea or experienced teaching, this may occur with little conscious monitoring, but newer activities may require much conscious reflection and reworking of strategy.

The cyclical nature of skill learning and the need to get into the action has also been very similarly stressed by a modern synthesizer, David Kolb (1984), who adopted from earlier work the idea of an *experiential cycle* in which one starts from concrete experience, proceeds to reflection on the experience, thus yielding conceptualizations and inferences which one then tries out in further active experimentation, which in turn yields another concrete experience on which to reflect, and so on. This is a very similar though slightly different-grained analysis from the skill cycle above, but those who have identified with Kolb's experiential learning concept, especially those from counselling backgrounds, have also drawn attention to the importance of the *feelings and motivational aspects* of 'putting oneself on the line' by 'getting into the action'. If getting into the action and utilizing the feedback and reflection is central to skill acquisition, then so must be the motivational aspects affecting whether one does or not and the emotions one undergoes as a result. Both cognitive and motivational types of consideration are therefore likely to be central in mentoring.

Equally important and closely tied up with learners' motives are their *perspectives* or *theories* about action and learning. If skilled action (like, say, tennis playing) requires us, as it does, to have an accurate awareness of what's involved (e.g. the rules defining tennis and how tennis balls behave), then it's perhaps not surprising that people do form reflective or 'meta' theories about the nature of action, skill and skill acquisition. Earlier, for instance, we considered a traditional 'brute action' view which seems to be implicit in much modern use of the term skill. Similarly, people may have their own views, perhaps implicit and taken for granted, as to how to learn. They may, for instance, think that a particular type of capability can be reduced to a particular set of procedures and may think training consists simply in being told what these are, so that they can be practised without thought or reflection. On the other hand, they may be aware that most open, complex actions require a variety of strategies and basic understanding, as well as systematic attempts. The effectiveness of learning is thus likely to depend quite a lot on the learner's personal approach and assumptions (whether espoused or 'in action'). Correspondingly, learners' (particularly adults') responses to teachers' and coaches' efforts may have much to do with how the latter match these assumptions.

Phases of skill acquisition

When people go through the repeated experience of the plan–attempt–feedback–reflect cycle described above, they tend to get better at the activity in question. But the path of skill acquisition has many features and involves various types of learning process; in some respects, it's gradual and progressive, in others there can be jumps and temporary regressions. However, studies of skill acquisition in the 1950s and 60s suggested that the learner typically goes through a sequence of three phases, traditionally referred to as the cognitive, associative and autonomous stages of skill acquisition.

- The earliest, *cognitive* phase is characterized by the need to get some plan of action to enable at least basic attempts, including knowing what to look for, what to do and when. At this point it's typically difficult for the novice to get it all together, mainly because we humans have severe limitations on what we can keep consciously in mind at one time. Actually, people usually bring quite a few chunks of strategy and know-how from their previous experience. Much of this may be well automated and applied intuitively, so that learning becomes a messy mixture of deliberation and 'letting it happen'.
- Nevertheless, in the following *associative* phase, with repeated efforts to remember strategy, to make attempts and to adjust their strategy on the basis of feedback, the learner tends to find things coming together and getting easier and more intuitive.
- Once the person can actually get it together and do the whole action more or less consistently, they're said to be in the *autonomous* phase, but the learning doesn't stop here. In this phase of skill acquisition, there tends to be a very gradual further automatizing (sometimes misleadingly called 'over-learning') of all that's involved – the reading of the situation as well as the responding, and not just responding, since virtually all skilful activity requires us to anticipate. This gain in intuitiveness and ease may also have its disadvantages, however, in that at the same time, paradoxically, we're losing conscious awareness of the details within our overall action. This may then get in the way of flexibility and adaptation, and it may make it more difficult for us to pinpoint what we're doing when we want to help someone else acquire the same capacity.

Hubert and Stuart Dreyfus (1986) put forward a theory of skill acquisition stages which is similar in many respects to the above, but also different in some important ways. It is richer than the traditional view, perhaps because the Dreyfuses started with the analysis of relatively complex forms of human expertise rather than simple physical ones. Although this also means that the validity of their view is more difficult to establish, their ideas can certainly claim some support (e.g. Benner 1984).

The *Dreyfus model* distinguishes five stages in skill acquisition, labelling them: 1) novice, 2) advanced beginner, 3) competent, 4) proficient, 5) expert. Central to this hypothesized sequence is the degree of intuition involved in the recognition of relevant features of a situation, the sense of what is important, the overall awareness of the situation and the decision as to what to do. Novices are held to do everything by virtue of conscious, general rules operated in an analytical, rational way (though the Dreyfus approach sees them as having no capacity to judge salience, i.e. importance of features).

Experts are held to do all of these intuitively, tacitly and holistically. My own view is that the Dreyfus–Benner approach nicely highlights some important aspects of the development of complex human capabilities and may usefully illuminate learning to teach. However, their position seems something of an overreaction to a traditional North American preference for procedural prescription, and yet also still anchored in it. To assume, as they do, that novices always have to start by being given rules to follow blindly, is hardly necessary and possibly undesirable. In other words, some quite large issues remain.

Assisted performance

Recently western educationists have been rediscovering aspects of the Russian psychologist L.S. Vygotsky's work which complement the material introduced above. Vygotsky (see Tharp and Gallimore 1988) pointed out that most human capacities are not learned in isolation and probably couldn't be anyway. They're learned with the help of other people, who assist the learner to perform actions in pursuit of outcomes meaningful to that learner. In everyday terms, we might put this view of teaching or skill development as 'assisted learning by doing'. It is interesting to note that both Schön (1987) and Dreyfus and Dreyfus assume that, realistically, the acquisition of systematic capabilities like teaching must be seen as requiring assistance from others.

Thus the specific functions in the skill cycle – awareness/planning, attempt, feedback monitoring and reflection/replanning – constitute the basic aspects on which any would-be coach or teacher (i.e. promoter of learning) must be able to offer effective help. The effectiveness of this assistance will then clearly depend much on how sensitively and skilfully such a helper relates to the personal motives and values of the learner, not forgetting the need to take into account the learner's own 'theory' of skill and how to learn it, as mentioned above. Given all this, then, we might say that the skill cycle and its elements and associated considerations provide a basic framework for specifying coaching/mentoring functions. These will be developed in subsequent chapters.

from others to develop the capabilities of their new role (the general absence of such assistance from traditional teacher education was, to put it mildly, found surprising and long lamented by those entering this role).

Learning teaching 27

Thus the ideas introduced here about skill and its acquisition should also have application to the development of mentoring capability. So also, with suitable adaptation, should much of what will be said in the remainder of the book about ways of helping student-teachers learn to teach. I shall offer specific suggestions in various places, but I should add that since the focus of this book is on mentoring, the main concern will be with understanding student-teacher learning of teaching and strategies for assisting this.

Further reading

In addition to the references already cited in the relevant further detail sections, the following sources may be useful in following up topics central to this chapter. Details will be found in the references section at the end of the book.

On the concept of teaching and much else in relation to teaching and teacher education, the handbooks edited by Wittrock (1986) and by Houston *et al.* (1990) offer a wealth of resources, largely North American in origin. Aspects of the interactive approach to teaching are developed by Tomlinson and Kilner (1990).

For common-sense views of action and skill see Hargreaves (1980) and Forguson (1989). On the modern psychology of human skill and expertise various chapters in Gellatly (1986) provide a very readable introduction, as do Bereiter and Scardamalia (1993). Other more advanced treatments include Chi *et al.* (1988), Colley and Beech (1989), Holding (1989), Anderson (1990) and Schmidt (1991).

For various views concerning the treatment of teaching as a form of skill see Berliner (1986), Griffiths (1987) and Tomlinson (1989a) and more generally on teacher development: Joyce and Showers (1988), Elliott (1991, 1993) and Olson (1992). For Schön's notions of reflectiveness as applied to teaching see Handal and Lauvås (1987), Calderhead (1989), Russell and Munby (1992), Calderhead and Gates (1993); and Gilroy (1993).

There are excellent recent collections on mentoring and the shift to school-based teacher preparation in the UK by McIntyre *et al.* (1993) and Bridges and Kerry (1993); another useful source in this area is Wilkin (1992).

Journals that are particularly likely to include articles of relevance to this chapter and the rest of the book include: *Journal of Education for Teaching; Journal of Teacher Development; Journal of Teacher Education; Mentoring;* and *Teaching and Teacher Education.*

The reflective coach: functions and forms of mentoring

Building from the teaching skill learning cycle

The previous chapter considered basic ideas and issues concerning the nature of teaching and the possibility of assisting student-teachers to become competent at this very complex, open form of skill. The present chapter will build from those perspectives. In particular, it will develop the idea of the teaching skill cycle to focus on functions and strategies in the coaching aspect of mentoring assistance. Although this gets us considerably closer to the practicalities of mentoring, this chapter therefore still has something of a ground-clearing role, in that it seeks to pinpoint the basic functions involved in helping student-teachers acquire teaching skill and then to indicate the main forms of doing this. That is as far as this chapter will go, because we also need to look at the motivational and counselling side (Chapter 4) before bringing these two aspects together with this and other material and applying them to concrete strategies for mentoring within school-based provision (Chapters 8 and 9). By way of introduction I am going to recall briefly and then extend some of the last chapter's ideas about the open skilful nature of teaching.

The artistry of teaching

Teaching is a contested activity
To recognize that teaching is a form of skill is not to deny that there are values involved; the opposite in fact, since we've seen that skill is inherently purposeful. In particular, the aims in any piece of teaching involve

issues of value. Should we be teaching this or that? Should we be aiming at a minimum or general achievement for all, or to maximize the learning of a few? Although in the UK the national curriculum may impose certain constraints, many issues of emphasis and priority remain and we therefore have to be careful about assuming that others share our particular values. In the context of school-based mentoring, therefore, it seems that teacher-mentors have a professional responsibility to assist student-teachers to think open-mindedly about the many basic values involved in teaching contexts.

As an open, complex skill, teaching admits of many 'right' ways
Typically there's not just one right or wrong way, but a number of alternative strategies with potential for achieving particular teaching purposes in particular contexts. So we shouldn't assume that there's necessarily only one 'good practice', even though we may have our own well-based preferences. It's rather a matter of helping student-teachers understand and acquire a repertoire of teaching strategies and tactics, along with understanding as to when best to adopt them. I suggest the same applies to mentoring.

In teaching a lot is usually going on at the same time
An effective teacher is usually doing a number of things at once and achieving a variety of functions through each action (cf. Doyle 1986). That is, as in any skill, the demands are complex and the best strategies are multi-purpose or multi-functional. Simply uttering a sentence by way of giving pupils information, for instance, also conveys attitudes towards them through the particular wording used, the nature of the context, the intonation, the accompanying posture and so forth.

Teaching capability has many tacitly embedded layers and subskills
Not only does teaching tend to be amongst the most complex of human enterprises, but its constituents have a characteristic embeddedness. Broad functions are achieved by combining more specific subfunctions at increasingly concrete levels of strategy and tactic. Managing pupil behaviour, for instance, may include giving instructions, which involves saying particular sentences, which includes finding particular words, and so on. The more embedded the subaction, the more tacitly or intuitively done by those with experience and the more difficult it is for those who observe it to pick it out.

Becoming skilled at teaching takes many types of learning
From this discussion we can safely say that becoming intelligently skilful at teaching requires a combination of various kinds of learning achievement by student teachers, including

- learning to *distinguish* and *unravel* the many embedded elements and processes that tend to be involved in any aspect of teaching, but also
- learning to *combine* and *integrate* these elements to get things together.

These two types of learning need crossing with two further forms of development:

* Learning *awareness* and *grasp,* learning how to read and monitor teaching situations, as well as
* Learning *what to do* in them, learning how to act, anticipate and respond.

Where these combinations of learning gains occur, student-teachers become more aware of the different aspects in the teaching situation which are often quite invisible to them at the outset. They become more sensitive to bits of information such as signs of pupil restlessness, facial expressions that signal misunderstanding of a given item, indications of pupil feelings, and much more. They also become more able to take such aspects into account, not just separately, but in combination. Similarly, they become more able to use particular classroom tactics separately and in combination. Perhaps above all, they become able to integrate these forms of awareness with their action, to deploy their strategies and responses more and more on the basis of the ways they read and anticipate situations. They will do all of this with increasing economy and efficiency (see Further detail section 3.1).

However, these forms of learning are far from inevitable, even when student-teachers are immersed in school teaching contexts. They need active assistance through mentoring and the remainder of this chapter is concerned with the major functions and forms this may take. In embarking on these considerations, a first thing to realize is that neither student-teachers nor their mentors start with blank slates.

What student-teachers bring to the situation

It's perhaps obvious, though it also seems easy to forget, that beginning student-teachers don't all start the same. Even more important, none of them starts from scratch. They will typically have strengths to apply and extend, but also gaps to fill and sometimes preconceptions and dispositions which need amending.

Students bring consciously espoused ideals and informal theories about teaching. These need to be allowed expression and examination so that they can be built upon and developed/amended as appropriate. It would be strange if those setting out in a profession hadn't thought seriously about what it involves, even more so in the case of teaching, which is something everyone has experienced as a pupil. Although we might expect those who choose teaching to have generally had positive experience and expectations regarding teaching, this isn't necessarily so in all cases; people do go into professions for all sorts of reasons. In any case, very many students have both positive and negative teacher models in mind, whose styles they wish respectively to emulate or avoid.

Student-teachers will thus enter their courses with some degree of

Further detail section 3.1
Starting points and development of professional knowledge

The idea that people start new activities with an existing reservoir of ideas and capabilities isn't totally foreign to everyday thinking, but it is perhaps sufficiently rare for it to have been particularly emphasized in recent years by educationists drawing on a variety of disciplines (cf. Meadows 1993). Modern psychology confirms that what human beings make of situations depends very much on an interplay of the data they're faced with and the ideas and frames they already possess. To some extent, that is, human perceiving and knowing is *constructive* (cf. Tomlinson, 1989b). In a now classic study of schoolteachers, Dan Lortie (1975) emphasized the power of the preconceptions student-teachers bring to their preparatory courses. More recently this was stressed by Theo Wubbels (1992), who pointed out that these preconceptions involve both explicit and implicit, often unconscious, stances. He suggested that the latter deserve particular emphasis, because they do appear to exert a more powerful influence on action and tend to determine whether incoming ideas on the subsequent course will 'make intuitive sense' to their holders (Hollingsworth 1989). These assumptions are very easy to miss, but as Elliott and Calderhead (1993) also point out, they may be important to challenge.

Dimensions of expert knowledge development

In so far as professional knowledge does develop, what does this entail? Quite a number of studies exist across different domains of expertise and they suggest a number of dimensions in its development. In the simplest terms: those who are more proficient and experienced just tend to *know much more*. More specifically, however, this includes their awareness and strategies becoming

1 *more differentiated:* they're more sensitive to detailed features and demands of relevant contexts and they have a greater range of strategies and substrategies available for deployment.
2 *more integrated:* they use economical 'chunks' both in their awareness and their actions. They have learned to recognize complex configurations of signs and they have automatized varying combinations of subskill components; they get things together more readily.

Both of these features are combined within expert *routines*. Notice that such routines aren't just automatic behaviour, but automated reading-*and*-reacting. Experts tend to say when asked that they 'just knew' to do a particular effective action; that is, they appear also to read situations without deliberate monitoring. This has strengths as well as weaknesses.

However, it's not just a question of what 'experts' have got, but also of how they apply it. Expert practitioners in a field are *quicker* and more *economical* both in reading and action on situations; they can take account of more at a time. As skill develops (Anderson 1990) another apparent trend is that whilst novices focus on *surface* features, experts map these features on to underlying *key ideas* and understanding (they've gone from 'what do I do if . . . ?' to 'what does it mean if . . . ?'). Similarly, novices tend to think of things only in one particular way, for example a particular model or terminology, whilst experts' representations are more independent of particular formulations and terminology; they've located the important aspects and may well be able to think about them in a variety of ways.

On the other hand, there are also two contrasting trends. The first is that as we've seen, expertise not only becomes language-independent, it also becomes *difficult to articulate* at all in verbal terms. The second is that in so far as experts do communicate with each other about their domain, they can use specialized and economically effective language which is closely dependent on their experience: to outsiders, therefore, such jargon is (for the moment) meaningless. So the value of jargon depends on who and where you are; it's useful when you've mastered it, a barrier while you haven't.

Coming from studies of the reverse side of skill (that is, forms of human error such as driving accidents, pollution disasters), Reason (1990) brings things together by suggesting that there are three types or levels of know-how in professional competence: *routine-based, rule-based* and *knowledge-based* (actually he calls the first 'skill-based', but is using the term in a narrower sense than I've been doing here). In a familiar situation we tend first to 'do what comes naturally', that is routinely read the situation and bring out actions intuitively in response. Should this not produce smooth progress towards our goal, we move to a rule-based level by consciously examining the situation to see if it calls up one of our 'prepackaged' response strategies. That is, the reading is deliberate, the reaction intuitive. If this fails we really have to think about it and deploy mental representations to work out solutions explicitly and guide our actions consciously. It appears that in general we humans prefer to do things in the above order, rather than think first and act later, as the rational assumptions of traditional western culture might have had us believe.

Teacher professional knowledge

Although it could be highly profitable to gain access to the professional know-how of the best practising teachers, this can be surprisingly difficult for a number of reasons. Perhaps most basic is the intricate and contested nature of teaching aims and their achievement (Olson 1992). It just isn't so easy to establish who is expert (as opposed to, say, merely experienced) at the second-order activity of teaching (as compared even to such complex first-order activities as flying aeroplanes). Another main reason is the sheer difficulty of getting at what's going on in an experienced teacher's action, given that it's 1) largely intuitive, and 2) embedded within an ongoing period of classroom activity which can hardly be interrupted so as to ask them there and then (cf. Calderhead 1981; Yinger 1986). Because of this, a variety of ways have been used to try to get at expert teachers' professional know-how, though each tends to have its own problems.

Nevertheless, there are indications that teachers' professional knowledge echoes the development of expertise found in other areas in a number of respects. David Berliner (1986), for instance, found evidence that experienced teachers took less time to process images of classroom scenes and that they focused on more relevant teaching themes (like grouping and apparent work concentration), whilst novices took more time and focused on surface features like clothing. Other work (e.g. that of Sally Brown and Donald McIntyre 1993) confirms previous findings that proficient teachers do indeed develop wide repertoires of action-chunks or routines, which are deployed flexibly and rapidly, but intuitively for much of the time. Brown and McIntyre found further that these teachers found articulation difficult, but were nevertheless 'surprisingly' confident of their judgements about classroom events and pupils (as were the experienced nurses regarding patients in Patricia Benner's 1984 study). This finding is perhaps ambiguous in its implications. On the one hand, it fits with all we've just seen about well-established intuitive strands in expert know-how. On the other, given the variability of classrooms and human pupils, there are clearly potential dangers in any over-confidence that would lead to an ignoring of feedback, especially from pupils.

In experienced teachers the language-independence aspect of expertise appears to take the form of their preferring to talk in terms of *images* (Calderhead 1990), though it could be that this finding may be partly due to the research methods used. The apparent absence of specialist language is difficult to explain, tempting one to think perhaps of the solitary 'my classroom is my castle' tradition, or perhaps that the perceived irrelevance of teacher education course 'theory' has confirmed common-sense separations of thought and action. My own view is that although experienced teachers tend to use everyday-sounding terms and expressions, like 'working in pairs' or 'group work', they actually mean quite complex sets of things, which they take for granted (like all the things one has to be alert to when using such methods). When they function as mentors they're likely to find this out, in that they will have in fact to explain these taken-for-granted aspects to the student novices for whom such meanings are not yet familiar.

Mentoring preconceptions and expertise

As this last point suggests, these aspects of the development of skilled expertise are likely to apply also to that of mentoring capabilities, though these and teacher education expertise generally do not appear to have been much studied to date. In particular, whilst teachers may not suffer (or gain) from having specialist jargon, new teacher-mentors clearly do not start entirely empty-minded or neutral, even if they're entering the role for the first time. If only from their own experience as student teachers and since qualifying, they will tend to bring ideas and ideals.

However, it seems important to remind ourselves how easily our well-established assumptions and substrategies can persist here, even though we may have called them into question at the level of conscious thinking. For instance, a recent survey by Saunders and Tomlinson (1994) suggested that at the level of consciously 'espoused theory', many secondary teachers do strongly welcome the move to school-based professional preparation and would like to get away from the shortcomings they perceived in their own courses (e.g. 'no real value till you got into teaching practice, and then it was the deep end'). Yet quite often their conception of new possibilities seemed restricted by persisting strands from the old model. For instance, some saw having students in school during the first term of a PGCE year as a way of 'getting them really ready for a good teaching practice second term' (rather than, say, seeing the year as an opportunity for longer term, systematically assisted acquisition of teaching capability and the avoidance of stressful 'deep ends').

Of course, this finding is only surprising if we still think in dualist terms of all knowledge and ideas as conscious and forget the importance of tacit 'knowledge-in-action'. However, even if we don't, there is a further caution when we also remember the general human tendency to prefer this level in the form of 'routine fixes' (Reason 1990), plus that of adult learners to seek confirmation of their existing abilities and resources (see Knowles 1978; Hunt 1987). That is, just as student-teachers' preconceptions need taking into account explicitly and may possibly require amendment, so also as mentors and designers of school-based programmes, we need to reflect and communicate sufficiently so that any unfortunate assumptions from our past do not become simply built into our new approach and routinized through practice.

preconception regarding teaching. Their ideas may often be relatively global, implying a choice between stark and simplistic alternatives (not uncommon amongst novices in any field). Other things being equal, however, students will persist with the preconceptions they bring, even though these might be based on idiosyncratic experience and hearsay. Sooner or later, therefore, such views need a chance to emerge and be discussed (and be checked at least as to their healthiness, let alone their wisdom – I once encountered a PGCE student who said, apparently quite seriously, that he believed 'pain to be an essential ingredient in effective learning'). How this might be approached is a topic I shall return to in due course.

Students bring explicit ideas and expectations about how one learns to teach. Not only do students have explicit ideas about pupils and teaching, they may have conscious expectations about the ways one learns to become a teacher. They may well share some of the dualist assumptions about action and skill acquisition discussed early in the previous chapter. In our culture, for instance, there's evidence of a prevalent view of 'learning by immersion', so that students often feel an urgency to get into the swing of class teaching practice (though particularly in traditional college-based courses, they also built up apprehension about going into the 'lion's den'). Some students may also expect that they should be told exactly what to do, how to teach. Once again, this type of viewpoint also may profit from open discussion and reflection (preferably sooner rather than later in this case), otherwise such unrealistic expectations may persist with widespread negative effects, as I suspect they often have within traditional courses.

Students bring taken-for-granted assumptions which can act as 'theories-in-action'. Whilst student teachers are likely to have these varying kinds of *explicit* outlooks and preconceptions, perhaps even more important are their *tacit* assumptions, the 'theories-in-action' (see Further detail section 3.1) which tend to be mixed in and under their consciously held views. Such assumptions are all the more important, first because these assumptions tend to be what will actually generate their actions when they're not thinking deliberately about it, second, because they are often entirely implicit and taken for granted, so that it's hard even for those who hold such ideas to get at them and examine their merits, and third, such assumptions tend to have become 'part of a person's identity'. So even if we do manage to become consciously aware of them, we tend to be defensive about our assumptions – they're part of us. It's equally important, then, to build on student-teachers' taken-for-granted ideas where feasible, but also to help change and develop them where necessary, whether they concern school teaching as such or their own learning as student-teachers.

Students also bring existing capabilities which include potential teaching skills and subskills. Student-teachers obviously bring with them a whole range of capabilities and knowledge which may be relevant in teaching. This range will vary from student to student, as will the ways these existing strengths can be related to their developing teaching capability:

- Very many existing capabilities can and will simply be *brought usefully into their teaching without them realizing it* (e.g. their command of spoken English, their subject knowledge/skills, much of their social sensitivity).
- Other existing subskills and strategies *may require assistance to be brought into the student's teaching repertoire.* For instance, subcomponents of students' everyday social capability may be central to teaching behaviour (e.g. intuitively recognizing the subtle signs that keep conversations going). Yet some students appear not to realize that they can use these strengths. Some even seem actually to assume they don't possess any, but that they need to learn something brand new by way of teaching tricks. Such sorts of outlook signal a need for assistance, both to arrive at a more adequate way of thinking and to build on the relevant skill strengths they do possess.
- Some of their subskills *may need adapting and amending* because they 'transfer negatively' to teaching. For example, the sorts of conversational subskills just mentioned may be vital in the typical one-to-one conversations student-teachers have been used to (where, for example, a considerable degree of eye contact is normal), but may actually hinder them in a group or whole class situation (where they need to scan around most of the time).

Of course, many specific forms of teaching strategy and tactic will not have been developed at all and students will need to be made aware of them and helped to develop proficiency at them (a typical example would be the classroom scanning mentioned above).

Each student intern is in some respects unique, so mentoring needs to achieve some degree of individual matching. This situation doesn't necessarily mean completely different treatment for each student intern, because they're not unique in every respect. However, their positions with respect to the above types of belief, assumption and capability, not to mention their personality dispositions and sensitivities, cannot simply be assumed to be similar. These individual qualities need to be given chances to emerge, so that we can adapt our mentoring approaches as far as possible to particular student strengths and needs. Although this can happen in various ways, as we'll consider shortly, some of their assumptions and existing skill aspects in particular may be difficult to pick out until we see actually the student-teacher engaging in some sort of teaching action.

Teacher-mentors too bring ideas, assumptions and resources

Appropriately adapted, the above points also apply to teachers taking up the role of school-based mentor. Given the considerable influence they're likely to have in this role, it seems particularly important for teacher-mentors to examine their own ideas and assumptions, but it may in fact be even harder for them to do this than it is for students. As with students, many of our relevant outlooks and values as teachers will be at the level of assumptions and implicit professional practices, and these are if anything likely to have become *more* ingrained through active experience of teaching. Moreover, what is involved here includes not only assumptions and capacities in relation to teaching and student-teacher forms of learning, but also regarding our own learning and performance as mentors.

I would suggest, therefore, that it's important for those taking on school-based mentoring to realize the potential implications of what has been seen so far about explicit and implicit forms of professional knowledge. Otherwise there is considerable danger that whilst we consciously espouse the possibility of improvements through school-based forms of teacher preparation, we also undermine them through old assumptions which still tacitly drive what we actually do. This might for example occur at the level of general approach in which we saw the shift to school-based mentoring simply as a matter of replacing thought by action (exchanging all that irrelevant 'theory' for some 'real' practice), or additionally, we might import specific practices from traditional arrangements without realizing it, thereby undoing the potential of those features we *have* managed to change (see Further detail section 3.1).

If mentors are to help student-teachers achieve worthwhile professional learning, therefore, they need to assist them to adopt the forms of reflective stance proposed by Schön and others. But because mentoring is itself a form of professional capability to which teachers bring all sorts of existing ideas, assumptions and capabilities, then teacher-mentors too need to adopt a reflective approach to their own activities and learning.

It must be admitted that opening one's mind to alternative possibilities does in some ways get more difficult the more experience one has at something (we'll return to this issue in Chapter 4). Nevertheless, for teachers starting out on the mentoring role such a reflective stance is likely to be more realistic, more effective and more satisfying. It will help them to realize, for instance, that they have much knowledge and skill which is of relevance to mentoring. Mentoring is, after all, promoting student-teachers' learning, thus a form of teaching, and the teaching teachers have done with school-age pupils has strong common strands with it. Whilst a reflective stance will involve thinking about the differences as well, an awareness of the intuitive aspects of professional capability should also help novice mentors see that they don't have to (and in fact can't) be *totally* clear and sure before getting into the action. What they do need is to think thoroughly enough in advance to be clear about what they will try, how and why, then to let their existing capabilities flow, and to improve these as mentoring capabilities by reflecting on and in such activities.

In so far as mentoring centrally involves coaching, therefore, I would suggest that in both of the senses indicated above, the mentor should aspire to be a *reflective coach*. Mentoring, like teaching, should involve a continual reflective cycle. However, since coaching is another idea we may need to amend in the light of modern understanding of professional learning, I now want to consider the basic functions it involves in school-based mentoring.

What student-teachers need: reflective coaching

In the previous chapter I pointed out that capability at something tends to develop when people engage in an experiential skill cycle of *reflective practice*. In the case of teaching this includes the teaching cycle functions of:

- *planning* the teaching on the basis of clear understanding of aims and context, and appropriate selection of strategies, then
- *engaging* in the teaching activity, whilst
- *monitoring* that action and its effects, then
- *feeding back* information from this monitoring into *reflection* and replanning of the teaching or particular subaspects of it.

Sooner or later, all these aspects have to be combined in repeated *plan–teach–reflect* cycles relating to meaningful units, such as whole lessons or syllabus topics. However, given the limits on human information processing, especially in novices, it may be necessary at various points to focus on particular aspects of the cycle and to attend to very specific subcomponents in the teaching activity. That is, we may need to 'unpack and focus on the bits', though we shall have at some point to reintegrate them with the other aspects of the overall action.

We also saw that complex human skills are typically achieved only with various sorts of assistance and clearly that is what mentoring is all about. The above elements in the learning-to-teach cycle therefore indicate the essential areas in which student-teachers' reflective practice will profit from assistance which, following Schön, may be termed *reflective coaching* (see

Table 3.1 Basic functions in mentoring assistance

---

1 Assisting planning by contributing to pedagogical understanding and grasp of a repertoire of teaching strategies
2 Direct assistance and support for teaching activity
3 Assistance with monitoring of teaching activity and its effects
4 Assisting analysis and reflection both during and after the action
5 Taking account of skill acquisition phases
6 Harnessing student motivation and commitment through interpersonal sensitivity and skill

---

Further detail section 3.2). In other words, taken together, these areas indicate the *basic functions in teacher mentoring*, to which mentors must sooner or later attend. I want next to consider these various mentoring functions at a general level. For ease of consultation, you will find them summarized in Table 3.1.

Basic functions of mentoring and their rationales

(1) Assisting planning by contributing to pedagogical understanding and grasp of a repertoire of teaching strategies
Planning is taken here to require and thus to include relevant *understanding*. This is because *all* skills include understanding of context and process, which with experience becomes increasingly intuitive. Open skills like teaching also require ongoing problem solving utilizing such knowledge explicitly. If intelligent planning is basic to teaching, then assistance with it is a basic mentoring function.

Understanding for planful teaching will centre on *pedagogy*, that is understanding of the nature of teaching-learning interactions. But this will extend from specifics to do with particular subjects, types of learning process and pupil, through to background awareness of broader societal issues required for responsible membership of the profession. Such understanding needs to be *critical*, in the sense argued for earlier, that it is appraised for its coherence, relevance and grounding in evidence. Students also need insights into their own learning and as part of mentoring they may need help to 'learn how to learn' intelligently and reflectively. Their commitment and intelligent participation are likely to be enhanced if the basics and rationale of such an approach are offered to them explicitly.

Well-informed awareness of a *range of teaching strategies* might be seen as part of pedagogical understanding, but appears important enough to receive mention in its own right. Student-teachers need introducing to a systematic repertoire of teaching strategies, along with rationales concerning their strengths and difficulties, suitability for differing pupils and contexts and so on. Such assistance will also need to extend into analysis and understanding

Further detail section 3.2
Basic functions in reflective coaching

For those who find visual diagrams useful, the basic functions of coaching for reflective teaching are summarized in Figure 3.1 using the system scheme previously presented as Figure 2.2. The coaching functions are indicated in the round 'bubbles' connected by dashed lines to the cycle of student teaching phases.

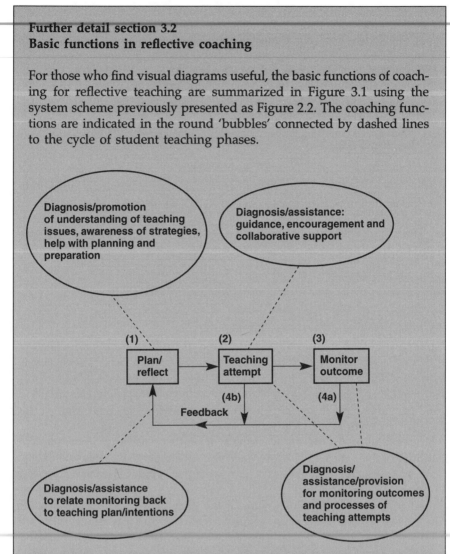

Figure 3.1   Coaching functions in relation to the teaching skill cycle

These functions will hopefully speak for themselves, but please note that the repeated mention of *diagnosis* is deliberate. It's intended to be a reminder that our mentoring action and advice needs to be based on an intelligent reading of the situation if it's to provide systematic and useful assistance. The mentor's diagnosis is all the more necessary in so far as student-teachers find it difficult to monitor their own thinking and action in the early stages; they have less idea of what to look for and less capability to keep track of it anyway. Like any such activity, mentors will tend to become intuitive at this, but as argued in Further detail section 3.1, we also need to remain reflective, reviewing our practices, preferably with others, at least from time to time.

The above cycle plus its coaching input functions can of course be applied at any level of teaching action unit, from a consideration of whole teaching periods at a time, through to focuses on particular within-lesson phases or actions such as transitions, to very specific events and interactions. What we do focus on will naturally depend on our diagnosis of what we witness at any given point.

Notice, then, that this view modifies the old dualist stance in which coaching tended to be seen simply as 'shouting instructions from the sidelines' (without attention, for instance, to the learner's perspective or rationale). That sort of direct guidance can of course be included within our broader view of coaching, especially if we get into the classroom and work collaboratively with our student-teachers (or use such innovations as radio-assisted practice – see the appendix). But this view of coaching also includes assisting other skill cycle aspects of the student-teacher's learning-by-doing: their understanding and planning, their monitoring of action and outcomes, their feeding back of the information gleaned into their further thinking and replanning. As such, therefore, this approach based on the cognitive psychology of skill acquisition very much complements the independently developed ideas of Schön (1987) on the educating of reflective practitioners. That is another reason why with him I refer to it as *reflective coaching*.

As I see it, this approach also illuminates two basic issues in teaching and mentoring. The first is concerned with the issue *of what is effective in helping teachers develop new ways of teaching*, whether they're new or experienced. The above view steers us away from any idea of a single secret 'key' to effective innovation and teaching skill development. It tells us that just in terms of individual learning functions alone (not to mention the motivational and social aspects we'll be considering in the next chapter), *a number of aspects* are necessary, with corresponding coaching assistance for each. This is very much confirmed by the work of Bruce Joyce and Beverly Showers (1988, Chapter 6) on staff development, showing that its effects on skill at implementing new teaching strategies increases as training programmes include more of the following: information provision, theory, demonstration, practice, feedback and coaching. It was notable, for instance, that staff training doesn't appear to assist teachers reliably to transfer their new skills into new situations until the training includes at least theory provision, plus demonstration, plus practice, plus feedback provision. If one really wants to make a difference, then coaching is needed as well.

A second issue is that of general *sequencing of provision* for student-teachers. This issue tends to be prone to the sort of polarization I lamented earlier, namely to be seen as having understanding/theory first, then application/practice, versus getting people into the action first, so that they actually have something to reflect on and theorize about. Apart from it being likely that different sequences will suit different student-teachers and teaching subjects, our present view of reflective skill learning and coaching suggests a subtle but important difference in approach. It does indeed fit with the skill psychology sources cited so far to say that student-teachers need to get into the action reasonably soon and that too much 'pure theory' and discussion before this is likely to achieve little. However, suggestions that student-teachers should first gain 'some mastery of their teaching skills, *before* they reflect on its links with pupils' learning (Maynard and Furlong 1993) appear to imply the sort of action–thought split I disparaged earlier (as these authors also do elsewhere). Whatever the sequencing of broad aspects of provision, however, what is surely needed is for the key purposes of teaching (i.e. promotion of learning) never to be allowed to disappear totally from consideration. Even if it is necessary to focus on specific strategies, tactics and events, it is central to the teacher-mentor's reflective coaching that they should assist the student-teacher to keep their practice meaningful and purposive.

of the *embedded subskills and tactics* (the 'nitty-gritty') within particular teaching strategies within the repertoire.

(2) Direct assistance and support for teaching activity
We saw that active, planful *attempts* at something are essential if one is to become skilled at it, and teaching is no exception. The sheer complexity of teaching even an average class and the stressful nature of the typical early phase of skill acquisition constitute strong arguments for direct, in-classroom support for teaching attempts. Such forms of assistance are traditionally associated with 'mere coaching' (see Further detail section 3.2) and sometimes dismissed as 'tips'. There is nothing wrong with tips, however, so long as such help builds on the sort of pedagogical understanding and planning just referred to in the previous section. It will need, for instance, to employ terminology already understood (though where feasible, new terminology may also be all the more meaningfully introduced 'on the spot'). We may therefore need to adjust our traditional concept of coaching and realize that help to understand and think about the issues is

actually a first aspect of coaching and that specific 'tips' need understanding within the context of other aspects thus covered.

Nevertheless, this aspect of mentoring, direct assistance with ongoing teaching, seems to have received little explicit consideration in traditional teacher education, though in recent years forms of it have appeared in such practices as paired teaching, small group teaching, IT-INSET collaborative work between teachers, tutors and student groups (Ashton, Peacock and Henderson 1989). The present shift to school-based arrangements appears to be a golden opportunity to take this function much more seriously and give support at whatever level of detail seems necessary. School-based arrangements appear to offer considerable possibility of getting into classrooms and working with student-teachers so as to share the demands of the situation with them, thereby helping them get their insights and planning into their action more directly and easily.

(3) Assistance with monitoring of teaching activity and its effects

The teaching skill cycle involves using various forms of *feedback* based on *monitoring of actions and outcome*, both within the lesson activity and after it. Here again, the 'written crit' of traditional teacher education paid little attention to the possibility of direct assistance for monitoring the details of mini-actions and episodes during the teaching action. Its 'post-lesson conference' (as the 'chat after the lesson' of traditional teaching practice supervision is now more impressively termed) illustrates at the very least problems of getting access to details embedded within a lesson and the need for sufficient time for monitoring and reflection.

Once more, school-based arrangements appear to offer possibilities for mentors to offer assistance both with overall monitoring of lesson and longer term outcomes (did the pupils learn?) and with in-class monitoring of detailed actions and their 'mini-effects' during the teaching ('what happened/ is happening because of your action?'). In doing this, the task of mentoring is to assist student-teachers to see what they *actually* did (as opposed just to what they *intended* to do or *thought* they'd done) and what *actually* happened by way of ongoing effects and overall outcomes.

(4) Assisting analysis and reflection both during and after the action

It's clearly important in systematic practical activities like teaching to plan specific strategies, but it's simply not enough merely to have fixed routines. A teacher's strategies and tactics need in the first place to be planned appropriately for the particular combination of pupils, intended learning outcomes, context and resources in question. They then need typically to be adapted flexibly as the action unfolds; when a teacher finds things not working on a particular occasion, any of a number of 'fall-back positions' may be needed. So 'knowing what to do' actually includes 'knowing why in relation to these circumstances'.

A major point of the current ideas introduced earlier on the skill cycle is that the development of a working pedagogical understanding can't come *solely* from abstract awareness of ideas and findings, however well established. Skilful teaching know-how comes from the combination of making a thoughtful attempt *and* thinking carefully about how it went, both during and after the action. This requires not just monitoring of what happened, but also *analysis* as to why. In contrast to the traditional (dualist) separation of 'theory' and 'practice', it's clear that the student teacher will build up *practical understanding* of the what, how and why of teaching strategy precisely through such planful action and its *reflective analysis* at various levels. In due course this thoughtful flexibility will tend to become embedded intuitively within the experienced teacher's 'craft knowledge' at least to some extent, if never totally.

Mentoring therefore also needs to assist students to analyse and reflect systematically, not just after the teaching session or series of sessions, but also during the teaching, whilst they're close to the action. Students need help not just to monitor, but also *explore, interpret* and *explain* the how and why of what went on. This then flows naturally into the next phase of the teaching cycle, namely the (re-)planning of the next piece of teaching.

The central importance of such reflective assistance bears particular emphasis here for at least two further reasons:

1 In so far as *mentors* become anxious about helping a student-teacher succeed, they may find themselves reverting in practice to the narrow dualist idea of skill as a set of correct but thoughtless procedures. They may not realize this consciously, but that's what begins to be implied if they get drawn into simply telling the student the right/good versus wrong/bad nature of what they've done, rather than assisting the student to *analyse* the nature of the effects and the *how and why*.
2 Reflection and analysis take time and time is always limited. The scarcity of such resources was doubtless a factor undermining the quality of traditional teacher education and few people think of it as a problem that is about to disappear under the new arrangements. On the other hand, the new school-based arrangements do seem to offer some quite new possibilities regarding reflection on and in action, which will be explored in more detail later.

(5) Taking account of skill acquisition phases
The kind of assistance mentors give students with respect to any of the skill cycle functions must take into account where the students are in their development. The well established phases of skill acquisition introduced in the previous chapter have sometimes been summarized by saying that learners start from *unconscious incompetence* (not knowing that they don't know), proceed to *conscious incompetence* (knowing that they don't know how), thence

to *conscious competence* (knowing in theory, but applying only with difficulty) and eventually to *unconscious competence* (knowing how to, but not being exactly aware of what they're doing).

This snappy formulation may be too crude in some respects (see the earlier section on 'What student-teachers bring to the situation'), but it does serve to remind us that in the early stages of teaching skill acquisition students are likely to have more need of assistance and monitoring by the mentor. These might take the form of *direct* person-to-person assistance with the different aspects of the skill cycle, but also of *indirect* support, including the arranging of contexts and the planning of a progressively more demanding set of cumulative experiences. Generally, but particularly in the early stages, direct support needs to be economical, so that it doesn't overload the student's capacities to take in and integrate.

As already emphasized, mentors need at the same time to be on the look-out to help students gain insights and skill not only in relation to teaching, but also with respect to their own learning and self-development as student-teachers. Such a function is of course closely related to the promoting of reflectiveness and interpersonal facilitation. In this connection it's also worth remembering two dangers of an inadequate understanding of skill and its development, which student-teachers have not been unknown to suffer.

A first danger is that when something goes well, the student may too readily think they've 'got there', that is, that they have achieved proficiency which probably will not in fact be gained until they've had a good deal more varied experience and practice. The course of learning any capability tends to involve spurts and relapses, the more so the more varied the factors in the situation – and in teaching there are very many!

Another possibility is that in so far as a student-teacher has managed to find 'something that works' and to get comfortable and intuitive with it, they may be tempted to cling to this as their only strategy, rather than risking the pains of building further strategies into their repertoire. The Nobel prize winning psychologist Herbert Simon called this 'satisficing', because it's a matter of being satisfied by what minimally suffices. When thinking of specific ways to assist student-teacher learning, we clearly need to think of helping them acquire not only proficiency but also a range of teaching strategies.

(6) Harnessing student motivation and commitment through interpersonal sensitivity and skill
Students-teachers are only human, they're involved in something that is usually very meaningful and important to them in a variety of respects and, as I keep implying, 'teaching ain't easy'. Moreover, like all teaching, mentoring is about promoting learning and this demands the student-learner's active participation. Part of mentoring assistance is therefore as far as possible to harness the motivation and commitment of student-teachers.

This isn't so much another function in the sequence of skill cycle assistance, rather something that needs to pervade *all* the mentoring assistance functions. Mentoring is more than just counselling because its aim is teaching capability as well as personal satisfaction. But, for the reason just cited, the interpersonal helping aspects associated so strongly with counselling are indeed central to mentoring; mentoring always includes a counselling aspect. Its importance is such that I shall devote the following chapter to it, so that when we come to look at concrete mentoring strategies, both the skill acquisition and the motivational-interpersonal aspects can be brought together, as they must.

Forms of student-teacher learning and their mentoring aspects

At this point it may be useful to recall the distinction I drew earlier between *functions* and *strategies* in skilful activities. The functions are the constituent purposes and subpurposes of the action: what it's about achieving. The strategies are the actual ways someone goes about doing it: what one does to achieve the functions. Thus in the previous section I was offering a functional analysis of mentoring, picking out its essential purposes, and this was based in turn on a functional analysis of student learning through aspects of the teaching skill cycle.

In practice, however, the basic coaching functions discussed above might be realized in a variety of specific forms, through different types of concrete activity. That is, there could be various forms of student-teacher learning, with corresponding forms of mentoring strategy to achieve the reflective coaching functions. I want to suggest, in fact, that there are four basic forms of learning teaching and corresponding mentor assistance, namely:

• students learning from others teaching;
• students learning through their own teaching attempts;
• students learning through progressively collaborative teaching with others;
• exploration of central ideas and broader issues.

These forms are summarized with their main components in Table 3.2, following which their major aspects will be considered. Detailed tactics and tips will be left until Chapter 8.

(1) Assisting interns to learn from others teaching
Power and pitfalls of direct observation
Learning by observing others has had a mixed history in teacher preparation. 'Sitting with Nellie' (a reference to pupil monitors in the earliest part of the century), so as to copy her teaching actions once enjoyed a central place in teacher *training*. But it fell into some disrepute in the post-Second

Table 3.2   Major forms of student learning activity and mentoring
assistance

---

1 Assisting interns to learn from others teaching by:
   (a) unpacking the planning,
   (b) guiding observation of the action,
   (c) modelling and prompting monitoring,
   (d) modelling and prompting reflection.
2 Assisting interns to learn through their own teaching activities by:
   (a) assisting planning,
   (b) supporting the teaching activity,
   (c) assisting monitoring and feedback,
   (d) assisting analysis and reflection.
3 Progressively collaborative teaching involving:
   (a) progressive joint planning,
   (b) teaching as a learning team,
   (c) mutual monitoring,
   (d) joint analysis and reflection.
4 Exploring central ideas and broader issues through:
   (a) direct research on pupil, colleague, school and system contexts,
   (b) reading and other inputs on teaching and background issues,
   (c) organized discussion and tutorial work on these topics.

World War era of teacher *education*, since it was pointed out that observers
can find it difficult to discern the important features of the action and their
interpretations may tend simply to confirm their own preconceptions and
prejudices (as Calderhead and Robson's 1991 research confirms more recently in the case of PGCE students on precourse visits to primary schools).

These and yet further dangers do exist, but there is also evidence to
confirm the traditional view that direct observation *can* be a particularly
powerful basis whereby humans acquire action strategies. We seem able to
take in (and reproduce) much more than we or others can say; 'a picture is
worth a thousand words', a video excerpt perhaps rates a million and 'being there' can be inestimably richer. In what follows, I am thinking particularly of the direct witnessing of lessons as they're being taught, since
significantly increased access to these is one of the most obvious features of
a school-based student experience. Nevertheless, the use of media such as
video or audio recording can also have similar functions and further advantages. They can also be used separately or in combination with direct observation of teaching. Video and audio recording will therefore receive attention
in the book's appendix.

In teaching skill cycle terms, studying someone else's teaching can allow
the student a way of 'going through the skill cycle by proxy', a form of
vicarious learning. They may witness everything from planning to outcome to reflection. This may not include the essential benefit of doing it

themselves, but taking in other people's teaching can thus provide a source of ideas and action plans to add to the student's store of potential strategies. In terms of our basic conception of teaching as skill, therefore, all the student-teacher gets from witnessing other teaching (in the first instance, at least) is the development of their plan/understanding. However, they can do so in an actively analytical way, rather than just passively and they then have at least one basis on which to try things out themselves in 'thought experiments' or actual teaching attempts. In other words, direct observation can be the basis for 'experimental imitation' rather than having to be 'mindless cloning', as long as certain precautions are taken.

The student-teacher needs assistance to understand all elements in the teaching skill cycle
Although learning from existing practice need not be just a matter of imitating observable surface features without assistance, it can easily degenerate towards this. 'Sitting with Nellie' can be a powerful experience, but is dangerous on its own. Novices don't tend to know what to look for and they find it difficult anyway to distinguish the different strands in the expert's smooth and fluent performance. And since the whole point is to gain insight into *purposeful strategies* and their *flexible adaptation* for teaching, the student intern needs some idea of the particular teaching purposes and rationale involved in the teaching they witness.

Ideally, therefore, the student-teacher needs assistance sooner or later to gain access to the *whole teaching skill cycle* in question, not just to observe the actual teaching action phase passively. The observed teacher's *planning and rationale*, the processes and subtexts embedded in their *actual teaching*, the ongoing and outcome *effects* involved and preferably also the teacher's analysis and *reflection*, all are relevant and important for meaningful practical learning. If you're not averse to acronyms, may I suggest PAMR (planning–attempt–monitoring–reflection) as a means of referring to this cycle.

This also means that these aspects need to be deliberately explained or at least commented on by a mentor, and if that mentor is the actual teacher involved in the observed teaching, there are some obvious advantages. They or another mentor need to 'unpack' their thinking and planning to the student. They may usefully *guide* the student's actual observation towards various strands in the teaching action. They can usefully *model the monitoring* of immediate and longer term effects by demonstrating how they check what is happening and how it turns out. Finally, they can equally *demonstrate reflection* and analysis through 'out-loud' analysis of their own teaching. It's important to note, however, that this PAMR emphasis is not proposing any woolly holism which denies attention to detail and subskill, far from it. What it *is* contending, however, is that the integral nature of any skill, teaching included, is such that sooner or later specific aspects have to be seen in relation to the whole activity. In the terms adopted here, that is, phase-aspects of the teaching cycle need to be related to each other within a total picture.

At the same time as being shown such aspects, students need to be given opportunity and help to *explore and examine actively* the what and why of such offerings. Student-teachers can thus not only be shown action, monitoring and reflection, but also be encouraged to monitor and reflect about the teaching for themselves as a basis for discussion with the mentor. Although mentoring style may vary just as much as teaching style, there is reason to think that this combination of concrete experience and context-relevant shared reflection has exceedingly powerful learning effects at a number of levels.

Finally, the teachers and teaching contexts they are given access to should be chosen to maximize relevance and to fit in with students' current learning progress. This will include the stage of proficiency and skill they have achieved, the particular teaching substrategies felt important for them, and any other individual learning needs which can be discerned at particular points in particular students. Learning teaching through witnessing other people do it can thus take many forms with corresponding variations in mentoring style. As a general form of skill learning it can make a very powerful contribution here, though it also needs combining with other forms we're about to consider.

(2) Assisting interns to learn through their own teaching

Power and pitfalls of learning by doing
'Learning by doing' has become a very fashionable slogan and as we've seen, systematic research confirms that active attempts at an activity are essential for the acquisition of capability. But we also saw that there's a bit more to this than just 'doing'; mere repetition of behaviours simply automatizes those actions in that context. Teachers need not *only* to get more efficient at particular subskills (though they do need this), as if these 'techniques' of teaching were all we were talking about. Rather, overall teaching skill includes ability to flexibly judge, select and combine substrategies. Thus these 'higher processes' or decision making are very much part of what a student-teacher has to get into by way of action.

Student-teachers need to carry out all elements in the teaching skill cycle
Consequently, what needs to be 'done' is the whole teaching skill cycle; attempts aren't enough without the other aspects, in fact, without any sort of plan or strategy there could be no attempt. For the development of intelligent artistry what is needed is repeated planning, active attempt, monitoring and reflection, both in and after the action. *Learning by doing* really should mean by repeatedly doing *all* of these (as referred to above with the acronymn PAMR).

As also indicated above, this doesn't preclude narrowing down on particular tactics and actions within the overall teaching, but even here the PAMR angle applies: one has to have an idea of what more specific sub-aim one is trying to achieve and how, and it may help to focus attempts on such subskills. But then it is equally important to relate these subgoals and actions to the other aspects of the overall teaching units. Given the history of polarized thinking in this area, moreover, it may therefore bear emphasizing that I am here calling for attention *both* to the part aspect *and* to the whole. The fact that one has to refer to both and that we haven't the information-processing capacity to deal with everything at once should not allow us to slip back into any sort of either–or assumption in these respects.

Student teachers need assistance with all these elements
Having re-emphasized these points, it's also clear that student-teachers therefore need mentor attention and probably active assistance with *all* features and phases of the teaching cycle. Particularly in their earliest ventures, they will have less idea of what they're trying to do or of how to go about it. What ideas they do have will be less firmly integrated into their action attempts and more easily disrupted by difficulties and resistances in the classroom context when they do try such strategies. And given the ease with which novice teachers are thus overloaded by the information demands of teaching, they will find it all the more difficult to monitor the various strands of action and effect that occur. Their analysis and reflection will be correspondingly impoverished. Clearly, they stand to profit from close assistance in all these aspects of planful teaching efforts.

So school-based arrangements offer an unprecedented opportunity to help student-teachers get into the action in supported ways that help them actually learn from that action. Two particular advantages are that:

- the *perceived relevance* of their tasks is virtually assured by their being part of the teaching on offer to real pupils in an actual school;
- it should be possible to *introduce students gradually* to aspects of teaching during the course of their school experience, which should make for more success in such aspects *and* for ability to monitor and reflect.

The traditionally passive view of teaching practice supervision probably means that the need for active mentoring assistance in the various teaching phases should now be strongly emphasized, otherwise teacher-mentors may possibly persist tacitly with assumptions from their own early histories. We mustn't forget, of course that such assistance is assistance for *students'* planning, action and reflection – we can't learn for them. In this respect school-based arrangements offer, in principle at least, major opportunities for close coaching support within the classroom and I will be looking at some of the detailed possibilities in Chapter 8. Nevertheless, for various reasons, not least to do with motivation and a developing sense of confidence, it should also be said that students profit from some degree of being allowed to make mistakes on their own, without someone breathing down their necks. But this is likely to be more useful *after* they've got their basic bearings through observation of others and close support for their own first efforts.

Increased importance of student motivation and feelings
It perhaps bears emphasizing that where students are putting themselves on the line in this way, through engaging in attempts at something new and public like teaching, it can be very threatening. This is particularly so if they happen to hold unfortunate assumptions about teaching capability and its acquisition. This prompts the need for 1) dealing with these sorts of background issues sooner rather than later, and 2) finding strategies and tactics to facilitate students' relaxation and openness. These latter aspects are sufficiently important, in my view, to merit a chapter (the subsequent one) to themselves.

(3) Progressively collaborative teaching (PCT)

It will probably be clear that whilst the above two forms of student-teacher learning may be useful on their own, they are likely to be all the more powerful when combined. Given the complex and gradual nature of teaching skill development, this will have a variety of advantages when students work closely with one or more teacher-mentors in a structured way over a period of time.

The expression *progressively collaborative teaching* (PCT) has been suggested as a name for this sort of approach, in which the student engages in teaching with another, usually a more experienced teacher-mentor, initially staying very much within the mentor's framework and undertaking limited aspects of teaching with support, but progressively trying out and taking on a wider range of more extensive aspects. The progressive nature of this arrangement is important to emphasize; the novice status of student-teachers means not only that they're not in a position to make a full contribution from the outset, but that they need various forms of assistance that are geared to their progress.

Thus in the early stages of such an arrangement, the balance will be that the student-teacher is let into the teacher-mentor's longer term and immediate planning and rationale, given the opportunity for guided observation of the actual teaching, and has the teacher-mentor's reflective analysis shared with them. They are encouraged to participate in a spirit of constructive exploration. They will begin to undertake limited aspects of planning and preparation, then of actual teaching. These tasks will grow over time so that the balance shifts more towards the student-teacher's initiative and control in more and more extensive aspects of planning, preparation and teaching activity. Analysis and reflection are shared throughout. PCT can involve more than one student working with the same teacher-mentor and there are some clear benefits to purely student–student collaboration, without mentors, which it can include at any point.

Some advantages of PCT

PCT appears to offer more than just the sum of the advantages of learning from other teachers and from students' own teaching. Amongst its specific advantages are that:

- It involves *repeated collaboration and assisted learning with respect to all aspects* of the teaching skill cycle, with respect to teaching whose 'reality' and importance are acknowledged and protected.
- It acknowledges and builds on typical phases of teaching skill acquisition by allowing gradual but flexible *'scaffolding'*: that is, support which can be provided but gradually removed as the learner becomes independently capable.
- It allows the student to learn progressively from their own *teaching in a real situation, yet without the full task demands* which make the early phase of teaching skill acquisition so difficult, stressful and inefficient.
- At the same time it gives the student a better reason and basis for *learning from another teacher*, because they share teaching goals and investment of effort with that teacher.
- It is *economical* in that it allows the mentor to assist students, potentially more than one at a time, as part of her or his own teaching time in her/ his own classroom(s). The presence in the room of more than one teaching personnel can also assist class management and allow a much richer and more flexible set of learning activities for pupils.
- It can *help mentors in their own professional development*, through giving a stimulus and time for reflection in and on their own classroom teaching, whether by themselves or stimulated by enquiry from the student-teacher.

Some cautions regarding PCT

Nevertheless, certain cautions need to be sounded regarding PCT, particularly in so far as certain traditional assumptions may creep in and affect it detrimentally.

- PCT needs *explicit planning* to be achieved in organized, economical and profitable ways and this takes time, especially in the early days. This is generally true of any collaborative or team teaching, but especially so in the case of PCT, which has a clear training function for novice teachers.
- The *mentoring function of PCT needs safeguarding* against simply exploiting the economic advantages of extra assistance. Whilst team teaching perhaps never took off as generally as its advocates would have wished, teachers have recently grown much more used to working with other staff in their own classrooms, particularly in the context of the integration

of pupils with special educational needs into mainstream classes. There is perhaps a danger of an unfortunate volte-face in this area. Namely, the resistance one now sometimes picks up to having students in the classroom may be based on old thinking, according to which students should somehow have been prepared for this 'deep end' before entering it. As the realization dawns that students can be delegated tasks so as to actually assist the teacher, there is a danger of the teaching profession falling into the traditionally decried practices in nurse education, where student nurses were treated just as 'extra pairs of hands' on wards and their learning relatively ignored.

- In so far as PCT may be a powerful way of 'letting students into existing teaching strategies and styles', such privileged access ought not to be restricted to one teacher-mentor. The student ought probably *to engage in PCT with at least two different teachers* with contrasting styles.
- For the same reason there do need to be *opportunities for students to engage in independent development of ideas and teaching*, i.e. learn from their own teaching outside a PCT arrangement, at least once the student has been eased into effective teaching through early involvement in PCT, but possibly before this, depending on such factors as student proficiency and confidence.
- PCT may pose learning opportunities for both students and teacher-mentors, but by the same token the closeness of such collaboration also offers *challenges to the openness and flexibility of both*, as we'll consider in some detail in the following chapter.

As some of the above suggestions indicate, these potential difficulties do not appear insurmountable in themselves. Whilst school-based teacher preparation is likely to need aspects of all the basic forms of student-teacher learning considered here, PCT appears to be the approach which can achieve a particularly strong combination of the sorts of factor seen earlier as promoting intelligent teaching skill development. It is at the same time probably also the most difficult form of student learning to achieve under traditional arrangements, but the most clearly feasible under a school-based approach. Its detailed tactics therefore need revisiting, as they will be in Chapter 8.

(4) Exploring basic and background issues

Although what we've seen of the nature of teaching skill and its acquisition has emphasized the importance of getting into the action, it has also constantly re-emphasized that skill is *purposeful action informed by insight*. Teaching doesn't just *include* 'skills' as conceived on the dualist/behaviourist model (see Chapter 2) as bits of behaviour plus some thinking and feeling sooner or later. Teaching *is* skill, which means that values, understanding and relevant knowledge are always involved, even if often embedded within the action.

The understanding needs to be *broader and deeper* than the immediate issues in teaching activity are likely to reveal, however. Such immediate classroom issues may well be the best prompt to student interns' realization of the need for deeper exploration, but even extended post-lesson discussion probably won't suffice to explore them adequately. For this we appear to require a range of further ways specifically designed to assist students to get to grips with what are typically quite subtle concepts, as well as with background knowledge and broader perspectives. In turn, they need help to bring these perspectives back into their teaching and professional lives.

This further type of student-teacher learning seems to require at least three subforms: direct investigation of specific issues and wider aspects of the school context, reading and other inputs on issues in teaching and its background context, and organized discussion of both of the above. Generally speaking, whilst the new school-based arrangements facilitate new and more extensive implementation of the first of these activities, the latter two tend to have been central to traditional arrangements. The school-based situation may offer possibilities for their closer integration into everyday student-teacher thinking, though this may pose a considerable organizational challenge, especially in school–higher education institution partnership schemes.

Direct investigation of wider aspects of the teaching context
As we noted earlier, there's evidence that just letting students loose on situations to 'observe' tends not to be very effective. Direct observation or research tends to require some sort of assistance to focus actively and selectively on particular aspects and issues. Such investigations are likely to yield even more useful effects if they're followed by thorough consideration and discussion with others. Topics of this sort of separate, focused research might include:

- *school pupils*, including their general experiences of lessons and school life generally through 'tracking' and interviewing pupils or classes, the experiences of particular subgroups of pupil, such as those with special needs, including high ability;
- *school provision for pastoral care and careers guidance*, including pastoral team arrangements and management, discussions with staff involved in counselling and pastoral work, form and tutorial and form period work if not already covered under the previous heading of teaching;
- *curriculum planning* at school and departmental levels, including *assessment* and *examination* arrangements, in liaison with relevant role-holders;
- *staff development and in-service training* arrangements and opportunities, including induction and appraisal;

- *school–community links,* including parental involvement and consultation arrangements, links with LEA, community groups, work experience programmes;
- *management and governing body* issues, including policies such as equal opportunities, finance issues at departmental and school level.

Reading and other inputs on aspects of teaching and its background context
Virtually all aspects of teaching can be explored by *reading* written material and research publications and informed through inputs such as *lectures* and *talks.* Topics which appear likely to need planned coverage in this way include:

- *pedagogy* and underlying aspects of teaching, including philosophical analyses of educational aims and assumptions; current insights into learning and teaching; pupil differences and development including special needs; trends in subject teaching; aspects of pastoral care and counselling; pupil welfare including forms of and response to abuse;
- broader *social and political* considerations relating to education, such as historical background and current issues about state educational policy on such topics as the national curriculum and testing, and professionalism for teachers;
- the ever-changing *legal and financial framework* of teaching in schools and colleges.

Organized discussion and tutorial work
The above sorts of activity and provision do need following up with discussion involving mentors at least some of the time. Formally programmed tutorials and seminars therefore appear a necessary part of all teacher preparation. The obvious pitfall to avoid is the traditional separation of this exploration of basic ideas from practical concerns. The advent of school-based arrangements appears to offer considerable advantage here, in that it should be possible to relate consideration of basic matters to the experiences of student-teachers in a particular school, as opposed to their relatively isolated treatment in traditional college-based courses. On the other hand, school-based partnership schemes might actually exacerbate this split, for instance by having such discussions in a higher education institution part of a partnership scheme and staffed by its personnel, but the 'real practicalities' of classroom mentoring being done by schoolteachers at the school end.

The obvious implication is clearly to think very carefully in setting up such schemes about ways in which such perceived separations may be countered and integration encouraged. It would appear highly desirable, for example, to involve school-based mentors in the college end of things and probably also to hold seminars in school, in which both college and school staff participate. Given the separate traditions and polarizations of the past, such collaboration may perhaps pose initial teething problems, but the potential benefits appear great. The LUSSP (Leeds University Secondary School Partnership) scheme in my own school of education, for instance, seems to have got off to a particularly good start precisely through having a weekly visiting link-tutor arrangement involving tutorial groups taking place in each partnership school (more of this in Chapter 8).

Further reading

Given that this chapter has largely involved an extension of the previous one, the Chapter 2 further reading suggestions are also applicable here. For those wishing to pursue the specific topics of the present chapter, you may find it useful to consult the sources mentioned below before proceeding to the specific references given in the text and the further detail sections.

For a beautifully written and well focused introduction to issues concerning teacher thinking and professional knowledge, Sally Brown and Donald McIntyre's *Making Sense of Teaching* (1993) is well worth the effort. The collection by McIntyre *et al.* (1993) also contains introductions with very useful further references to many aspects of mentoring, of particular relevance to this chapter being the contributions by Elliott and Calderhead; Feinman-Nemser, Parker and Zeichner; Frost; Smith and Alred; McIntyre and Hagger; and Tickle. On mentoring through collaborative teaching see Burn's chapter in Wilkin (1992).

For the relevant psychological literature on skill and training, once again Gellatly (1986) and Bereiter and Scardamalia (1993) provide very readable introductions and other more advanced treatments include Chi *et al.* (1988), Colley and Beech (1989), Holding (1989), Anderson (1990) and Reason (1990). For a thorough consideration of support for teacher professional development, Bruce Joyce and Beverly Showers' *Student Achievement through Staff Development* (1988) should not be missed. Journals relevant to mentoring were indicated at the end of the previous chapter.

4

The effective facilitator: interpersonal aspects of mentoring

In the previous chapter we looked at basic aspects of reflective coaching, that is, ways of assisting student interns to acquire intelligent teaching capability through engaging with the teaching skill cycle. The focus was on the acquisition of know-how, but it was clear that this involves getting student interns to engage actively in various sorts of process. In other words, mentors have to relate to and help student-teachers as persons and to influence their actions, which means engaging with their values, motives and feelings. These interpersonal aspects are nowadays often referred to as the counselling aspects of mentoring, with good reason, though I shall also suggest that this may carry some assumptions which need some adjustment.

In this chapter I want to concentrate on these aspects of mentoring. This means in the first place considering perspectives on what it means to talk of mentoring as a form of interpersonal skill. It then also means examining the basic functions and strategies involved in promoting students' motivation and commitment to reflective learning and in combating the stresses that this can evoke.

The chapter therefore starts by considering views on helping as a potentially skilful type of activity, as something which may be attempted in systematic ways and whose strategies may be usefully analysed and reflectively applied. This will call up previous material on the nature of skill and the functions of coaching. We will then look at some basic aspects of dealing skilfully with people, including issues of motivation and stress, and will link these to what have been termed the 'core conditions' for effective counselling. I shall hope to show that much of this material has relevance not only for the ways mentors relate to student interns, but also for mentors' own coping and development.

Mentoring as interpersonal skill

Helping as a form of skill

'Getting on with people', helping them and working with them are activities that people (perhaps especially the British) have traditionally tended to take for granted. They haven't typically been seen as activities one has to think about or plan for systematically. In fact, attempts to approach them in a deliberate fashion are sometimes called unnatural, unwise, even foolhardy, and one may be seen as scheming or told 'you're dealing with people, not machines'. Even teachers and teacher-educators who are happy to talk about the pros and cons of different strategies and styles of teaching are sometimes found to resist an analytical approach when it comes to the 'personal side' of teaching. Personality and personability are assumed, even more often than the knack of teaching, to be qualities one either has or hasn't got, not something one can decide to get or learn.

Perhaps this stance can be traced back to the fragmented, dualist view of skill inherent in much everyday talk, to which I referred in Chapter 2. On the other hand, it's also to some extent consistent with the more developed recent views we saw in the same chapter. Namely, interacting with people is something we do from birth, starting with our parents and caregivers. Whilst even the very early interchanges between mothers and babies have been shown to involve systematic features such as turn-taking, reacting differentially to different voice tones, and so on, these ways of going about social contact and the purposes they fulfil tend to have become almost totally intuitive. We've been doing them, and thus automatizing them, since our earliest days, and much of what we've learned to do and attend to has itself been picked up implicitly. Little wonder, then, that social interactions seem so natural and apparently unlearned. This doesn't stop such actions being purposeful and strategic, however, even if their early acquisition and present intuitiveness make this hard to see; that's exactly how very well established skill always tends to look.

In keeping with what we've so far seen about the nature of skill, therefore, I would want to say that helping people is another case of a very open sort of skill. People vary in how good they are at it. It is purposeful, though its goals are often difficult to discern. In fact, it's part of the concept of helping that the helper targets their efforts towards the realization of the helped person's goals and this is usually through assisting their action rather than 'doing it for them'. Thus effective helping is not likely to admit of simply trainable, sure-fire procedures because the demands vary so much. As well as occurring informally, however, it can be attempted in more systematic ways and in this sense, there are indeed many 'helping professions'. Finally, relating to and trying to help other people does appear to be something in which well-grounded understanding and experience can yield strategies for doing so more effectively and in which reflective practice tends to help one improve. There seems to be no reason why this shouldn't also be true of the inevitable interpersonal aspects of mentoring, which certainly qualifies as a helping activity with the potential to be done more or less skilfully.

Counselling approaches

The last few decades have witnessed massive expansion and development of systematic, strategic approaches within what are known as the *helping or person-oriented professions*. These ideas and approaches came originally from *counselling psychology*, itself an area that has undergone considerable developments (see Further detail section 4.1). They have in fact already had considerable impact on various areas of education, originally in career advice and pastoral care, then in management and staff development, and more recently in teacher appraisal and to some extent in class management. So they're likely to have relevance and certainly ought to be considered with respect to mentoring.

The major concern of these approaches has tended to lie with the alleviation of psychological problems, that is problems with behaviour and feelings. Following their founder, Carl Rogers, the psychological assumptions adopted by counselling approaches tend to be that people generally have positive motives and ability to control their own action, but that they may not behave that way, particularly when they're anxious and stressed. To counter this, the non-directive counselling tradition has emphasized the provision of three *'core conditions'* by anyone who would help someone get to grips with personal problems. These are:

- an *accepting stance*, in which one doesn't make one's assistance conditional on the other person behaving in any particular way and one certainly doesn't moralize or prescribe;
- *sensitivity* to the feelings and experiences of the person being helped and the communication of this sensitive awareness or *empathy*;
- *genuineness*: without imposing their values on the other person, the counsellor may express their own feelings.

It's worth recognizing that there can be considerable tension between these three aspects, but I will leave dealing with this until the more practical and detailed focus of a later chapter. In the last few decades the counselling field has become very eclectic, drawing on a range of different types of psychological approach. A major development has been the systematic approach to 'skilled helping' developed by Gerard Egan in the United States, which involves three stages:

Further detail section 4.1
Developing perspectives in counselling and the helping professions

The historical origins of counselling approaches lie in the period between the two world wars, in the USA, when Freud's theories dominated psychotherapy. Growing reaction arose against the Freudian idea of unconscious mental forces blindly driving human behaviour and its requirement that people's psychological problems needed lengthy unravelling by trained experts (i.e. Freudian psychoanalysis).

In the face of this and the other dominant theory of the time, behaviourism (see p. 125), a group of American psychologists including George Kelly, Abraham Maslow and Carl Rogers developed what they termed a *humanistic psychology*, insisting that human beings are in charge of their own destiny to a considerable extent and that at their deepest level, human motives are positive (see Medcof and Roth 1979).

Rogers is known as the founding father of psychological counselling in that he sought to replace the Freudian model with a *person-centred* or *non-directive* approach, whose essence was one of *facilitation*. The counsellor should be helping their client find their own solutions to their own problems, rather than telling or directing them. In this early stage, therefore, counselling was contrasted with advising. In due course the research of Rogerian psychologists revealed just how difficult it is to be totally non-directive and ideas moved on somewhat. One of the persisting emphases, however, is on what Rogers termed the core conditions of counselling, which came out of early research on effectiveness in psychotherapy and which well express the humanistic stance. These were:

1 *Acceptance* or 'unconditional positive regard', a stance in which one maximizes client commitment and participation through not imposing any conditions to be met by them. One stays 'neutrally warm' towards them. This has to be understood and deployed in combination with the other two conditions.

2 *Accurate empathy*, the ability to gain a sense of how things appear and feel to the other person and to communicate this to them. One lays aside for the moment the views and values one holds for oneself, as Rogers put it, in order to enter another's world. This fitted with his *phenomenological* stance that what matters to a person is the way *they* perceive things, not necessarily the way things actually are (which also accords with the constructive nature of human awareness noted in Further discussion section 3.2).

3 *Genuineness*, also called *authenticity* or *congruence* (between one's values and actions). A counsellor may have certain relevant feelings,

in which case they may express those feelings, but as feelings. If one has a problem with the client's behaviour or stance, for instance, then rather than condemning the client or prescribing what they should do (a condition-setting approach), one may express oneself authentically and say, literally, that one has a problem or negative feeling about what the client is doing. The extent to which this sort of expression has in fact become part of everyday vocabulary is perhaps indicative of the widespread influence counselling ideas have now achieved in English-speaking culture.

These core conditions are important and general enough in their relevance to mentoring for me to return to them further in the main text. Meanwhile, the developments that followed Rogers brought other psychological perspectives into counselling (cf. Nelson-Jones 1982), so that his non-directive approach is now one amongst many, though for a great many practitioners, it continues to be central.

Egan's model of skilled helping

A good illustration of a development which has had widespread recognition and application in recent years is Gerard Egan's work (Egan 1990). This 'systematic approach to effective helping' presents a 'three-stage problem-management model', as follows:

1 *helping the client to identify the problems and possibilities of their present situation*, which tends to involve subaspects of 'helping clients tell their stories', finding focuses and aspects they can do something about, helping them understand the nature of situations and their reactions and feelings, identifying and challenging blind spots and unfortunate assumptions. It next proceeds to:
2 *helping them to construct new scenarios and to set goals* to which they can commit themselves, including the creation of viable agendas of action. And then to:
3 *Helping clients select and implement strategies for action*, including brainstorming and choosing strategies, and turning strategies into a plan.

Egan's work seems to me a good example of a practical, but reflective approach, in that he has retained his basic framework, but refined and amended particular strategies and tactics over the years in the different editions of his book. In his latest (1990), for instance, he particularly emphasizes the general point that he is offering principles, not formulas and that skilled helpers need a variety of insights which can come from many sources. Helping, (like teaching and mentoring), he points out, is generally dependent on the interaction between helper and client. What helpers need to bring to the situation is as much open-mindedness and flexible strategy as possible. Coming from a somewhat different background, then, Egan's message is strongly consistent with what I was suggesting about reflective coaching in the previous chapter. In other words, the reflective coach also needs to be an effective facilitator.

- helping the client to *identify the problems* and possibilities of their present situation;
- helping them to *construct new scenarios and set workable goals;*
- helping clients *select and implement strategies* for action, including brainstorming and choosing strategies, and turning strategies into a plan.

There are obvious similarities between this and the reflective coaching functions I derived in the last chapter from the systems view of skilled action. In both cases there's the idea of progression through a series of phases. They also share the idea of embedded subskills and strategies within broader functions, although they use slightly different terminologies. It might therefore seem relatively straightforward to map some of the insights and suggestions of counselling approaches into the coaching aspects of mentoring. However, I do not see it as adequate simply to 'bolt on' these counselling ideas into student-teacher mentoring, partly because there are also other ideas which appear powerful and relevant and partly because whilst mentoring overlaps considerably with counselling, they aren't actually quite the same.

Mentoring is more than just counselling

Whilst mentoring may include counselling aspects, in some ways it involves more, or at least a somewhat different emphasis. The focus in the helping/counselling tradition has tended to be strongly *client-centred*, in so far as *the person being assisted* (*not* the counsellor) is themselves seen as the source and arbiter of purpose and direction. The counsellor has tended traditionally to be seen *only* as a facilitator of self-development based on the client's own goals and preferences. In a word, counselling tends to be concerned with achieving client satisfaction and contentment.

However, we need to remember that by definition in mentoring, as in teaching generally, *the goals have already to some extent been set*. The goal in mentoring isn't *just* to end up with clients who feel happy and in control (though it hopefully includes this), it's also to equip them with *teaching capability*. Basic aspects of teaching and teaching competence may be contestable and teaching strategies are certainly argued about, but in school-based teacher education in the UK, for instance, we've already taken on a relatively specific set of purposes: our goal is to turn out people who are capable of teaching their subjects in British schools. Recently, in fact, the British government has attempted to spell out the nature of this capability in more detail than ever in the form of competence statements which we'll be considering in Chapter 7.

Our student-teachers are therefore not completely free to specify their own goals, nor to judge when they have achieved the capability at which they should be aiming. Nor are they likely to be able to, at least at first. As the study of skilled expertise has shown, part of being a novice in any domain involves not having a detailed awareness of its goals and therefore of one's own goals as a learner of that skill (for instance, like the jazz enthusiast who is reputed to have asked Louis Armstrong whether she, the enthusiast 'had rhythm', and was told that if you have to ask, then you don't). In more positive terms, student-teachers might be taken to have already opted for the goals of their teacher preparation course by the fact of entering it. But their grasp of these goals may not only be relatively vague and based on the outsider perspective of their own experience as pupils. It may, as indicated earlier, actually involve preconceptions that are in considerable need of amendment.

All this suggests, then, that mentoring cannot be *simply* a matter of the non-directive facilitation of student-teacher contentment. It has also to involve processes whereby students are likely to acquire effectively intelligent teaching capability.

Nevertheless, having made this point, we also need to be clear that it is not a matter of simply pitting mentoring against counselling as two distinct possibilities on the same level. Mentoring involves engaging the motivation and commitment of students towards achieving such capability and to those processes likely to be effective for their acquisition. This may require the possibility that forms of interpersonal influence sometimes need applying. Thus, mentoring and counselling are different in that one is more inclusive than the other; mentoring includes aspects of interpersonal facilitation and influence, whilst counselling does not necessarily involve the learning of capabilities.

There are also some further commonalities between them which further indicate the benefits of considering interpersonal aspects of mentoring in their own right. One is that counselling specialists have long since recognized that *pure* non-directiveness is virtually impossible in dealing with people and the area has developed over the years to include perspectives which entertain forms of direct influence. On the other hand, the skill psychology we reviewed earlier sees persons as planful and reflective decision makers generating their own action, even if it rejects the traditional rationalist view that people are always totally aware of all they think and do. This means that modern skill perspectives fit strongly with the traditions of counselling and helping when, as we've seen, they view coaching very much as a matter of facilitating student-teachers' critical examination of ideas and purposes and their reflective participation in the teaching skill cycle.

Mentoring therefore includes purposeful interpersonal dealings with student-teachers. Rather than simply bolting on counselling perspectives, however, I want to pursue the approach I announced at the outset, namely of first attempting to analyse what appear to be the basic constituent functions in interpersonal influence and working systematically with student-teachers. That is, the question is: what is always involved when working to influence persons? Having done this, I will return once again to the issue of the status of core counselling conditions in relation to basic functions in mentoring.

Basic functions in the interpersonal aspects of mentoring

When attempting to deal with other people to some purpose there appear to be three irreducible functions needing consideration. In mentoring, they pervade all dealings with student interns, whatever phase of the skill cycle the mentor is focusing on and whatever type of mentoring strategy they're employing. Because we need to check these aspects in the planning and carrying out of mentoring activities, it may be useful to refer to them via a mnemonic formed from their initial letters – DAM:

- *Defining/doing:* how are we shaping the situation, what are we doing to influence the course of events?
- *Active awareness:* how are we tracking and understanding what's going on?
- *Motivating:* how are the other person's motives and feelings being affected, so that they engage themselves in the action with more or less commitment?

These three functions appear to be involved in what goes on in any purposeful interpersonal activity such as mentoring, and like most areas of skill, they involve subaspects and background ideas. In looking at them a little more closely, however, I'm going to reverse the above order and devote major attention to the motivation and feelings side of mentoring, since these are what the defining/doing and active awareness functions are largely geared towards.

(1) Motivating

The force of habit
Just as we saw in Chapter 2 that everyday views of skill may need some revision, so also this may apply to everyday theories of why people do things. Just as common sense tends to overplay the role of conscious

deliberation in bringing about action, so it also tends to assume that such deliberation is in the service of satisfying consciously held motives and values. In fact, this assumption that every action has its motive or reason is built into the very word we use in connection with the regulation of behaviour, namely *motivation*.

However, as has been pointed out, everyday life isn't in fact characterized by conscious decisions at every instant. In turn, not all human actions are directly driven by intended values or motives, still less by explicit ones. An apparently large proportion of our actions are intuitive and habitual. Sometimes we may be tacitly seeking particular goals, but there are also indications that particular behaviours can be just a matter of automatic response to events and contexts. In such cases, when a whole action unit gets switched on, one might say that skill has become habit.

The point in the present context is that if the automatized aspects of student-teacher action can have such power, then in getting them to do things that will help their teaching skill acquisition, we need not only engage their motives and values, but also harness their habits and assumptions. I want to return to this below under the 'D' function of the DAM trio, defining/doing, but given that this aspect seems to be neglected both by common sense and by the freedom emphasis of the counselling movement, I thought it worth highlighting at the outset of this section. However, this is far from denying the importance of motives and values as such, so let us look at these now.

The power of motives and values
Our wants and needs clearly play an important role, not only in our conscious decisions, but also in unconsciously guiding reactions and governing feelings. There are a variety of sides to such motives and it's probably important to keep sight of all of them. In whatever terms one does see human motives, it's clear that in any interpersonal activity in which human participation is an aim, *engaging the motives* of those concerned is vital. This is relevant to the interpersonal aspects of mentoring, where it seems important to keep at least the following points in mind.

Student interns' values and motives are likely to be many and wide-ranging, with differing emphases and priorities within different individuals. To harness their commitment, it's important to take account of each intern's concerns and priorities. An influential general theory of human motives (that of Abraham Maslow) contends that some human motives are more basic than others in that people tend to require some needs to be satisfied before they'll be motivated to pursue others. According to Maslow, physical needs and security are in this sense more basic than attaining acceptance by other people, and in turn, gaining this sense of belonging is the condition to be fulfilled before people will try for achievements that gain particular respect and esteem. The person who is secure in this sense may go on to venture something new and original.

Maslow's particular hierarchy may not apply identically to every student intern, moreover people can have quite different preferences and motives, but they do tend to have priorities amongst their values and concerns. Taking account of interns as persons therefore means not only seeing what capacities they bring, as I emphasized earlier, but also taking seriously the particular concerns and value priorities they have, consciously or unconsciously, in relation to teaching and all that learning to teach may involve.

Interns' motives and feelings have to be understood in the context of their perspectives and assumptions, particularly about pupils and teaching. It may be the assumptions rather than their motives as such that need amending. People's values depend on their assumptions, in that what they 'go for' depends on what they assume possible. So when they appear to have unfortunate preferences and goals, it may be their assumptions that need attention. For example, not a few beginning teachers wish to be 'pally' with pupils, some of them because they assume (and don't perhaps even realize they assume) that this will simply liberate a benign Utopia in the classroom. Others strive for an impossible degree of complete control and tightness, because they appear to assume that pupils have nothing positive within them that can be harnessed. In both of these sorts of cases it's probably more a matter of showing the student-teacher that something different is more realistic, rather than just attempting to dissuade them from their stance. This is another reason why thorough discussion of background features is important in school-based provision.

Experiencing the immediate and intrinsic values of significance and interest in the activities they undertake in learning teaching is important for enhancing interns' commitment and effort. Most of us tend to do what we're told by those we take to be capable people charged with assisting us, even when the only payoff seems to be well beyond the present activity. This tends to apply to student-teachers too, but what makes things more interesting and engages their intrinsic commitment is:

- when they see an activity as *significant and relevant* in relation to their particular motives (which means that mentors may need to draw out relevant connections and meaning for student-interns),
- when they experience some degree of *success* in achieving what they see as significant goals (which may require various forms of assistance by mentors), and
- when they experience a medium degree of *novelty and uncertainty*. Providing these isn't perhaps likely to be as much a problem as assisting success in the case of student-teachers learning to teach. On the other hand, one can easily have too much novelty and uncertainty, since they can also produce stress.

Motives related to interns' sense of security and self-esteem tend to be centrally important for their full participation and need to be catered for. The Rogerian counselling tradition adds to this the point that in social situations of the sort student interns will find themselves encountering (amongst the most important being classrooms and staffrooms), their own feelings of security regarding their self-esteem and reputation as capable beginning teachers are likely to be very sensitive. Like all of us, interns want to feel and to appear *competent, consistent* and *in control.* Mentors therefore need to be alert to the degree of threat students may feel on particular occasions regarding these values and to judge the likelihood of success or otherwise so as to provide appropriate assistance when needed.

The nature of stressors and stress
Psychological stress and distress are internal states which are influenced by the same factors that produce curiosity, interest and commitment; they appear to do so through the mechanism of nervous system arousal. It's not a question of the more the better or the more the worse. Too little stress is distressing in that it makes for boredom, even depression. Too much produces the distress of anxiety and a feeling of being overwhelmed, with various likely reactions as well as possibilities for coping. Intermediate levels of stress tend to be found comfortable, even stimulating, though the relevant level will vary according to the temperament of the individual. Three basic sorts of factor combine to act as *stressors* affecting *stress level* and comfort in this way: the involvement of significant values, the degree of novelty and uncertainty experienced, and the intensity and complexity of task demands.

- *What's at stake: the significance of potential costs and benefits* – The values and potential payoffs in an activity raise the stakes, particularly when they're the sorts of student-teacher fears mentioned above. The stronger the motive or value involved, the higher the stakes and the emotional arousal. Here the way the student-intern *perceives and reacts* to the situation is particularly important. This in turn may depend on their general anxiety dispositions and the coping reactions they've evolved over their lifetimes, but also on their underlying assumptions and 'theories-in-action' concerning teaching and what's expected of them, which may need amending (e.g. their perceived need to perform perfectly from the outset).
- *Degree of novelty and uncertainty* – The more novelty and uncertainty facing a person in a task, the more arousing. By definition, student interns tend to be novices to teaching, so they're faced with relatively more novelty and uncertainty from what is anyway one of the most open and unpredictable types of human activity. Indeed, many teachers can still remember the feelings of apprehension or stronger from their earliest teaching days, though in various ways, some may have forgotten it (it may be the subject of *denial* – see below). Although school-based arrangements allow considerable scope to alleviate this sort of stress and make for more gradual

and supported phasing of demand, mentors need not to lose sight of the likelihood that a good many student-teachers will experience considerable degrees of stress in the face of their particular uncertainties, especially at the outset.

* *Intensity of physical input and complexity of task demand* – The complexity of a task and the sheer physical intensity of what impinges on a person act in a similar way to produce arousal. Clearly, then, large, boisterous and noisy classes make for more difficulty and stress, but experienced teachers can easily underestimate both the complexity and the novelty even of reduced teaching activities.

These types of stressor tend to act in combination in the sorts of situation student-teachers will face. Thus, for instance, the typical student-teacher is highly concerned to succeed in terms of their own planned goals, but also in the eyes of their mentor and the pupils, before whom they don't want to 'look daft'. As well as these intrinsic values in the immediate situation, there are extrinsic ones to which present success is instrumental, like eventually getting a job. But as novices they are by definition under considerable uncertainty about what to aim at and how to go about things, having particular worries about the control aspects of teaching and whether pupils will accept their authority. Moreover, when they get into the actual teaching situation, they will experience its complexity of demand with particular acuteness, particularly where their own preconception of a simple, natural set of processes has not as yet been brought out and examined.

Traditional 'block teaching practice' arrangements have if anything tended to exacerbate the combination of these stressors, but by contrast, the forms of school-based provision proposed in the last chapter, in particular progressively collaborative teaching, offer the potential for considerable improvements in this respect.

Effects of stress

Whilst it's possible to have too little stress for comfort and effectiveness, it's much more likely that student interns will experience being over-stressed by the above sorts of stressors involved in their early experiences in teaching. This sort of stress experience tends to have various types of effect and to elicit certain kinds of related reaction. These include:

* *negative feelings* of varying strength, usually including anxiety, from which they will wish to escape (traditionally termed 'distress').
* *restriction in capacity to deal with information*, making them neglect aspects in the situation, miss parts of the message, have 'tunnel vision', think in simplistic terms, jump to conclusions.
* *energizing of well-established responses*, often done relatively automatically. Under stress interns may find themselves *impulsively regressing* to precisely those limited teaching tactics they thought they'd now replaced

with more effective ones (e.g. shouting where they'd vowed never to), an effect probably also involving the above information-processing restriction.

Reactions to stress: coping versus defending
The best response to a stressful situation is to avoid the above types of reaction and *cope* objectively, strategically and with suitable energy levels for that individual, but the response that so often occurs is to *defend* in ways that are actually extensions of the above sorts of reactions, versions of *fight* or *flight*. Such reactions may make sense as short term removers of nasty feelings, but they tend to deal only with the symptoms and not alter the causes of the stress, which is why they actually tend to get people into vicious circles of further pressure.

Worse still, people may have become relatively skilled and habitual at deploying these forms of defence *intuitively* and *without realizing it*, and may actually be adopting *initial stances* that are defensive from the outset, making them more fearful and reticent in the first place and priming them ever more strongly towards defensive reaction. Student-teachers are no exception to this possibility, so mentors need to consider the typical forms of defensive reaction, including:

- *Impulsive or unreflective action:* these are often an outgrowth of the response triggered by sheer arousal and by the restrictive, tunnel vision-like effects it also has on conscious thinking. A typical reaction is to 'Do something – anything!' but actually it's likely, as indicated, to be some well practised action, like withdrawal or getting angry. In more introvert personalities, the reaction may be more one of withdrawal. An extended version which combines both withdrawal and doing something is *busy-ness*: keeping the negative feelings and frustrations at bay through engagement in something easier and more habitual.
- *Selective ignoral:* this can include self-serving *distortions* in the perception or memory of what is being raised and even, in extreme cases, total *denial* ('I didn't actually hit him'), but perhaps more often *normalizing*: 'Oh yes, I did notice that' (so there's no need to discuss it).
- *Deflection and selective attention:* possibly combined with the above, *deflecting* focuses attention away from the centre of perceived stress on to other things the person is happier to deal with (as in the above example of busy-ness). Other more conversational versions of this may include *contrasting* ('It would never happen with 8A, you know'), *reminiscing* ('Do you remember how much worse it was with 9B two years ago?'), or *fantasizing* ('Of course we could easily avoid that sort of problem if we had . . .'). Detailed tactics for countering such defences will be dealt with in Chapter 8 (a case of defensive *procrastinating* on my behalf?).
- *Reinterpretation and defensive attribution:* here the actual events may be recognized, but reinterpreted in selectively defensive ways, including the

self-favouring *attributional bias* ('They have failed to learn' whereas 'I have succeeded in teaching them', rather like 'He is bloody-minded' as opposed to 'I have independent judgement'), *disowning* the event ('It wasn't actually my fault'), generally *rationalising*: finding a plausible (but invalid) reason or excuse ('That kid was really angry, so I was forced to shout very loud at him'), which may also include *projecting* one's own negative feelings and causes on to others ('That kid was really angry' as opposed to 'I was angry at that kid').

In all of the above motivational aspects one can, as usual with human beings, expect considerable individual differences amongst student-teachers. At the specific end, the particular concerns that individuals can have will easily match the uniqueness of the particular 'bees in the bonnet' teacher-mentors may have experienced amongst school pupils. At the general level, as with pupils, one may expect systematic variations in stressor susceptibility and coping style, for instance as between student-teachers with more introvert personalities (more likely to go for self-blaming, worry or withdrawal) and extrovert personalities (overt reactivity, action rather than withdrawal, fight rather than flight).

These motivational aspects of interpersonal skill (including stress and its effects) therefore need bearing in mind when thinking about systematic strategies for an activity like mentoring. What we monitor and what we do in the situation has partly to be geared towards student interns' motives and values, and their likely reactions. This is so that mentors can as far as possible harness that motivation, in addition to making the whole student experience as positive as possible. However, this material doesn't just apply to students, it also applies to teacher-mentors, especially in so far as they're new to the role.

All of this also applies to mentors
Teachers too are human beings with values, goals and feelings, including needs to protect their self-esteem and reputation. This will be particularly in evidence as they take on new mentoring roles, which are likely to offer their own challenges and stresses of the kinds listed above, but corresponding to the particular situation of new teacher-mentors. These will, for instance, face new demands and tasks requiring the development of somewhat new skills (though I have already argued that there are also some basic communalities between teaching school pupils and mentoring student interns which can probably be transferred from the former to the latter without very much adjustment). Insights into the nature of human skill and its acquisition will therefore hopefully form a sound basis not only for teacher-mentors to assist interns, but also for their own intelligent efforts to be informed by realistic expectations, rather than over or underoptimistic ones. In this teacher-mentors may need to review their existing assumptions and concepts. I offer the following for consideration.

Mentoring may appear daunting, but actually it's a challenge with considerable benefits. New teacher-mentors should realize that the novelty and signifi- cance of the task of helping student-teachers with something one has long taken for granted may make their role feel particularly daunting and deskilling, and may therefore provoke various defence reactions from them. This isn't surprising, but nor is it actually so problematic as it might at first seem. Actually mentoring is full of positive potential for teacher-mentors' own interest and fulfilment, but only if approached open-mindedly and thoughtfully.

Analysing and communicating teaching strategy is a different skill from deploy- ing it in practice. As was mentioned very early in Chapter 2, the understand- ing and know-how that constitute skills tend to be much more specific than our cultural traditions assume. Carrying out something is one kind of skill, for instance, talking sensibly about it is another.

The mistaken dualist assumption that action is always guided by con- scious thinking would have teachers assuming that as mentors all they have to do now is reveal to interns the conscious thinking that's been guid- ing their teaching activities. However, they may anticipate or actually find that this is difficult, since as we've seen, modern insights into skill would suggest that experienced practitioners tend to become intuitive at their ac- tivities. Nevertheless, if teachers experiencing this difficulty of articulation were to interpret it on the traditional dualist view, they could be pushed towards thinking they hadn't actually known what they had been doing as teachers ('perceived threat to self-esteem', I hear you murmur). Now they're going to be found out when student-teachers ask them for whys and where- fores ('anxiety concerning social reputation', you diagnose). Before they know it, they may find themselves deploying the defences: possibly some good old-fashioned *denial* mixed with *magical attribution* ('This theory stuff is irrelevant, just tell' 'em what to do'); perhaps a bit of *busy-ness* mixed with *deflection* ('The main thing is to plan what they'll be doing on the morning of day 58 – I'm doing the worksheets now'), a little *contrasting* ('It's never been done that well before anyway'), perhaps some *rationalization* ('Being thrown in the deep end never did *me* any harm'). Such reactions are not unknown (to me, anyway).

In fact, the traditional dualist view is also too rationalistic, though to the extent that professional teaching capability *is* deployed reflectively, which as a very open type of skill it probably needs to be, we might expect teach- ers to be capable of explaining their teaching insights to students. However, the modern insight is that expert capability actually tends to involve much intuition, so that being good at something may in many ways makes it *more difficult* to articulate and discourse about how one does it. Realizing this takes new teacher-mentors off the 'false hook' of rationalism, but does pose them with another challenge. Namely, it faces them with the task of ex- ploring their own intuitive action and its rationales. This too can appear daunting to a profession that has never enjoyed the time and encouragement to be reflective and whose experience of training under traditional arrangements has if anything probably encouraged an 'anti-analytic' stance.

Articulating teaching skill is different from deploying it directly, but teacher-mentors are likely to have the resources within them. Systematic capability *has* to be informed by know-how otherwise it wouldn't be reliable and systematic capability, which means that teachers have in some sense the wherewithal within them. No one knows everything or has perfect teaching skill, but it's likely that even someone with two or three years of reflective teaching experience – let alone ten or more – has far more stored up by way of know-how than they realize. In so far as this has become intuitive, new mentors will now experience conscious uncertainty when trying to make it explicit. However, 'bringing it out' isn't just a matter of waiting till the right words come (we almost certainly don't store most of it verbally anyway). It tends to require us to:

• *Think about specific teaching situations*, whether our own or those of our interns.
• *Allow our responses to emerge naturally and intuitively;* ask ourself 'what would be my way of dealing with this?' Our responses are not going to be random, but will tend to arise out of our stored know-how.
• Nevertheless, *monitor and check* these inclinations and their rationales consciously before offering them for student interns' consideration.
• Remember that in something like teaching, even though we may have strong dispositions and preferred strategies, it's seldom a matter of telling them the one right way, but mostly a question of *offering them a potential strategy and its rationale* to add to their repertoire. The rationale aspect is important, both in terms of promoting student reflectiveness and by way of establishing one's own credibility (but more of this in Chapter 8).

Put simply, then, teacher mentors are not going to get by without thinking explicitly about teaching and this may pose initial challenges, but they do have considerable resources within them on which to build. In doing all this, mentors also need to realize that:

Thinking explicitly and reflectively about teaching is likely to be both interesting and useful, but one needs to guard against deskilling possibilities. Teacher-mentors in UK school-based partnership schemes for Articled Teacher typically wax lyrical about the effects of their mentoring activities. They often report them as having rekindled their interest in and commitment to teaching by reminding them of why they originally became teachers. Indeed, just as one really only gets to understand something when one teaches it, so analysing and talking about teaching with interns is a golden, natural opportunity to deepen our own teaching sensitivity and skill. But we have to be alert to the possibility of *deskilling* ourselves. One familiar form of this is when we try to perform consciously and deliberately actions and subskills that have become more or less automatized and intuitive through experience, like the centipede who tripped over when he thought about the action of his fifty-fourth leg, There are two basic dangers here, which can both be combated.

- We may *actually disrupt our existing artistry*, like the centipede. This may apply to our own teaching, when we start to examine it and perhaps decide to amend aspects we suspect we've been wrongly taking for granted. A well worn precaution here is to change only small aspects at a time, though this is sometimes difficult, depending on the extent of the intended revision. We should remember, anyway, that we still have our old strategies to fall back on, in that they had at least seemed to work until now.

  With respect to teachers acquiring new mentoring capability, the same principles apply here as to student-interns (except that it's actually much easier for the mentors), in that teachers bring existing capabilities which transfer positively into mentoring. Teacher-mentors will be aware that student-teachers and school-pupils differ in significant respects, but they need not assume that the differences are total. For instance, as novices, student-teachers will profit from the sort of clarity of arrangement and explanation teachers are more likely to associate with the needs of younger pupil learners. Again, application of these existing capabilities and knowledge to modest changes is intrinsically easier, it allows our other capabilities to take care of remaining matters and, anyway, we always have our previous strategy to fall back on.

- As people who have developed considerable skill at teaching, we may *expect too much of ourselves* when we try to adopt something new as a result of conscious analysis and reflection, whether it involves new teaching strategies or aspects of mentoring approach, perhaps the latter being the more important consideration in the present context. Experienced teachers have usually become used to things running relatively smoothly and intuitively, but now they're putting themselves somewhat into the position of novices and so need to realize that things may improve much more slowly than they would normally expect. Nevertheless, even here, our other existing capabilities are likely to make the learning more specific and efficient – though this too depends on how radical a change of approach is involved.

Unfortunate assumptions and defensive reactions by student interns may push mentors towards defensiveness, but clear awareness of these issues will help avoid succumbing to this and the vicious circle it brings. Above I suggested that mistaken assumptions about skill and the new challenges of mentoring are particularly likely to evoke defensive reactions in new teacher-mentors. However, this isn't the only source of such a possibility. When students take on such defensiveness, to some extent they thereby tend to pressure mentors towards the same unrealistic quick fixes and surface dealings they're scrambling for, and towards a similar defensiveness in the face of such pressure. Ultimately, mentors' best basis for resisting this and the vicious circle it's likely to bring is a firm understanding of precisely these issues. As with all human resources, of course, this understanding will only become useful and reliable to the extent that it is developed, deployed and tested in practice. At the outset, then, the present set of considerations are therefore important to bear in mind.

Having given motivation and feelings considerable attention both as regards students and mentors, I now want to return to the other main functions in the interpersonal aspect of mentoring. The second such basic function is active awareness.

(2) Active awareness

In the previous section we have been considering the motives, feelings and reactions that may be involved in any interpersonal dealings between humans and certainly those between mentors and student-teachers. If catering for these motives and feelings is a central function in systematic helping activities like mentoring, then another major function must be keeping aware of them in practice. An essential subskill within any overall skill is always *reading the situation*.

Awareness as a form of skill
It may seem strange to talk of awareness as a form of skill, because common sense in western culture tends to assume that awareness is something passive, it just happens to us, whereas by contrast, skill means doing something. This receptive aspect of perception is only part of the story, however. Modern psychological experimentation (not to speak of other disciplines from physiology to philosophy) confirm that human awareness and perception are to some extent *actively constructive* and do have basic features of skilfulness (see also Further detail section 3.1).

What this means is that what we pick up from our surroundings depends not just on what's available there, but also on what *we* contribute. This is because:

- *Our awareness is limited and therefore selective* – Our senses and memory can't take everything in at once, they can only manage to register a small portion of the available data. At an *unconscious* and 'out-of-the-corner-of-the-eye' level, this can still be quite a bit of information. However, we can deal *consciously* with only one thing at a time (though that may itself be complex: one sentence, one word, one letter, etc.) and then only at a finite speed.
- *We help to actively construct the elements of our picture* – What we perceive is partly dependent on our existing concepts and knowledge. We don't

attend to every aspect of the world around us, because as indicated, we wouldn't have time anyway. Rather we use the key bits as signs to indicate the whole: something red and round is the bowl of cherries we're seeking until closer inspection reveals otherwise. As Anne Brown puts it, we *'headfit'* the world into our existing pigeonholes: we assimilate and interpret it in our terms and this goes on *largely unconsciously* within the inaccessible processes of vision, hearing, and other forms of awareness (Brown *et al.* 1983).

If this is true of our awareness of the physical world, then it's if anything even more relevant when it comes to our perception of people. We tell a lot from a smile and read a face without thinking much about it or often even realizing what signs we're using, but this is still essentially going beyond the information given on the physical surface. However, our perception and awareness are skilful not only because they're something we *do* in this way, but also in that they develop with experience.

• *We learn what and how to perceive* – We've probably all had the experience of being in a familiar setting, like a street in our town, and becoming aware of a feature we hadn't noticed in all the years we'd been visiting the scene. Such accidental forms of *perceptual learning* need to be made deliberate when we set out to become capably skilled; we need to learn what to look for. Given that much of what we are interested in (such as motives and feelings) isn't on the surface, we need to find ways of becoming aware of the signs and reading them. As indicated in Chapter 3, this is an area where even the average person brings a host of existing social skills which are usually so intuitive they're not even thought of as a learned capability. However, as fulfillers of a systematic role and function, like student-teachers, new mentors may need to extend their capacities actively and strategically to gain relevant awareness. Like any skill, repeated reflective practice is the great teacher.

Strategies for active awareness
Having argued that interpersonal awareness requires active commitment, what are its possible forms and strategies? We can distinguish between two relatively broad forms of active awareness, *direct or immediate awareness* and *strategic and indirect eliciting of information*, each with their more detailed subcomponents.

Direct or immediate awareness tends to take the major forms of:

• *Listening* – It sounds rather obvious to say that mentors should listen carefully to their student-teachers, but human perception does tend to be selective, people become skilfully economical at picking up only a minimum of what's said; *our* self is the interesting thing for *us*, the other person can seem boring if not an actual pain (and mentors are certainly going to come across that problem). So we hear the easily noticed bits and unconsciously fill in the gaps with our own interpretations and agenda. In the face of this, then, it's worth emphasizing that *effective listening* needs to be more thorough and open-minded, giving *time, opportunity* and *encouragement* for the person's actual message to get through.

In particular, there's a need to listen out for *verbal* and *non-verbal signs and indicators of mood and reaction*: *what* student-teachers say, but also which particular words they use that may emphasize personal investment and involvement; and *how* they say it: voice tone, firmness/tremor, volume and so on.

- *Looking* – However obvious, it bears repeating too that visual awareness can also be particularly important in reading people's reactions and stances. Non-verbal indications such as facial expression and posture are of known importance, though their global nature means that here too we need to be particularly careful not to read things in too readily. This latter point is especially important to remember in view of the indications that non-verbal awareness tends to be firmly and unconsciously embedded within our intuitive reactions to people from a very early age.

- *Integrating the information* – Much of what's just been said amounts to the recommendation that as mentors we need to put together as much of the information as time will allow. To the extent that time and opportunity are limited for gaining awareness of anything, including student interns' personal states, then we need to make our conclusions correspondingly provisional and tentative. This is not something that most humans find very easy, given their long term unreflective participation in social situations, where feedback is often difficult to get and sometimes harder to interpret.

Strategic and indirect eliciting of information

The above considerations relate primarily to the nature of our listening and looking as forms of information gathering. It's also clearly the case that the way we behave towards our interns will help influence how openly they reveal their states and stances. In fact, this social influence aspect is nowadays very much seen as part of listening skill by the counselling/helping tradition. In terms of the set of basic interpersonal functions I've distinguished here, this stretches us from active awareness into the other two aspects: *motivating* student-teachers to be forthcoming and communicative through what we *do* and how we do it. To anticipate the treatment below of the third doing/defining function and the details of Chapter 8, it's clear, for instance, that whether or not interns 'give us access' to their thoughts and reactions is likely to depend very much on whether we ask them. This is another of those obvious-when-stated points, which nevertheless does quite often tend to be forgotten or omitted through being taken for granted within a group. This is perhaps particularly likely in the early days of a mentor's experience, when they may be feeling under some stress.

Thus *strategic elicitation* may include *directly* asking and exploring intern reactions, but it may also involve bothering to prompt and note *indirectly* what sorts of reaction particular suggestions and situations seem to elicit, sometimes perhaps even setting these up for the purpose. Such things as diaries may be useful forms of longer term reflection by student interns and may be useful for mentors to consult, yet often the best occasion is the informal one when they're busy at some relatively mundane activity, perhaps relatively soon after the event (like clearing up after a lesson). In such a situation they're able to also talk as they do the activity. This is of course not to deny the general need for formal reflection after lessons and at other points, but mentors need to think systematically in advance as well as opportunistically of using such occasions strategically (but obviously subtly, or the informality will disappear).

In keeping with all I've been suggesting, however, interns also *need their own space and time* to think and react for themselves, which includes the possibility of trying things out on their own and of retaining their own private reflections if they wish.

(3) Defining/doing

This third aspect of interpersonal skill is perhaps its most obvious one, given the dualist tradition of emphasizing skill as 'doing'. Here we've seen that skill, including forms of interpersonal helping like mentoring, also involves understanding and awareness of the situation, in particular of the other person being helped. We've also just seen that this reading of the situation is something we have to approach actively, it's a form of subskill in its own right. However, we now return to the more obvious action function within mentoring to consider *what sorts of activity a mentor may actually do* to influence and affect student-teacher participation and feeling.

We have of course to remember that we're dealing here with persons. It's not just that there are ethical criteria of respect for persons, their rights and needs, though we must obviously remember these. More pragmatically, it's also that we're faced with the basic question of how one gets independent human beings, in this case student interns, to do things that are sooner or later beneficial to them and their teaching capability, but whose point they may not see at present. Building on what was said above about the nature of human action and its regulation, I want to propose that it's useful to think in terms of two general forms of interpersonal influence. The first is more familiar and traditionally emphasized and the second more subtle, but potentially just as powerful. They were earlier labelled as *engaging motives* and *harnessing habits*. As so often in human matters, these functions can be distinguished, but in reality both forms intertwine all the time, shade into each other and may be strategically combined in various ways.

Engaging student-teachers' motives

In this mode the basic premise is that people have values and motives and they tend to do what they perceive will satisfy their motives. Traditionally, this rationalist viewpoint has seen people as consciously in charge of their own actions and has therefore tended to assume that once the basic 'contract' is clear (e.g. 'We're the trainers, you play your part and you'll get the competence you want'), all else will follow. In general, such traditional assumptions also seem to have favoured the power of negative sanctions and fear as powerful motivators, though teacher education contexts have probably been the more enlightened exception to this. Similarly, whilst teachers and school cultures may still use the negative sanction approach to a considerable extent, they seem unlikely to transfer such stances to the young adults they're now faced with inducting into their own profession. So what does this leave them with? Modern evidence suggests two amendments to the 'negative-rationalist' approach to influencing other peoples' actions:

- *The power of positiveness* – What people want and enjoy appears to govern their actions at least as powerfully and consistently as their fears and dislikes (though these can be very powerful in particular cases). This bears particular emphasis in the face of a British culture which, varying types of evidence suggest, has heavily favoured negative forms of control. By contrast, praising achievements, giving credit for effort, expressing appreciation and other forms of positive reaction can have considerable power to affect people's feeling and commitment. It must be admitted that the existence of a negative cultural tradition can in *some* cases get in the way of students taking such positive reactions seriously or, more likely perhaps, of mentors feeling able to express them. Nevertheless, mentors need not be dishonest or false about this, they need only remember that positive reactions do indeed tend to have positive effects and that student teachers tend to be in particular need of this form of feedback.
- *The role of association and non-rational processes* – As stated previously, by no means all our behaviour appears to be governed by conscious decisions. Behaviourist psychologists talk in terms of people simply going for what they associate with positive experience and reward, which is said to reinforce the actions it immediately follows. Others talk of unconscious wishes. Earlier we saw how deliberate actions become unconsciously intuitive and that we actually pick up more information than we can consciously deal with. We can add that the limitations of human attention and memory are such that a purely rational view of persons won't actually get us far (though it can perhaps help with our defences when we project responsibility on to others!).

Taking these points on board leads to a particular emphasis on the importance for harnessing student motivation and commitment of providing *positive experiences* by way of actively enhancing student experience of the sorts of values reviewed earlier: security, assistance, encouragement, opportunity for and celebration of successes, medium levels of novelty and variety, consultation of student intern perspective and preference. This applies whether we're talking about a student trying a major new initiative or 'just' getting them to give their point of view on something ('active listening' includes interpersonal facilitation). We need to remember, therefore, that these approaches are part of mentoring. It means that we will not tend to rely on negative motivation which acts just through excluding the undesirable, though there may be limit situations in which safety and well-being, for instance, do require boundary-setting and prohibition. More typically, rather, we'll want to accentuate and reward that which is desirable in students' action.

Harnessing their habits and assumptions
The other mode of influence links with what sociologists call *'defining the situation'* and it can also be seen to flow from what we've seen about the skilful nature of everyday action. As I've repeatedly said, everyday action isn't characterized by conscious decisions at every instant, but this can provide potential opportunity for interpersonal influence.

When people enter an everyday situation, they tend naturally to act in keeping with it, because they read the signs that *define the situation* in question. That is, they perceive what is possible, what is expected, both by way of values and ways of acting. But as we've seen, they tend to do this intuitively, and this tacit reading and anticipation of cues as to what's at stake tends equally to switch in the more or less unconscious patterns of action and subskill they've learned in such situations. So when we enter familiar situations we don't actually have to think how to behave. In a shop, for instance, we find ourselves behaving as a customer; in a church we behave 'church' rather than 'party'. This sort of thing also occurs at a more individual level too, as when a well-groomed stranger addressing us politely puts us at ease and perhaps elicits our 'telephone voice' and cooperation, or a punk outfit has us feeling uneasy before anyone opens their mouth (depending, of course, on our allegiances).

The other side of this coin is that situations may be relatively undefined, with unclear expectations. To the extent that someone is aware of this, they may strategically gear their behaviours and communication to offer signals as to the nature of what's expected, 'what it's all about'. That is, people may attempt actively to define the situation, thereby tending to get others (and themselves) to behave and function in that sort of setting. They may do this explicitly (e.g. they shout explicitly that there's a fire), but it's likely to be far more effective if they can harness any corresponding behaviour patterns that may have become habitual (i.e. intuitively assumed) for the participants in that situation, by initiating *actions* that would be normal (e.g. they reach for the fire buckets and hand them round). This may relate particularly to the beginning of an encounter, but with respect to the open-ended aspects of situations it's ongoing and dependent on the participants continuing to behave in particular ways. Thus the definition of the situation and the ensuing behaviours get 'negotiated', typically at an unconscious level, through the various 'moves' people make. Let us look more systematically at this process in the mentoring context.

• *Explicit definition and influence* involves clearly articulated messages of which participants are consciously aware; they know what is being said/asked. In a mentoring situation, one way or another, the mentor tells the student-teacher clearly. This may involve anything from *requests and recommendations* in the immediate situation to *longer term directives and guidelines*: setting the ground rules, forming a detailed plan of events over time. Explicit definition is perhaps more likely to be in a verbal form in mentoring situations, whether in written documentation or oral communications, but in an immediate context non-verbal gestures can sometimes be extraordinarily clear! As regards the likely contents of such messages, these may obviously vary considerably. But not only will mentors need to make particular arrangements, information, goals, rules and expectations clear to student-teachers, they will also need to be explicit about their own openness and approachability.

• *Implicit definition and influence* most typically involves *direct/immediate* interaction, when it tends to include *non-verbal communications* through facial expression, posture, voice tone and volume, etc. But it may also involve *implicit verbal* communications, where it's not the obvious content of what is said that counts, so much as the implications (e.g. something 'meant to be overheard' by one's target person, or a conclusion left to be drawn by the recipient). Such subtle aspects sustain the situational definition over time and may change it equally subtly.

However, implicit definitions can also include *indirect/strategic arrangements*. One can try to arrange the whole context by planning particular sequences of events or by engaging in systematic strategies, for example, of attending to and rewarding positive achievements, but ignoring negatives unless necessary.

Given our traditional assumptions about conscious decision making, it's perhaps these implicit aspects of situational definition that deserve most emphasis here. Generally speaking, the way one behaves directly in a situation sets an implicit and powerful role-invitation for others. Indeed, explicitly defining acts will still tend to have their implicit aspects. When a mentor confidently and pleasantly asks a student-teacher what pros and cons he or she sees in a planned teaching strategy, for instance, the explicit message is obvious, but there may be many implicit messages, including for example that reflectiveness and reasoned action is a good thing, that the teacher-mentor is in a position to call for and react to such rationales. Correspondingly, when a teacher-mentor volunteers such reasoning to a student-teacher witnessing their teaching, they are likely to be similarly conveying the appropriateness of reflection and the naturalness of their subsequently asking for the student's rationale, as well as their own openness and approachability.

Thus mentors' implicit definitional attempts may relate to any aspect of their role, but are perhaps particularly suited to the communicating of positive expectations and encouragement, of openness to issues and a reflective approach to one's own teaching. In other words, one behaves not just in the way one wants one's student-teachers to behave, but also in ways which are likely to elicit such styles in response.

• *Implicit and explicit situational definitions need to be consistent.* Considerable confusion and unease can result when student-teachers get conflicting messages from important reference persons such as their mentors. Although I am suggesting that mentors can deliberately attempt to project implicit aspects of situational definition, these are by their very nature prone to occur without monitoring. It therefore behoves mentors to make sure, for instance, that there is no 'non-verbal leakage' (in voice tone, facial expression, posture, etc.) of messages conflicting with what they wish to project and, in particular, with what they have conveyed explicitly. If there is, then the indications from social psychological research are that it's the implicit signals that will tend to be effective.

At this point it's also relevant to remind ourselves that one respect in which student-teachers vary is the ways they read such signals. Their backgrounds and experience, their temperaments and current moods may all combine to produce interpretations and responses different from what mentors intended or thought likely by way of effect. Even if mentors in their turn cannot be expected to be able to monitor every aspect of their action and communication, this does alert them to the need for reflectiveness and self-monitoring, especially in the early stages of adopting such a role.

There are of course *ethical issues in situational definition and influence* involved here. The person who is aware of the potential power of implicit definition may be in a position to influence, even manipulate others to some extent. Much of what's involved, for instance, in successful selling and negotiation appears to involve this type of implicit 'soft sell' technique. The issues can turn out to be pretty intricate in particular circumstances, but I would offer two general considerations.

A first notion relates to purpose. Mentors' actions ought obviously to be directed towards positive outcomes for student-teachers and their well-being during the process of achieving these outcomes. Since this process occurs over a period of months and through a variety of different experiences and settings, it's unlikely that everything can be realistically expected to always proceed on an onward and upward track. But even when a mentor feels they have to influence the student-teacher in a direction contrary to the student's immediate inclinations, in fact particularly at such points, they need to be clear that their own strategies are indeed likely to benefit the student in the longer run and not actually damage them at any point.

A second point is that although in the above sort of situation especially, mentors may wish to make things very clear and explicit so as to address students in their freedom, it is probably impossible, given the nature of human information processing, to avoid some degree of implicit definition and influence. It just does not appear possible for us to raise every possible aspect of a communication or situation to conscious awareness. Skilled, intuitive processing seems to be a basic feature of human competence. Correspondingly, since the actions and inputs of mentors will inevitably have some degree of tacit influence, we have little choice in that role but to *attempt to define the situation and influence our students in effective ways.* This does not preclude mentors from laying out clearly their general values and assumptions and their particular reasons for actions and recommendations, nor does this take away the reality of implicit processes; it just requires them to be consistent with the explicit messages. In a word, as mentors we either abdicate responsibility or try to make virtue out of necessity. For anyone who is aware of this issue, the latter is surely the only choice.

The integral nature of the three basic functions

Having separately examined these three 'DAM' functional aspects of inter-personal capability, I ought now to emphasize how intertwined they tend to be. Our ways of doing and defining will also have direct motivational impact; making a suggestion in a firm but pleasant way is itself providing a positive social experience whilst at the same time conveying that one cares and is there to help. Similarly, ways of maintaining an active aware-ness of student-teachers' feelings and progress are likely to have definitional and motivational impact. Again, moves that we make explicitly to motivate and encourage will bring us into forms of contact which yield an awareness of student perception and feeling which will tend in turn to have their own definitional impact. In fact, of course, what mentoring involves is not sepa-rate actions to fulfil these basic functions, but multi-functional strategies which combine more than one at once. That is what Chapter 8 will focus on.

Before doing that, however, the tendency of quite a few educationists nowadays to think of interpersonal aspects immediately by reference to counselling and the importance of the core counselling conditions we saw earlier make it relevant at this point to consider how these relate to the 'DAM' analysis just offered.

Core counselling conditions and 'DAM' functions

Ever since it was found that effectiveness depended more on counsellors showing certain qualities than on the particular theoretical approach they employed, counselling/helping circles have emphasized three basic aspects of what the counsellor communicates to the client. I introduced these 'core conditions' earlier in the chapter, but they're worth considering not only for their own value, but also for their relationship with the 'DAM' analysis just presented in this section. Let us examine each briefly.

Acceptance or unconditional positive regard
This is a matter of accepting another person 'warts and all', as a human being to be helped, without imposing conditions to be met for that help to be offered. One *doesn't* take the stance towards one's student that 'if you want my help you'd better be nice/stop picking your nose/pull your socks up/agree with me/do it my way', etc. Rather, we try to find out where they're starting from and in particular to see how they perceive the situation.

In terms of the DAM analysis, at base *acceptance* seems to address a combination of the *motivating and defining* aspects. One minimizes the chances of student-teacher defence and avoidance through communicating a stance that minimizes threat. This amounts to requiring mentors themselves to be as free as possible of problems and anxieties that might get in the way of the intern's effective participation, perhaps particularly mentor anxieties about challenges to their ways of working. Thus for instance, someone with a dogmatic belief in a particular teaching strategy as the only right one and whose authoritarian insecurity made them need agreement by others (particularly their 'youngers and inferiors') would hardly be likely to make a good mentor from the viewpoint of the *acceptance* aspect. Their own 'needs' and defences would be likely to compete with those of the intern.

Accurate empathy
This refers to the ability to *gain and communicate* that one is gaining *a sense of how things appear and feel to the other person*. A very important part of this is through skilful perception, 'being a good listener', which includes an awareness based on undistorted attending to what the person offers, by way of both explicit and implicit messages. One also needs to *check and communicate* this awareness, through such techniques as 'reflecting', which essentially means making clear to the person what one is picking up from them. This can of course be done more grossly (e.g. just repeating their actual words) or more subtly, but people using such strategies explicitly for the first time are often amazed at how readily they can unleash others' views and feelings (perhaps because generally speaking in our culture, we're normally so bad at listening effectively in these ways).

In DAM terms, then, accurate empathy appears to be mainly a combination of *active awareness* and *defining/doing*. The former is oriented in mentoring towards the student's perspective, whilst the defining is about establishing that this is indeed a helping relationship in which the student can feel confident in sharing their viewpoint and in particular any worries. Once more, such a message is also likely to have a reassuring *motivational* effect.

Genuineness or authenticity

Even in the counselling tradition, tension is recognized between the condition of *acceptance* and that of genuineness and honesty on the part of the counsellor. The Rogerian view, however, is that honesty shouldn't be used as an excuse for defensive attributions of a judgemental nature. It can be maintained, he held, by saying literally what *you* feel, though there arises the issue of how long in particular cases one should persist in communicating acceptance and empathy before expressing one's own feelings. Given that we all have some degree of natural self-protective tendency, we perhaps ought to err on the side of being patiently positive.

The Rogerian stance arose out of a self-consciously positive view of human potential and the stance that counselling was for individuals who chose it entirely freely. On the other hand, mentoring is assistance for interns who may have chosen the course, but don't have the freedom about continuing on the session by session basis that characterizes counselling. A teacher preparation course is also confined to a limited period and finite resources. Crucially, its goals are certain specified teaching capabilities and criteria.

This certainly doesn't mean that counselling ideas and strategies are irrelevant to teacher preparation and mentoring – far from it. In this connection we have already noted that in recent years workers such as Egan have developed the approach into a more systematic one (see the earlier part of the chapter) so that the Rogerian facilitative emphasis is seen as relevant particularly to the first, 'stock-taking' stage of a helping process.

However, it's perhaps in this particular aspect of *genuineness* that the difference between counselling and mentoring goals makes itself most felt. Namely, mentors not only happen to have values which they may feel a need to express to students, they have as part of their role to entertain criteria of teaching competence and of progress towards it, which they're charged with promoting. Importantly also, they carry out this activity in a school to whose pupils they also owe basic concerns with respect to educational achievement and general well-being.

Whilst the counselling condition *empathy* may be relatively unproblematic in its translation into mentoring, therefore, the balance of *acceptance* and *genuineness* is likely to shift somewhat. This will be in the direction of regular, if not constant, reference to the teaching skill and its proficiency criteria with which mentoring is after all concerned. This should also be reflected in the explicit and implicit defining of the mentor-student relationship, as it doubtless also will be from the student side, if anything more strongly. Students have after all come to be helped to learn to teach and the problem is often to get them to see that to do this they have actually to think and take indirect routes, since universal recipes are not feasible. This does not mean that the mentor is any the less concerned with the student's motivation and well-being; this whole chapter has sought to begin dealing with these aspects. But as I suggested earlier, mentoring, like teaching, is different from counselling in the nature of its eventual and therefore ongoing goal of promoting specific capability.

Further reading

Numerous introductions to counselling are now available, amongst which the books by Richard Nelson-Jones (1982, 1988) are authoritative and well-written. Guy Claxton's books *Being a Teacher* (1989) and *Teaching to Learn* (1990) are very relevant for their inclusion of motivational and stress aspects of teaching; the book by Handal and Lauvås (1987) combines counselling approaches with a concern for reflective practice.

5

Classroom strategies and their learning potential

Why bother with pedagogy in a book for teacher-mentors?

It would be reasonable to ask why a book intended for teachers who are likely to have considerable experience should include a pair of chapters on pedagogy, i.e. the nature of teaching and learning, particularly when I've kept saying that experienced teachers tend to possess a wealth of teaching 'craft knowledge'. I ought therefore to make clear the reasons behind this and the following chapter.

- *Teacher-mentors and their student interns require a valid framework and common vocabulary within which to communicate about and reflect on aspects of teaching.* As well as needing help to pick out and communicate about relevant aspects of teaching activity, student-teachers will (or should) be asking about the rationale and justification for adopting particular strategies and tactics in particular circumstances. Even if applied only narrowly and instrumentally, any form of reflectiveness merits positive response and encouragement in my view. This doesn't require a totally exhaustive and definitive framework of ideas about teaching (nor could it probably ever get this). But it does needs *some* framework and one that is adequate in coherence, relevance and grounding to be of use in decision-making and the communication of specific ideas, many of which are likely to come from teacher-mentors themselves.
- *Such a pedagogical framework would help teacher-mentors articulate their existing craft knowledge of teaching.* I've repeatedly referred to the finding that

the know-how of experienced practitioners such as teachers tends to be tacit to a considerable extent. Part of the value of a valid framework of ideas and a corresponding vocabulary of aspects of teaching and related issues is that it should actually assist mentors to 'unpack their practice' for the benefit of student-teachers. This is likely in its turn to strengthen mentors' own reflectiveness and perhaps, as many teacher-mentors report, enjoyment of their craft.

• *A common pedagogical framework and vocabulary provides for consistency and flexibility within any particular teacher preparation scheme.* Given the complexity of what's involved in teaching, it's probable that it could be portrayed equally well using any of a number of frameworks, though they would probably show considerable overlaps. Corresponding to this and surely even more important, ideas from any quarter should be permitted critical examination by those involved in teacher preparation. Nevertheless, however paradoxically, we can both remain open to the benefits of such pluralism and encourage a quite basic degree of reflectiveness precisely by having a common working model. Its central benefit is namely as a common reference frame which will help student-teachers to get their 'mind maps' of teaching clearer more quickly, with the assistance of the above sorts of articulation from their mentors. In addition, however, this not only allows the proponents of particular ideas and emphases to situate their views in relation to it, it also provides a basic formulation about which there could and should be continuing debate, and doubtless long will be. And of course, such debate ought to include the possible revision of the pedagogical framework itself.

• *A sound, clear pedagogy is a necessary base for generating valid and consistent assessment procedures for student-teachers, in particular through competence profiling.* If we're going to judge student-teachers' teaching capability as part of their certification of qualified status, as we in fact have to, then we need to base such assessment on our best insights into what we believe the nature of teaching capability to be. In the UK, the Department for Education has made it a prerequisite of approval that the new school-based schemes should use competence statement profiles (DFE 1992). I shall argue in Chapter 7 that the version the DFE offers as a starting basis actually does deserve amendment, which to its credit, the DFE document did foresee as a possibility.

Ways of analysing teaching

How then does one build such a view of what teaching involves? That is, a view which is on the one hand clear and accessible, yet on the other also does justice to the myriad of rich details that may be relevant at a host of levels and from seemingly infinite numbers of angles? Doubtless not easily, but one has to start somewhere. There are different kinds of approach, each of which yields some sort of insight deserving consideration. Since I've already introduced some of these approaches in earlier chapters, in this first section of the chapter I'm going to start by recalling the general analysis offered in Chapter 2. I shall then go on to consider different levels of functional analysis, and round off by seeing how teaching strategies relate to the functions and subfunctions in teaching. This will let us focus in the second section on classroom strategies and their potential to bring about pupil learning.

I should make clear that in all this I do not see my task as the reviewing or recommendation of classroom teaching strategies as such. For one reason, such strategies would need to be related to and illustrated in terms of particular areas of the curriculum. This would be well beyond my scope and in any case, there exist many useful sources on the teaching of particular subjects and age-ranges. A further and in many respects more important consideration is that specific teaching methods and their constituent activities are what practising teachers are most familiar with. School-based teacher preparation profits precisely from this. What the present chapter is mainly about, then, is the building of a pedagogical framework within which teacher-mentors can bring out and pass on their expertise in ways which promote intelligent skilfulness in their student-teachers. If the ideas within this chapter also promote the development of teaching strategies as such, that would of course be a welcome bonus.

General analyses

If we start with the question that is central to the profession and to preparation for it, 'what is teaching basically about', then one approach is to examine the essentials of the concept as such and to combine this with description of what the teaching profession actually takes on.

In Chapter 2 (see Further detail section 2.1) I pointed out that conceptual and systems-type analyses together indicate a basic generic meaning: teaching is essentially a purposeful interaction in which a teacher attempts to promote learning by getting learners to engage with them in activities likely to result in intended learning gains. From this we saw that, whilst one needs to take all the elements in the interaction into account, the paramount and defining *aim* in teaching is to end up with a gain in pupil capability, that is, *learning*. We can add that it equally shows us that, particularly in the case of compulsory school systems, teaching tends to involve an *interpersonal* or person management aspect, in that the teacher is charged with 'getting the pupils to engage in the process'. The extent to which these two aspects are actually intertwined is nicely summed up by characterizing teaching as *the management of pupil learning*.

Looking at the realities of education systems, we also see of course that teaching actually takes place in a social setting whose immediate context is usually a school, and that schools have a broad range of social functions, both explicit and implicit. Teaching, then, involves a range of roles, including pastoral ones, participation in the school's organization and functioning, and relations with the world outside the school.

A further aspect of the real-life social setting of teaching is that it takes place in a time dimension. As a member of a profession, a teacher is expected not only to show proficiency, but also *development*, whether in respect of basic teaching capacity or in career moves into new functions and responsibilities in schools and the wider education system. Mentoring within school-based teacher preparation is becoming just such a role and career step.

At a general level, then, 'what teaching is about' is commitment and capability in managing pupil learning, in fulfilling wider professional roles, and in professional development in all these respects.

Functional analysis of teaching

Another approach to the characterization of teaching is *functional analysis*, which is particularly likely to be evoked when the question is put in such terms as 'what does a teacher actually have to be able to do?' In pursuing this line, in Chapter 2 I also proposed that provided we understand the nature of skill adequately, then 'doing teaching', like any purposeful activity, involves a skill cycle of:

- planning and preparation with respect to aims and process;
- actual teaching activity, conduct of the process;
- monitoring of outcomes and process;
- feedback use in reflection and replanning;

Can we distil this any further and get at even more basic subfunctions of teaching activity? Looking at the above teaching skill components and remembering the basic functional analysis of interpersonal skill offered in the previous chapter, then it can be noted that, as in all action, teaching requires the teacher to

- do actions which define and affect the situation;
- maintain active awareness of what goes on.

There's also always some purpose in mind, however. So in addition to these two basic components of teaching action (which you may recognize as the *D–defining/doing* and the *A–active awareness* of the previous chapter's 'DAM' analysis of interpersonal skill), we have to add two further components.

Inasmuch as teaching is by definition geared towards promoting learning, then we need to add this element to the two basic subfunctions. These three aspects can be denoted by the acronym DAL (doing/defining, active awareness, learning promotion), so that examining the way a particular piece of teaching involves these functions may be termed a DAL analysis. Equally, in so far as teaching is a social activity in which teachers need to manage learners into appropriate activities, we need to add a motivating function. This gives us the acronym DAM, and the possibility of the kind of DAM analysis already seen in the last chapter with respect to interpersonal skills in general.

What DAL and DAM functional analyses should achieve is to pick out essential purposes or functions which need to be achieved within teaching. In this way they can provide a reasonable answer to our original question: 'what must teaching involve?' in that they point to features we always need to take into account when considering teaching in any context. These functions may apply at different levels of detail and may be broken down further (as suggested in the second part of this chapter), but they must also be understood within the overall context of the piece of teaching being considered. A functional analysis of the learning promotion and management aspects of teaching can thus provide a basis for judging the suitability of particular teaching strategies and tactics. However, specifying such subfunctions and purposes does not in itself tell us precisely what to do or what strategies to select in order to achieve them.

Strategies for the management of learning

We might imagine that we could get even more specific about teaching activities by extending the functional analysis to consider more and more specific levels, but at this point we really have to take another approach and talk about concrete teaching strategies and tactics in their own right. This has much to do with the fact, noted in Chapter 2, that complex skills like teaching require so many functions and subfunctions to be achieved simultaneously that they can't rely on a different action to achieve each. Rather, they demand *multi-functional strategies* which fulfil many purposes at the same time. Thinking about such strategies appears to demand a slightly different, more concrete sort of focus.

These are of course the terms in which practitioners tend to think. If one asks teachers what teaching involves, then as studies of teacher thinking cited earlier show, it's natural that one finds them talking in terms of concrete classroom strategies and tactics, the forms of pupil task and interaction they actually conduct in their teaching. They will refer, for example, to such things as explaining, questioning, boardwork, doing worksheets, arranging group discussion, doing projects and so forth.

When student-teachers want to know 'what to do', they too are doubtless expecting something in these concrete sorts of terms. Clearly, any pedagogical view that is going to be of use in helping them must indicate how it relates to classroom strategies. To omit any reference to these in mentoring would be a bit like a playwright offering a play with absolutely no script, just a general summary of what the actors should get across.

Reflective teaching and mentoring mean linking strategies and functions

On the other hand, *just* dealing in terms of particular classroom strategies and tactics, whilst omitting any reference to teaching functions and subfunctions would be a bit like only providing elements of the script, with no indication of their order and still less of the plot!

The appropriateness of particular classroom actions and pupil tasks depends on the particular purposes and functions involved at that point in the teaching/learning process. It is part of any effective action, teaching no less, that one's means should be likely to promote one's ends. This implies that in teaching, possible classroom strategies and tactics need to be chosen in the light of the particular set of goals and subfunctions the teacher (or whoever is deciding) has in mind. In turn, this means that a student-teacher needs to gain not only a considerable repertoire of teaching strategies and substrategies, but also an understanding of the different levels of purpose and subfunction at stake in the enterprise of teaching. This functional awareness provides a justificatory basis for the selection and intelligent execution of particular strategies. This is important particularly because activities in classrooms have to be flexibly adapted on the hoof, so as to remain likely to achieve their purposes in the face of changing circumstances.

However, one of the paradoxes of skill referred to earlier is that expert performers often give the impression that they do *not* indulge in such reflective thinking. Experienced teachers, for instance, do not tend to refer explicitly to intended learning outcome goals when talking about the ways they go about their teaching and there is even evidence that when asked to teach with aims in mind, their teaching suffers by becoming more rigid (cf. Clark and Peterson 1986; Calderhead 1987). Given that these are the people who are now to be involved in mentoring novices, this exposes an issue deserving our attention. Why should this apparent lack of thoughtfulness occur and what, if anything, is its relevance to mentoring? This is definitely an issue whose many sides demand a treatment beyond my present scope and on which only a fool would claim to have the final word. Nevertheless, the two major sets of background ideas so far introduced may help illuminate it.

The skill psychology perspective: What we learn from the psychology of skill seems highly relevant here. For instance, the limits on our human capacities for conscious information processing make it typical that constant (or 'redundant') features in a situation are dealt with in a more automatized fashion, with conscious attention being reserved for the irregular and unpredictable, the problem sources. Just as we don't notice the motorway barriers so much as the antics of the road-hog ahead, so experienced teachers think about pupils and their reactions more than about the subject-topic they've so often taught (cf. Brown and McIntyre 1993).

Likewise, this and the embedded nature of skill strategies mean that action is *localized*. Although when expert at something we're usually doing a lot at once, we're seldom doing it *all* at once. We deal with the subtask in hand. Just as we don't think much over the horizon to Glasgow when driving there from London, but more about keeping on the road and getting across the lanes to the next service area, so according to the research by Brown and McIntyre and others, teachers don't think about ultimate learning goals so much as about maintaining 'normal desirable states' of pupil activity and task-related progress within lessons.

Furthermore, there is a tendency of the processes in action to become automatic or *routinized* with experience and practice. As we've therefore seen, in addition to the above effects, it does get more difficult to declare one's procedural know-how explicitly, particularly in words.

I think that the main point to be made here in relation to mentoring is that these features may be all very well in the established artistry of experienced teachers (in fact there they appear essential), but in mentoring we're talking about the early stages of teaching skill development. Even if we would like student-teachers eventually to become intuitive in their skilful action, what gets automatized should be not just the overt behaviours (and could not, according to cognitive skill psychology), but also the decision making that goes into their selection and execution.

This means that at least in the early stages, novices need to constantly consider the rationales and functions of teaching actions, at whatever level of globality or detail. I also think we have to go beyond this. To the extent that one is dealing with an open, complex type of activity like teaching, a consciously reflective, open-minded stance shouldn't be restricted to novices (and saying just when student-teachers cease to be novices isn't exactly easy anyway). This is in fact the emphasis in Donald Schön's writings about professional action and learning. It may be noted that this does appear to be at odds with contentions by theorists such as Hubert and Stuart Dreyfus and Patricia Benner that the highest levels of expertise are completely intuitive in nature (see Further detail section 2.3). However, although this raises issues which are of considerable importance in relation to later teacher professional development, here I am going to pass them over as being beyond the scope of my present focus on student-teacher mentoring.

The recommendation for mentoring, then, is that student-teachers need to be exposed to all the relevant considerations entering into the choice and application of particular teaching strategies, from their functional rationales, through to tips on what it takes to 'make them work in practice'. How much we do try to consider at once and when to do so are further issues which I shall deal with later.

Motives and attitudes: To return to the issue of teachers' apparent failure to articulate their teaching rationales, the possibility needs to be entertained that this is due more to a lack of motive than of capacity, mainly because until now teachers have had little occasion, time or encouragement to do so. Indeed, given our general culture's dualist contrasting of theory against practice, not to mention the shortcomings of traditional college–school separations in initial teacher training, it's hardly surprising if teacher culture has sometimes tended to adopt a defensive anti-intellectualism in the face of 'useless educational theory'. There are actually some indications (Tomlinson and Swift, 1992) that a similar lack of reflectiveness has characterized teacher educators with respect to the nature of their offerings. In both cases it may be a case of fish being the last to discover water!

However this may be, it does seem imperative that teachers taking on mentoring roles should recognize the importance of a thoughtful, reflective stance. This does *not* mean espousing the opposite traditional pole and embracing abstract 'theory' in isolation. To do that would be to restrict the new school-based opportunities by thinking in the either/or terms of the old college–school separation. What it does involve is teacher-mentors taking a thoughtful approach to the practice with which they are in touch, so as to help student-teachers understand that practice and become intelligent, self-developing professionals themselves. This means helping students not only to see *what* is involved in particular classroom strategies and arrangements, but also to understand *how* these work and *why* they should be used, i.e. what functions they are likely to fulfil. This may possibly involve exploring issues to quite deep levels within the school-based programme, but the great opportunity of these new arrangements is precisely to keep such reflection always in touch with the action, indeed, to make reflectiveness more relevant because it *is* in touch with that action.

Having made the case that mentoring requires communication by reference to a pedagogy which does more than just describe classroom strategies, I want now to offer a framework which links such strategies with their goals and considers the nature of their potential to achieve those goals. It also offers a further analysis of the subfunctions that tend to be involved within such strategies: how they get deployed and what they target in the actual classroom. Although I shall go on to consider how they are closely intertwined, the promotion of learning aspect of teaching will be introduced separately in this chapter and the pupil management arrangement aspect in the next.

Classroom strategies and their learning potential

The perspective being proposed is as follows. One of the basic goals of teaching is to promote learning. In this respect, teaching strategies or methods and the classroom activities they involve are chosen for their capacity to bring about learning gains. These intended learning acquisitions include various kinds of concepts, knowledge, understanding and skills within and across a range of subject disciplines. Moreover, there exist various kinds of learning process and a variety of factors influence their effectiveness. Teaching methods and their constituent activities don't necessarily guarantee any particular sort of learning will result. Rather, they have differing sorts and degrees of potential to achieve particular learning goals and this depends on how far they allow operation of the basic learning processes and factors influencing these. So teaching strategies need choosing for their relevant *learning potential* (also with class management in mind, but we'll look at that in the following chapter) and then implementing intelligently so as to maximize the realization of that learning potential.

On this view, a pedagogical framework needs to consider a range of matters. These will constitute the parts of this section, namely:

* kinds of learning that teaching may aim to promote;
* factors that influence learning effectiveness;
* the idea of analysing teaching strategies for their learning potential;
* the further subfunctions in any teaching method which contribute to whether it does in fact achieve its learning potential on particular occasions.

Promoting what learning?

When it comes to what teachers are trying to help their pupils acquire, the major categories are often listed as:

* skills;
* knowledge/understanding;
* concepts.

One might add *attitudes* to this list, but these are really more a matter of motive than capability and so should come in the next chapter.

The above list has become increasingly familiar within 'educator-speak' in recent years, particularly with the introduction of the national curriculum. This doesn't mean, of course, that everyone shares clear, well-grounded conceptions of what they entail. The very fact that such terms are common currency can actually make it less likely that we unpack them and check our underlying conceptions, though of course, this is hopefully seen as a necessary part of teacher preparation courses. It's also particularly necessary because, as seen earlier in the case of skill, our language and culture seem to have built into them some rather unfortunate assumptions which can be the source both of confusion and needless controversy.

Since this book is aimed at people who are likely to have had training and experience in teaching, it doesn't seem appropriate to go into the nature of concepts, knowledge and understanding, and skill in the main text. Readers will probably be familiar with these at least in the context of their own teaching subjects, which is where all this has eventually to be applied. In case you do wish to renew your acquaintance with these basic ideas, however (and there have been a few notable developments in recent years), I offer a brief treatment of them in further detail sections and further reading is suggested at the end of the chapter. The material on skill already covered in Chapters 2 and 3 and their further detail sections are also relevant here, applying generally to the kinds of intellectual and practical skills we're trying to teach pupils in school. In the present chapter, Further detail section 5.1 will deal briefly with concepts, knowledge and understanding. Suffice it here to add the following point.

Skills, knowledge/understanding and concepts are distinct but overlap. Given the dualist tradition in common-sense assumptions, it bears emphasizing that concepts, knowledge, and skills may be distinct, but this isn't to say that they're each totally different. The relationship is more a matter of inclusiveness. That is, *skill*, being able to achieve purposes in context, requires cognition. Skill relies on *knowledge* of those contexts and their workings (doing simultaneous equations, for instance, relies on knowing how aspects of algebra 'work'). In turn, knowledge tends to be framed in general terms and to refer to classes of item, whether real or symbolic. Knowledge thus uses relevant *concepts* (e.g. doing simultaneous equations requires the ability to recognize algebraic and numeric symbols). The less well-known recent classification of learning into tuning, accretion and restructuring (see Further detail section 5.1) to some extent cuts across all three members of the traditional list.

What promotes learning?

A great many things appear to influence how effectively people acquire the above sorts of capacities. We can divide these influences roughly into two types. *Direct factors* are central in that in themselves they tend to produce learning. *Indirect factors* are background influences on how far the direct factors actually get brought into play and they may moderate their effects. In these terms we could say that teaching is attempting to promote the action of the direct factors. In this sense, teaching has surely to be seen as the most important of indirect factors. What student-teachers *should* therefore be particularly interested in knowing about is direct factors, so that they can gear their teaching action accordingly (though as was said in Chapter 3, they are likely to bring many implicit preconceptions with them regarding this).

Skill learning
Whatever the skill, including those involved in school curricula, we've seen that its acquisition requires *getting a plan* which includes an idea of the goal

Further detail section 5.1
Skills, knowledge/understanding and concepts

Skill, as we've seen, is ability to achieve a purpose in a context, knowing how to do something. Skilled action tends to require flexibility based on knowledge, but skills can vary in their complexity, their openness-closedness and their content, hence many of the skills school teaching is concerned with are intellectual or cognitive capacities.

Knowledge is a more or less lasting representation of reality. Humans may possess it in a variety of forms (e.g. visual, verbal, concrete, symbolic), but the modern psychological assumption is that sooner or later these are to do with brain states and processes. When the representation is of 'surface' or individual items, we're inclined to call it just knowing.

When it's a knowledge of processes, 'how things work' in some domain, we tend to call it *understanding*. Knowledge/understanding and the skills that use them tend to have some degree of general application, i.e. to be conceptual.

Concepts involve identifying and dealing with things, events or abstractions as members of categories or groups. They involve and enable generalization. Two major aspects of concept meaning are their:

- intension/connotation/definition: the criterial or qualifying attributes for membership of that class of item, 'what makes an x an x';
- extension/denotation/exemplars: the actual instances of the concept or class.

Levels of concept use: mastering concepts isn't a case of all or nothing, rather, levels of concept use have been distinguished (by Klausmaier and colleagues amongst others). We may be able only to identify a particular exemplar (identity level) without being generally able to classify instances and non-instances of a concept (classificatory level), and when we can do this, it doesn't mean we can formally define the criteria involved (formal level). Sometimes we can even manage the formal level, without actually being able to use the concept at the classificatory level (sometimes called verbalism or formalism). In fact, whether the formal level is achieveable at all seems to depend on the type of concept we're talking about.

Natural concepts are those which we acquire through exposure and use in our culture; we don't tend to be able to use them at a formal level. Their criteria are implicit, their possible definitions often contested and they are acquired mainly through implicit use. They tend to abound in the humanities. *Artificial concepts* are those which have been deliberately and explicitly defined; they tend to characterize systematic disciplines of study and in particular the sciences.

Concepts may vary considerably, for instance, in their *content*: whether to do with physical things, living beings, actions and functions, relationships, or other abstractions, including the idea of concept itself. They also vary in *complexity*, with some concepts having more defining attributes than others, often because they include them as subaspects. Another form of variation, very important in teaching, is their *abstractness–concreteness*; this seems to include a combination of content and complexity. A concept such as 'war' seems more complex and less restricted to the physical than, say, 'battle' or still more so 'fight'.

Tuning, accretion and restructuring

There is another way of classifying the learning that's being aimed at by teaching, which cuts across the skill–knowledge–concept classification. It was proposed by the psychologist Donald Norman (1978) and talks about:

- *tuning*: getting more efficient, economic and faster in deploying particular items, whether concepts, knowledge or actions (e.g. getting more efficient at basic multiplication or using a particular modern language vocabulary);
- *accretion*: extending existing concepts and skill chunks to further material and contexts (e.g. extending one's knowledge of an historical period). This is alternatively called transfer;
- *restructuring*: acquiring new concepts or action-schemes, or new organizations of existing ones (e.g. acquiring the idea of differentiation in calculus).

and a strategy for action, *making attempts* to carry out the plan, *monitoring* the outcome and attempt, and *feeding back* and replanning as necessary. This whole cycle typically needs to be engaged in *repeatedly*. Given the cognitive limitations of learners, the type of activity in question may need *task analysis* into subtasks and aspects, at which subskill levels the same cycle of skill learning will apply (see Further detail section 5.2). Where this sort of decomposition has been used, then there will need in due course to be reintegration of the separate subskills. In skill acquisition, as in virtually every other form of learning, learners bring existing capabilities and subskills, which need recognizing and building upon.

Further detail section 5.2
Factors influencing learning

Acquiring skill

Different curriculum subjects involve different skills, but we saw previously (Chapter 2 and Further detail sections 2.2. and 2.3) that in general the acquisition of a skill requires the learner to go through a reflective or experiential skill cycle which includes a number of components. In turn, where learners do not possess or have difficulty with a component, they need assistance to acquire or cope with it. The skill cycle components are:

1 a plan or strategy indicating the aims, nature of context and selection of actions;
2 attempts at engaging in the action; with
3 monitoring of the action and its effects; and
4 feeding back their monitoring into reflection and replanning of aspects of the action;
5 practice: repeated engagement in this reflective cycle of purposeful action.

Engagement in intelligent practice of this sort tends to help the learner proceed through a typical sequence of phases of skill acquisition, though progress can be relatively irregular at specific points. In particular, the limitations on learners' information processing capacities may mean that tasks need breaking down into manageable subtasks and this is helped by the embedded nature of most skills. The purpose of *hierarchical task analysis* (Gagné 1985; Patrick 1991) is to achieve a picture of the component functions and subtasks in a skill. An illustration is provided in Figure 5.1 of a possible task analysis of the relatively simple, closed arithmetical skill of adding two three-column numbers.

Two further points are important here. The first is that sooner or later there is usually a need to recombine and *integrate* the separate strands, and subskills which need combining thus will need at some point to be combined in actual attempts at the portion of the task in question.

Second, any particular task analysis gives only one of what may be many possible breakdowns of the activity in question. It is not easy to achieve a task analysis which goes beyond mere logical decomposition to provide something psychologically useful for skill acquisition. Teachers and trainers need to remember this, especially because the existing capabilities, ideas and subskills learners bring to the learning of any skill are likely to fit into some task analyses and corresponding learning routes better than others. You may, for instance, be able to think of alternative analyses for the arithmetic task below. A final point is that even psychologically useful task analyses do not imply, as they're often assumed to, that one has to teach from the details to the whole. Rather they provide one way of indicating what one has to have covered or 'got' in acquiring the overall skill, whichever route one takes into it.

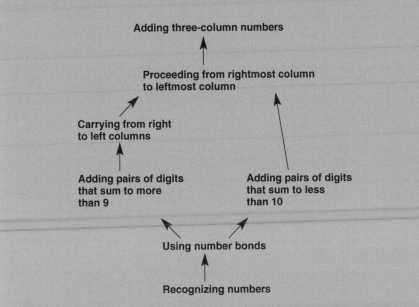
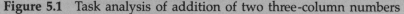

Figure 5.1 Task analysis of addition of two three-column numbers

Cognitive learning: knowledge/understanding and concepts

Research confirms the importance of the following features of experiences and inputs from the viewpoint of establishing cognitive resources such as knowledge, understanding and concept grasp.

1 *Meaningful grasp:* the learner has to be able to 'get hold' of the relevant information in two senses:

(a) *Quality:* what the learner makes of the input, which depends both on what they encounter (perception is 'data-driven' by what's outside pupils' heads) and, more importantly than often realized, the ideas they the learners bring to it (is also 'concept-driven' by what's inside their heads). Linking the input with ideas they already have is called 'meaningful' processing by writers such as Ausubel (1978) and 'deep' processing by Marton (1984). The point is that such linkage makes for robust and usable storage of what one has taken in, whereas surface or 'rote' processing (e.g. just of the words as sounds) is much more easily lost.

(b) *Quantity:* how much the learner picks up of the input; you can't store what you didn't get! We all have hefty limits on our immediate storage capacity, particularly with unfamiliar items. The younger the child, the more limited this working memory, partly because they're just more unfamiliar with most things.

2 *Practice:* repetition strengthens long term storage (i.e. robust learning), particularly when it's practice of meaningful processing as opposed to mere rehearsal of surface formulas (rote learning), though massive rehearsal can sometimes make up in some respects for meaningful processing.

3 *Interest:* impact, personal significance and novelty combine to consolidate the establishing of long term memory records directly (as well as indirectly influencing our engagement anyway). In this sense, interest and arousal aren't just icing on the instructional cake, they actually make it more effective. We all tend to store longer and more easily remember that which we find significant, novel and intense.

Concept learning

In the case of *concept learning*, the above factors also apply, but so do certain further requirements that are specific to concepts and their usage. For instance, keeping to a smaller range of clear instances helps speedy acquisition of concepts, but early variation in such exemplars makes for more transferable concepts, though it slows the acquisition somewhat. In turn, capabilities to apply and manipulate concepts may be seen as forms of intellectual skill, to whose acquisition the features of the skill cycle apply. Concept learning is another large domain, which has been well reviewed in relation to teaching by Howard (1987).

Indirect factors

Hitherto I've been mainly considering factors that directly affect learning of different kinds, but what about indirect factors? What sort of factors are they? The distinction is, as always, to some extent arbitrary, but the way direct factors were defined earlier was in relation to the actual process of learning. It was a matter of what forms or aspects of learning activity affect the robustness and utilizability with which information or strategies are stored. In this sense, indirect factors would include background considerations such as classroom context and resources, home influences, even pupil ability and interest to enter into the act of learning. From the viewpoint of action that the teacher can (try to) get the pupil to engage in, they may be considered indirect compared to the range of direct factors considered above. Nevertheless, they will certainly need consideration in the broader context of planning teaching, since one plans for particular material, particular pupils with particular abilities and dispositions, and with certain resources available.

Cognitive learning
The acquisition of the representational capacities of knowledge, understanding and concepts appears to depend directly on three main types of factor: *meaningful grasp* or 'getting hold' of the relevant information, *repeated processing* of the information and nervous system *arousal* (traditionally thought of in terms of interest). These three types of factor interact: what gets repeated gets learned, so the learner needs to repeatedly exercise their meaningful grasp, not just their retention of surface features. Here again, the importance of the ideas learners bring with them and typically use in assimilating new inputs cannot be overemphasized. A somewhat finer-grained presentation of these ideas will be found in Further detail section 5.2.

The learning potential of teaching strategies

I pointed out earlier that the most concrete sort of concern a teacher is faced with when planning their teaching is 'what activities do I actually get pupils to do?' What teaching involves, in the most obvious sense, is classroom activities which, generally speaking, the teacher designs and in which they manage and assist the pupils.

Characterizing classroom teaching activities
What do I actually mean here by 'teaching activities'? This is yet another of those cases where it sounds straightforward, but when you get up close, the details aren't so simple. One is perhaps inclined to answer the question by referring to familiar classroom activities such as teachers explaining, individuals doing worksheets, groups conducting experiments in science classes, class or group discussion, pupils taking notes, a class doing a project, role-play in modern languages or drama, and so on – your own examples will immediately come to mind.

When experienced teachers come up with such examples, they do so in the style typical of experts in a domain by referring economically to a whole set of features. That is, they may use everyday words, but actually it's a form of specialist language in that they tend to be referring implicitly to a whole range of specifications which have to do with the constituent details of the particular approach. These in their turn often have to do with conditions for its feasibility and success. For example, when an experienced teacher refers to 'group work', he or she probably has in mind a particular sort of size of group, an arrangement of classroom furniture, perhaps even an arrangement relating to a particular classroom, a particular set of roles for herself or himself in monitoring and assisting the group activity, perhaps a duration of the activity and possibly much more.

This is a good illustration of the sort of economical 'chunking' of ideas and actions that characterizes experienced practitioners. This (or some other) rich set of further details are embedded within their thinking and language regarding any teaching methods the experienced teacher uses. The important point when it comes to mentoring is that student-teachers are not yet likely to appreciate all these implicit elements in the concept. For them, for instance, 'group-work' tends just to mean 'putting them into groups'. On the whole they will not yet have differentiated and integrated the various component details needing consideration.

The same point emerges from the examples I mentioned two paragraphs above. These classroom activities can be seen to vary in complexity, time-span, number of pupils involved, etc. The implication seems to be that we need sooner or later to be able to characterize strategies for classroom learning activity in terms of a number of aspects or dimensions. It seems to me that these must include at least the following four *essential aspects of teaching strategy* (the illustrations given for each are not intended to be exhaustive):

- *what the pupils are doing* – e.g. listening, reading, writing, drawing/designing, interacting with a computer, making, doing practical work, watching, discussing;
- *how the class is organized* – e.g. as a whole class, in groups, in pairs, individuals working separately;
- *the nature of the pupil task function* – e.g. information finding, information intake, information recording, analysis, application, evaluation, problem-solving, practising;
- *what the teacher is doing* – e.g. directing, prompting, information giving, explaining, eliciting/questioning, listening, watching, demonstrating.

Three further points are important here. A first is that strategies of course have aims, but I'm dealing with that under the heading of function. Second, the above dimensions may not be the only important ones, but they do seem the minimum. I've found them useful to focus on in getting a closer idea of student-teachers' planning and teaching, but a different breakdown might be equally useful. The important point is that novices are likely to need help to get to grips with important details of classroom practice, certainly when planning teaching themselves, but even when trying to discern what matters in teaching they're observing.

A third point is that I am in no way implying that all of us should always try to think about classroom strategies analytically, in terms of their components and functions. It may be possible to distinguish these, but seldom to separate them. For instance, even though it may appear in the above set of aspects as if teacher and pupil activity can be separated, many of the terms suggested are themselves implicitly *inter*active; a teacher doesn't just 'give information' or 'listen' in a vacuum, for example, he or she gives information or listens *to* a pupil or pupils.

Equally, teachers with differing degrees of experience will tend to think about teaching methods in different ways, which will doubtless also be affected by their experiences and personalities. People will arrive at ideas for classroom strategies in their own styles, some holistically and inspirationally, others more analytically and painstakingly, most through some sort of mixture of both of these. However any particular student does arrive at an idea for classroom activity, nevertheless, their mentor needs to check these different aspects. Whilst experienced teachers may well be able to do this relatively intuitively, as they might in their own approach to teaching, they will, nevertheless, also need to communicate their comments and rationales for them to students in relatively specific terms such as the above.

The idea of learning potential

We do of course need to pay full attention to these details of concrete classroom activity. However, in spite of the concrete focus revealed by studies of teacher thinking, perhaps because of this, it needs emphasizing that considerations cannot stop here if it's actually educating pupils that we have in mind.

The major point of classroom tasks and activities is of course to bring about learning. It makes no sense to characterize any such arrangements as some sort of universal 'good practice' in and of themselves. What ultimately makes particular teaching methods and the teacher–pupil activities they involve 'good' or otherwise is the extent to which they promote learning gains of the sorts intended in the particular context. In passing, of course, it should be recognized that they also have to be feasible and useful in terms of pupil management and control. However I'll be devoting the subsequent chapter to a consideration of that aspect.

Issues as to the worthwhileness of particular classroom activities are not all-or-none matters, at least partly because any given teaching approach may support a number of forms of learning and partly because any approach may be applied more or less effectively. It seems therefore that we need to think in terms of the *learning potential* of specific classroom strategies. By this I mean the extent to which a classroom activity is likely to promote particular aspects of learning when done well, because it allows the operation of factors that positively influence those forms of learning. The idea, then, is that we should be assisting student-teachers to think ultimately in terms of the learning goals they wish to promote. In thinking about and planning their teaching, they should then be thinking *strategically* about possible classroom activities with their pupils. That is, rather than focusing just on the details of procedure, they should equally if not primarily also be thinking of such activities as strategies for achieving the desired learning outcomes (for the particular pupils in the particular circumstances). This does of course fit with the view noted in Chapter 2, that effective teaching requires not just capability to perform teaching actions, but also to *judge* when to adopt and how to adapt these.

Bases for judging learning potential
How does one judge the likely learning potential of particular teaching strategies? There appear to be two possible bases. Neither can give total certainty of course, but their combination is desirable. One basis is systematic, formal theory and research in pedagogy and in particular the psychology of learning. The factors I introduced above are of this sort. The background justification for this type of source lies in a critical appraisal of the validity and relevance of the underlying evidence. Giving readers access to this is of course one of my reasons for providing further reading suggestions in this book.

The other basis has to be the evidence of one's own experience, particularly if one is a teacher with considerable experience of the subject, pupils and setting in question. This experience base of craft knowledge is undoubtedly richer for most teacher-mentors, and more influential on *their* teaching. This importance is not lessened by its suffering two potential problems.

The first of these problems is that even for teachers with such experience, it's difficult, even for them, to check the validity of their intuitive inclinations, to be sure they're not selecting on the basis of how it felt rather than whether it worked, of particular local circumstances, and so on. The second and more important problem is in relation to mentoring. This is the difficulty we've seen teachers seem to have in articulating their experience into cogent responses and explicit reasons. The sort of formal framework being introduced here may go some way towards assisting this, but it isn't for nothing that this has been called one of the paradoxes of skill.

Not only should formal research ideas be brought into the applied situation and assayed for their fruitfulness, but general principles of learning need applying to the teaching of *particular subjects*. Humans have only so many basic forms of learning mechanism, and I would argue that the ones I have referred to here are basic and general in their relevance, as I hope the illustrations below will show. I am restricting myself here to these particular illustrations, since any attempt to do justice to the range of teaching subjects and national curriculum levels would clearly make this a very different book.

Nevertheless, sooner or later pedagogy ought to proceed into the specifics of teaching particular subject matter. This is important for a number of reasons, perhaps the most important being current research findings that the currency of human thinking is relatively concrete and context specific much of the time, and this applies both to pupils and student-teachers. There is also the additional reason that at least at secondary school level and beyond, teachers tend to exhibit a strong subject identity, seeing themselves as chemists, historians, and so on.

In keeping with this, the influential American educationist Lee Shulman (1986) has coined the phrase 'subject pedagogical knowledge' to refer to the importance of teachers possessing not only a knowledge and capability in their teaching subject as such, but also an awareness of how pupils tend to learn it: which concepts they find difficult, which misconceptions are particularly likely through which sorts of presentation, what's more difficult than what, and so on. In the terms I've been dealing in here, Shulman's position seems to amount to an interactive pedagogy (see Chapter 2) which takes the subject or nature of the learning content really seriously. This will tend to require mentors to go beyond the application of general learning principles; they will also need to consider formal research based in the teaching of specific curriculum subjects and even of particular topics and skills within them. It also highlights the importance of rich teacher experience in particular subjects and the importance of student-teachers encountering such specialist experience in at least some of the mentors they encounter.

Illustrations of learning potential analysis
Some examples of learning potential analyses are offered in Tables 5.1 and 5.2 with respect to a number of general classroom strategies and tactics. Table 5.1 does this with respect to the teaching of skills and Table 5.2 for cognitive learning. Being general, these analyses can only be based on the general learning influence features outlined above. In each cell there is consideration of two teaching aspects corresponding to each learning function or factor, namely *promoting* and *monitoring* it. The idea of these general subfunctions has already been introduced, but I will return to them below more specifically when considering the teacher actions required *within* particular teaching strategies and tactics.

One thing these examples illustrate is that the simpler and more specific the teaching tactic, the more it may show uneven potential in different respects. For example, *explanation* may have considerable potential for influencing/assisting the meaningful grasp, practice and interest factors of cognitive learning (Table 5.2). As such, it may also have potential in assisting the plan and feedback usage aspects of a skill cycle, but on its own it has virtually no potential in relation to the monitoring/assessing side of any of these. Indeed, explanation may even be likely to hinder learning (have 'negative potential') in some respects, for example, if offered during actual attempts when the learner needs all their concentration.

Table 5.1 Skill learning potential analyses of three illustrative teaching strategies

Teaching strategy / Learning function	Planning – replanning	Attempt	Monitor effect	Feedback use
Oral explanation (on its own, e.g. 'lecturette' as introduction to topic)	*Promote/assist:* positive; can offer explicit plan, including rationale and background knowledge for flexible and intelligent action, but limits on grasp and retention.	*Promote/assist:* possibly supports flexibility during action, but also negative potential through overload.	*Promote/assist:* possible support of monitoring/check by learner, but also negative potential through overload.	*Promote/assist:* considerable potential to help see connections between actions, strategies and outcomes, to inform replanning.
	Monitor/assess: no opportunity as such to assess grasp of input, let alone utilization/application in practice.	*Monitor/assess:* no opportunity as such to assess usage of input, let alone utilization/application in practice.	*Monitor/assess:* no opportunity as such to assess usage of input, let alone untilization/application in practice.	*Monitor/assess:* no opportunity as such to assess usage of input, let alone utilization/application in practice.
Pupil completion of worksheet task (following teacher input and with book and other resources available)	*Promote/assist:* may provide or require pupil planning for skill/activity in question, assisting skill/know-how and problem solving in the domain, but negative potential if too difficult.	*Promote/assist:* direct worksheet instructions may assist attempts at tasks required; activity offers.	*Promote/assist:* worksheet may instruct pupils how to check outcomes against criteria of correctness or progress.	*Promote/assist:* as such, low. Guidance for reflection on how monitored effects brought about, thence replanning probably not conveyable in general written form on worksheet, unless very specific, but can be base for further teacher help.

Pupil-pairs role play (no direct teacher involvement) e.g. Modern language learning				
	Monitor/assess: pupil written product = basis for direct assessment; activity for additional teacher diagnosis of understanding/progress.	*Monitor/assess:* doesn't involve teacher monitoring as such, but gives good opportunity to teacher to diagnose individual attempts and progress (cf. 'going round and seeing how they're doing').	*Monitor/assess:* doesn't involve teacher monitoring as such, but gives chance for teacher to monitor whether learner is monitoring own progress.	*Monitor/assess:* ditto re teacher monitoring.
	Promote/assist: none as such by teacher. Pupils may assist each other with aims and modelling of strategy and know-how, but may compound errors.	*Promote/assist:* none as such by teacher, but pupils may assist each other's attempts, but again danger of misleading.	*Promote/assist:* none as such, but pupils provide each other with check/feedback in so far as they possess relevant knowledge.	*Promote/assist:* low potential for similar reason to cell above and problem of recording monitoring (so use tape recorders?).
	Monitor/assess: offers an indirect opportunity to infer/diagnose understanding and strategy through witnessing the attempt/performance.	*Monitor/assess:* possible teacher monitoring 'from sidelines', getting at actual performance of skill.	*Monitor/assess:* doesn't involve teacher monitoring as such, but teacher may observe 'from side' whether learners are monitoring progress.	*Monitor/assess:* as next cell left, but probable need for teacher to continue indirect monitoring of a sequence of cycles to see if feedback being used.

Table 5.2 Cognitive learning potential analyses of three illustrative teaching strategies

Teaching strategy \ Learning function	Meaningful grasp	Practice	Interest
Oral explanation (on its own, e.g. in 'lecturette' introduction to topic)	*Promote/assist:* considerable; can make connections and offer rationale, put in different ways to cater for individual differences; but negative potential through overload and passivity. *Monitor/assess:* no opportunity as such to assess grasp of input, possible misapprehensions, etc.	*Promote/assist:* positive, can repeat statements in same and varied ways, but negative with respect to learner actively and overtly applying insights in practice, discussion or writing. *Monitor/assess:* no opportunity as such to assess whether recipients stay attentive, think about/use ideas.	*Promote/assist:* positive to some extent, may be linkable to issues of intrinsic significance to learners, use of humour, novel angles etc., but risk of inactivity/boredom. *Monitor/assess:* little opportunity as such to assess impact of input, let alone further interest and utilization.
Pupil completion of worksheet task (following teacher input and with book and other resources available)	*Promote/assist:* worksheet relatively low: inputs probably from teacher and text resources.	*Promote/assist:* high – one of the more obvious ways of arranging for meaningful practice of concept and knowledge usage, allowing differentiation to some extent.	*Promote/assist:* may be linkable to issues of intrinsic significance to learners, use of humour, novel angles etc., but not so powerful as 'live interaction'.

Pupil-pairs role play (no direct teacher involvement) e.g. Modern language learning	*Monitor/assess:* work sheet completion doesn't involve monitoring *per se*, but does give bases for teacher assessment of progress directly and/or through conversational diagnosis. *Promote/assist:* none as such by teacher. Pupils may assist each other with information and understanding, but may compound errors. *Monitor/assess:* offers an indirect opportunity to infer/diagnose understanding and strategy through witnessing what they say to each other.	*Monitor/assess:* again, gives a basis for judgement of task and learning progress. *Promote/assist:* high in that pupils are utilizing ideas and terms, and perhaps explaining them, but error possibility, although: *Monitor/assess:* offers opportunity for indirect monitoring of amount and quality of practice (whether accurate, checked, thought about, revised, etc.).	*Monitor/assess:* very little evidence potential as such, but again, a basis for interaction to monitor this aspect. *Promote/assist:* may be high where pupils are comfortable with each other; independence and freedom may be welcome; content may have potential for signficance (e.g. language games). *Monitor/assess:* offers opportunity for indirect teacher assessment of degree of interest and involvement operating.

Combining strategies

If only for this last reason, realistic teaching strategies generally need to involve suitable *combinations* of specific types of concrete teaching/learning activities (e.g. those mentioned above under the subheading 'Characterizing classroom teaching activities'). Conversely, it's also possible to have poorly balanced combinations within quite complex and well-established teaching approaches. For instance, a complaint against traditional whole-class teacher 'chalk and talk' approaches is that overall there may be little provision for assistance and monitoring of actual learner *attempts* at a skill being taught. That this may be more to do with the ways such teaching has been carried out, rather than a basic limit on its learning potential is suggested by the findings of major British research projects on teaching styles (see Tomlinson and Hodgson 1992). Another item which can easily slip by, particularly in larger classes, is monitoring of the typically varied ways in which learners *interpret* even the best textbooks and the most careful teacher explanations.

So whether a particular piece of teaching is approached through a consideration of basic teaching aims and functions or by starting from possible concrete teaching/learning activities, a *learning potential analysis* can help establish an effective balance within the teaching strategies actually adopted. It therefore appears to be something student interns should be inducted into by way of promoting a flexible and systematic approach to the planning of their own teaching.

Potential is only potential, feasibility may be something else

I want to conclude this section by emphasizing that learning potential is only potential. Even where our existing knowledge and experience allows a relatively full idea of the potential of a particular teaching approach for a given set of learning purposes and context, the reality may turn out otherwise. The best laid plans may still fail in some respects.

An open-minded appraisal of the learning potential of a range of plausible teaching approaches will probably reveal a messy picture. Different teaching strategies may fulfil similar functions and thus constitute alternatives to each other. Some teaching methods may be multi-functional, serving a number of teaching/learning purposes and subfunctions at the same time. In fact, particularly for student-teachers, the idea of learning potential takes on something of the meaning of an Olympic diving tariff. The teaching method equivalent of the 'three-and-a-half-reverse-twist-somersault-with-delayed-pike' may carry the promise of very powerful learning (as indicated, perhaps, by the student's observation of an expert teacher using this approach), but is probably so difficult that for the moment it would be better to play safe and do something corresponding to the good old simple jack-knife, where one can virtually guarantee achieving the lower tariff!

Student interns tend to realize this in principle, though without help to examine the precise nature of particular teaching strategies (using something like the four *essential teaching strategy aspects* offered a few pages back), they may well fail to perceive the complexities inherent in the high potential teaching methods they have observed being deployed so well and try them with disastrous results.

Making teaching strategies work for learning: DAL analysis

Having pointed out that teaching strategies enjoy a certain degree of independence in the pedagogical realm in that they aren't simply derivable from teaching purposes and subfunctions, an obvious question arises which may at first seem to have an equally obvious answer.

The question is, given that all this pedagogical analysis is supposed to be in the service of successful mentoring, can we now say anything useful by way of helping student-teachers to succeed in their use of the classroom activities and methods they choose as their teaching strategies? In relation to the learning promotion aspect of teaching, this becomes, how can we help them realize the learning potential of these strategies?

The seemingly obvious response might be that since teaching strategies are so different, then no, one can't say anything general, one just has to talk about the particulars of each type of classroom method in its own terms. My own view, however, is that once again, it's not an all-or-nothing issue. To some extent one does have to deal separately with what is specific to each type of teaching-strategy (and with respect to particular subject topics, for particular age groups, moreover). Likewise, sooner or later, student-teachers do need to get into the teaching of their subject to a particular set of pupils. But to some extent I suggest that it *is* possible to deal in general terms which may be useful to bear in mind when using any particular teaching method, though these general ideas will of course need applying to the specifics of each teaching method a student-teacher gets into.

This does in fact bring us back to the idea of *functional analysis*, that is of specifying functions one always has to think about when using strategies to realize purposes. This seems to apply here to two closely overlapping aspects of teaching strategies.

First, we're still interested in the achievement of *learning*, since these are after all teaching strategies. That is, we're interested essentially if not primarily in such strategies promoting curriculum goals, i.e. forms of learning. Thus within any teaching action, what I earlier nicknamed the DAL functions are important, namely: what the teacher is *doing* (by way of defining, assisting, influencing) and what the teacher is *monitoring* (assessing, staying aware of) to check the achievement of *learning* (including progress). There is also the question of *how* the teacher is achieving these.

Second, there is the more immediate question of the *task or activity* the pupils are supposed to be engaged in, which is designed to result in learning gain. What is the teacher *doing* to promote and *monitoring* to check progress in the execution of the classroom task? So here too, there are doing/defining and monitoring functions and they occur within a skill cycle, but the goal is task completion, perhaps with a task product.

Learning and task achievement aren't quite the same, though they're closely related and some people find them difficult to disentangle. The difference is important, however, because ignoring it can lead to considerable confusion in approaches to teaching.

Learning outcomes are capabilities (skill, knowledge, concepts) the (successful) learner now has 'in their head' which they didn't have before the learning activity. Learning progress is thus gain in respect of concepts, knowledge and/or skill (e.g. tuning, accretion, new structures of knowledge or action plan). The goal of the *task*, on the other hand, is the product of the activity as such. It is most easily seen when it takes the form of, say, a written answer to a maths problem, a history essay, the write-up of the science experiment, the group picture or the class collage, now on the wall. But it could equally consist of the conclusions conveyed orally by the individual or group who solved the problem, whether recorded orally or in writing, and so on. These products are not the learning gain as such, though they may sometimes be expressions and therefore indications of it.

Learning process and task activity are closely related in that task activity is meant to be learning activity; one learns through that activity, if it has the learning potential in question. But this may not happen ('I've explained it three times and he still hasn't got it', 'She's cooked those five times, but never remembers you've got to let them rise'). In such a case, the priority is in principle clear: teach it some other way, through some other form of teacher–pupil interaction.

DAL analysis for task completion and learning progress

I am suggesting that it would be useful if a pedagogical framework for mentoring were to specify the sorts of subfunctions involved in deploying teaching activities in the service of learning. Apart from giving a framework within which to think and communicate about teaching, this may also help as an *aide-mémoire* in observing and diagnosing student-teachers' teaching and progress. One of the problems here is that the embedded nature of actions means that as one tries to specify more of the details that may be involved, clear and easily accessible representation becomes more difficult. In this respect the technique of concept mapping appears to offer some advantages and may be used to build a progressively more detailed representation of teaching functions and subfunctions.

Figure 5.2 represents a relatively global level of analysis, showing the two main subfunctions in the learning promotion functions of teaching as the major 'nodes' or bubbles, with the learning function implied in the central node. To recap, the first two functions are:

Figure 5.2   Main DAL subfunctions

- *Doing/defining/influencing/assisting:* That is, what the teacher actually *does* by way of actions which will influence what occurs so as to promote pupil learning activity, 'helping things happen', in other words. It includes communicating requests and more generally 'defining the situation' (see Chapter 4) as well as particular forms of assistance for pupils to carry out activities.
- *Monitoring and assessing:* Keeping track of what's actually going on by way of learning activity.

These two main functions can be specified more closely. Anything approaching adequacy by way of this sort of representation must, for instance, show two further aspects of what they always involve, namely *how* they may be done and *what* they target. These in turn can be unravelled into further aspects; for instance doing/defining may be achieved *explicitly* or *implicitly* and correspondingly, monitoring/assessing may involve *immediate awareness* or also *strategic eliciting* of information.

The learning-related *targets* of the teacher's doing/defining and monitoring are the representation in this mode of the specific learning aspect of teaching functions and they too may be detailed further. These targets have to be seen to include: the curriculum or intended learning aims in question, the learning tasks or activities chosen, the pupil organization within the classroom, and the various teaching resources to be used in the activities in that context. This increased detail may be included in the form of further subnodes in the concept map network, as shown in Figure 5.3.

Further detail in teacher doing/defining/assisting functions for learning
Assuming we do decide to go in for such progressive functional analysis (whether or not we use this form of representation, though that may itself make a difference), then how far it's worth proceeding into the specification of subdetails is a matter of debate. It will depend on circumstances and purpose, but my own view is that generally for mentoring purposes it's useful to proceed still further than Figure 5.3, because there are further aspects and subfunctions which tend to be involved in any form of teaching strategy. Their addition does of course tend to extend concept-map diagrams somewhat. The further detail levels of the doing/defining and monitoring/assessing subfunctions are therefore shown separately in Figures 5.4 and 5.5. The additional items will hopefully speak for themselves to a considerable extent, but some commentary may be useful.

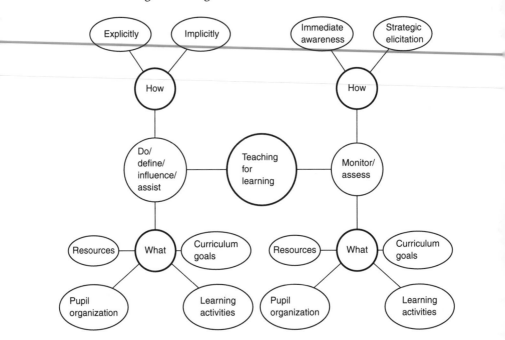

Figure 5.3 Intermediate detail concept map of learning promotion functions in teaching

What does teaching define, influence and assist? In Figure 5.4, going down to the *targets* of teacher doing/defining and assistance (the *'what'* node), the first two major subnodes on the right and their subnodes echo the discussion presented a couple of pages ago about the distinction between curriculum goals and task goals. As the concept-map indicates, *curriculum goals* will largely involve *learning goals*, i.e. capacity acquisitions such as concepts, knowledge and skills (including perhaps 'higher-order' skills like strategic study capabilities), but they may also include *values and attitudes*, like interest in the subject, open-mindedness and so on. Teachers clearly need to define and influence the nature of the learning goals and to assist progress towards them, though whether they actually communicate the learning goals to the pupils is itself part of the issue of teaching methodology.

Teachers certainly need to define and influence the actual classroom *learning activities* or tasks designed to bring about learning. This will include them defining the *task goals* to pupils ('what they're to do'), communicating the *constituent activities* of these tasks and assisting their carrying out, whatever they may be, including assisting pupils with the prerequisite *knowledge and skills* necessary to carry out these tasks. Together with and at the same time as all this, they will need to be defining and influencing the *organization of pupils* and the *deployment of resources*, from books, worksheets and

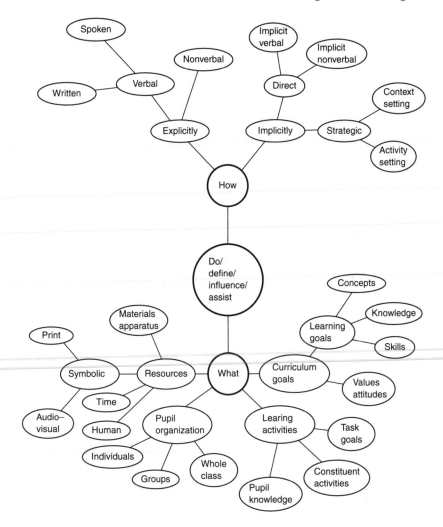

Figure 5.4 Further detail concept map of doing/defining learning functions

other print-based media, through to the 'use' of other teaching colleagues and assistants.

How does teaching define, influence and assist? Turning to the *ways* in which they may do this, the 'how' node and subnodes in the upper part of Figure 5.4 concept map, it can be seen that the proposed analysis foresees both explicit and implicit, direct and strategically indirect modes of achieving definition, influence and assistance. Perhaps the most important aspect to highlight for student-teachers is the possibility and power of indirect, background arrangement factors in promoting learning. Here the 'how' tends to shade in to the 'what'; as for instance, when teachers set tasks which will actually require further activities that involve the direct learning in question (e.g. 'call my bluff games' as a means of achieving dictionary use for learning spelling and dictionary use).

Further detail in teacher monitoring/assessment functions for learning
The further specification of the *monitor/assess* area of teaching-for-learning functions is shown in Figure 5.5. As is to be expected, there is a rather similar structure of further subfunctions and many of the terms are either general or have already been introduced, so relatively little extra needs to be said here. It is perhaps worth adding in the case of monitoring/assessing that, even more than in the doing/defining case, progressively focused functional analyses like this do tend to drive us towards particular forms of concrete strategy, i.e. what one actually has to do as a teacher in these respects. This is perhaps most obviously illustrated in the case of forms of *immediate awareness* in Figure 5.5; there are only so many forms this can take (though scanning is something to which many student-teachers need alerting, since they don't discover it on their own).

Once again, given its centrality, the issue of monitoring learning progress as opposed to task progress perhaps deserves comment. Since learning occurs through learning activities and experiences, the monitoring aspect of teaching clearly has to target both the execution of and progress in the relevant *activity* (whether it's listening to the teacher, holding a group discussion, or whatever) and the actual *learning* that's taking place.

Regarding the task activity, it's clearly important for the teacher to check on pupils' grasp of what is entailed in the task and their progress in fulfilling this. For instance, this checking on pupil task progress featured centrally in the approaches reported by Brown and McIntyre's (1993) effective teachers. In addition to this, however, a teacher needs to check, as far as possible, on the nature and extent of the *learning* that seems to be accruing. When a teacher circulates a class who are getting on with their worksheets, for instance, this is a very useful opportunity to see not just 'which bit they're up to', but what they're getting out of the activity by way of learning gains. Of course, worksheets will normally have been designed with learning in mind and experienced teachers have the basis for building in features likely to enhance their learning potential, and even when they might say that they were 'merely' checking on progress in the task, 'what's been covered', they're probably taking in other aspects too. This is because amount covered is only at best an indirect indicator of learning gain, and that is the basic goal. Student teachers, for various reasons, often fail to realize this and even more often to do it.

A note on functional analysis concept mapping: In my view, this sort of functional analysis in progressively more detail can form one useful part of an explicit pedagogical framework for use in mentoring. It doesn't do

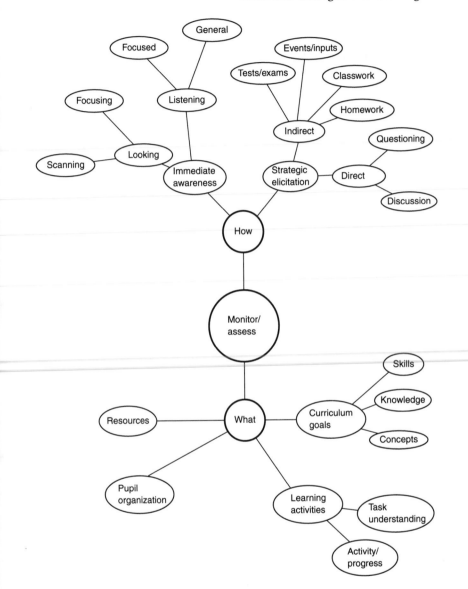

Figure 5.5 Further detail concept map of monitoring/assessing learning functions

everything; it certainly needs augmenting by a consideration of the particulars of a range of teaching methods and tactics, including the classroom activities they involve. It need not take the form of the concept maps just illustrated and other possibilities will be introduced in a later chapter.

However, since the present chapter has already become rather long, I propose to return to a consideration of the pros and cons of this mapping approach towards the end of Chapter 6, which will apply it to pupil management aspects.

Further reading

Useful works of relatively recent vintage covering learning and pedagogy include the books by Shipman (1985), Gellatly (1986), Edwards and Mercer (1987), Howard (1987), Pollard and Tann (1987), Tharp and Gallimore (1988), Claxton (1990), Edwards and Galloway (1991), Stones (1992).

6

Classroom strategies and their pupil management potential

In the previous chapter I argued for the role of an explicit pedagogical framework in mentoring and considered the learning potential of teaching strategies in the light of their capacity to involve factors that influence learning. The idea of representing functional analysis of this aspect through concept mapping was introduced. The present chapter extends these ideas to the pupil management side of teaching, since at the very least, choice of teaching activity depends not just on how well it promotes learning, but also how feasible, positive or negative it's likely to be in terms of pupil reaction and behaviour. In other words, we need also to consider the pupil and class management potential of classroom strategies.

Classroom strategies and their pupil management potential

As already recognized, class management is the other inherent aspect of teaching, insomuch as teaching is about getting learners to engage in activities and experiences designed to promote learning. The importance of this 'getting them to engage' aspect is generally recognized (if anything, over-emphasized, especially by students). But achieving good class management isn't always helped by the ideas and assumptions surrounding it. This is particularly true of some of the preconceptions held by student-teachers, which can contribute considerably to the worries they have about 'discipline' (or rather 'indiscipline').

They include the tendency to *separate* management of pupil behaviour from promoting learning, as tends to be implied by such sayings as '*first* you've got to achieve discipline and order, *then* you can teach them'. Another is the use of expressions like '*class control*', which may appear to suggest both the desirability and the possibility of exercising complete influence over groups of young human beings. Connected to this, one sometimes finds the further magical-technical assumption that there exists some simple secret of how to control and influence.

Student-teachers differ considerably in the ideas they arrive with and by no means all of them bring views such as the above. To the extent that they do, however, they're also likely to harbour exaggerated expectations of their courses ('tell us the secret of unfailing discipline'), and to be all the more recriminating when these presumed goods aren't delivered. These kinds of viewpoint can also hinder their own development of teaching craft, as they look in vain for the 'simple fix' and perhaps decide that lessons that went well were due to single factors (which were probably only part of the story). Or perhaps worse, failing to attain perfection, they may conclude that they themselves don't possess the required magical charisma and give up making the effort.

As usual, it's not that the above kinds of ideas are *totally* invalid. Rather, I would suggest that they need to be seen in relation to other aspects and considerations. More positively, I should make clear my working assumptions in this area.

Influencing pupils is an inherent aspect of promoting learning and vice-versa. It's not just a bolt-on, separable part of teaching. As I've been saying, to promote learning one has to get the learner doing what it takes to learn. In this sense, teaching is by definition managing learning, but equally the nature of the classroom activities used for this also have their effects on pupil response and behaviour. This is perhaps particularly true of the ways teachers relate to pupils in the course of such activities.

Class management isn't just a matter of behaviour control, but it does include influencing pupil actions. Teaching has been called a 'moral craft' in that it involves working with human persons and therefore respecting their freedom, values and well-being. There have of course always been deep debates about the balance between these values in the context of teaching. A teaching situation is *ideally* one in which there is mutual cooperation between learners and teacher because they share the same learning goals and an understanding of the processes. But this ideal clearly can't be presumed, even if it should be striven for, and this applies particularly in a compulsory education system. Entering the teaching profession therefore means participating in something which recognizes a limiting of pupil freedom and corresponding rights and responsibility to actively influence their behaviour (partly in order precisely to respect the rights and promote the well-being of such pupils).

Influencing pupil behaviour doesn't have to be negative or confrontational.

Ultimately, it's a matter of trying to get pupils to *participate* actively and intelligently in the teaching/learning process. It's *their* participation and this means utilizing the influences on *their* actions, which boils down to their motives and habits. Quite apart from respect of persons and if only for instrumental reasons, teachers generally wish to do this in a positive and economical way. Student-teachers not infrequently have particularly strong concerns to be positive and respectful towards pupils, sometimes based in part on their own negative experiences of schooling, though the times are changing in these respects.

In spite of this, even student-teachers holding such ideals tend also to share the peculiarly British emphasis (compared to North Americans and the rest of Europe, for instance) on *control of action through explicitly negative means*. Deterrence and negative sanctions are two typical watchwords here, with authority orientations also a widespread form of concern ('Will they respect mine?'). These emphases can put them into various types of painful dilemmas, particularly when under stress they find themselves regressing to the negative stances of which they so disapprove. Student-teachers therefore need insights into the full range of factors and processes that influence pupil action and strategies for applying these intelligently.

Other things equal, teachers and pupils want the experience and outcomes of teaching to be as positive as possible. This surely sounds obvious, but is worth stating, because some of the above negative preconceptions and cultural values actually tend towards a negative type of stance which can get in the way of positive effectiveness (the 'it's not doing any good unless it hurts' type of sentiment). Engaging the positive motivation and harnessing the habits of pupils therefore appears an obvious teacher strategy for the management of pupil learning activity.

The art of managing pupil behaviour is a particularly open, subtle type of skill. As we saw in Chapter 2, *open* skill is that which tends to achieve its goals in the face of relatively unpredictable, usually complex, subtle contexts. It doesn't lend itself to simple procedures or guaranteed routines and for this reason it isn't easy to learn or teach. Yet people show more or less proficiency at it and I hope I succeeded in showing in a previous chapter how dealing with people to some systematic purpose has the features of open skill. Similarly, pupil and class management may be seen as a closely related type of interpersonal capability and much of what needs to be said here can build on the material of Chapter 4.

Promoting the positive and preventing problems

Therefore, the position to adopt regarding pupil and class management seems similar to the one I espoused at the beginning of the preceding chapter with regard to the learning function of teaching. Namely, classroom activities and the ways that teachers go about relating to pupils have the potential to influence pupils' reactions and behaviour in various ways. They have *class or pupil management potential*. Teaching will function most effectively and least stressfully, perhaps even enjoyably, when we can use this to promote the positive and thereby prevent the negative, or, failing this, at least limit the problems.

As with the promotion of learning, so with the promoting of positive involvement. A pedagogical framework that is useful in mentoring student-teachers will be one that pays full attention to the concrete specifics of classroom action, but its understanding of these strategies will be informed by an understanding of how and how far they are likely to work for effective pupil behaviour and relations. As in the previous section, then, it seems logical to proceed by asking first about what we're actually trying to promote through the management aspect, then what factors seem to influence pupil behaviour and reaction. I will then reverse the order of the previous section and consider further functional analysis using the DAM trio for the management aspects and their illustration in concept maps. The section will then round off by analysing some examples of classroom strategy for their pupil management potential.

Class management for what?
Just what is it that we're trying to promote by way of our management strategies? The answer to this surely has to be that it's basically *pupil learning*. Teachers aren't charged merely with managing pupils as custodians (even if most of us can remember occasions when it seemed like that!), they're supposed to be getting pupils to engage in learning. Following the analyses of the previous chapter, this indicates not only that we want to promote their achievement of certain learning outcomes, but also, as a means to these, their effective involvement in the various classroom activities and tasks designed to bring such learning about. In other words, when thinking about the aims of the management aspect of teaching, we're not thinking about something separate from the learning promotion aspect.

However, this is not to espouse a purely instrumental view of teaching. It doesn't prevent teachers from also wanting the social situation in which all this occurs to be as positive as possible for all concerned or from wanting to promote the interest in a particular subject area and the enthusiasm for learning in general which they themselves hopefully experience – or to be able to limit damage to their own and their pupils' well-being from negative behaviour when it does occur.

What teachers wish to promote through their management strategies has, then, either already been articulated earlier or is relatively obvious. Also, once again, as with the learning promotion aspect of teaching, teachers themselves are well aware of and able to talk about the concrete strategies they employ and there is anyway now a host of books dealing with the particulars and background to class management strategies. As in the earlier part of the chapter on learning, therefore, I shall not be focusing on the consideration of concrete classroom management strategies. Rather, the concern is to build a coherent pedagogical framework which will in particular help teacher-mentors to articulate and discuss their own and other strategies available in practice or in the literature. It should also allow them to examine rationales with their students, so as to assess the class management potential of teaching approaches and teacher stances. Correspondingly, therefore, we need to consider what factors do tend to influence pupil motivation and behaviour.

Influences on behaviour and reaction
We have already considered some basic ideas concerning the nature of human motivation and interpersonal influence at some length in Chapter 4 and I shall introduce some more angles in a further detail section here. These ideas will only be summarized here in the main text, therefore, but if you're reading this chapter on its own, you may feel the need to consult the Chapter 4 material at some point (see the section on motivating in particular).

Much pupil behaviour is not generated rationally by motive, but implicitly through habit. This is admittedly putting it in crude terms, but my point is to counter the mistaken tendency of common-sense assumptions to suppose that human actions are always done for a reason (i.e. the fulfilment of a motive or value) and done consciously. To the contrary, much of our action, particularly the control of its details, is done more or less tacitly and unconsciously. In skill terms: well-practised substrategies tend to get run off automatically when we encounter the relevant contextual signs (which we also read intuitively). This is at least as likely to be true of school pupils as of adults, including teachers and student-teachers.

Conversely, therefore, one way of influencing action is to 'define the situation' in ways that will be read and responded to appropriately. We may attempt to do this implicitly as well as explicitly, with the former being particularly important to emphasize, given student-teachers' common-sense tendencies to think of class management in terms of the overt exercise of authority. In my view, the power of this 'harnessing of their habits' is sufficient to make it one of the central functions in class management approaches, but it does also raise ethical issues, which were briefly considered in Chapter 4.

Pupil motives and values are nevertheless centrally important influences on their behaviour and feelings. Nevertheless, the common-sense emphasis on people's behaviour being led by their motives didn't arise from nowhere. Most human action is or was originally driven by the intention to achieve what people value, even if much of this has become habitual or is pursued tacitly. There is indeed much evidence that the most important aspect in people's perceptions and reactions has usually to do with how it relates to their values. Do

I like it or dislike it? How strongly? On this view the other main class management function is to 'engage their motives'. Given traditional reliance on punitiveness and deterrence, the considerable power of *also* enlisting positive values and enjoyment seems important to emphasize.

Pupil motives are many and varied, but in the classroom some are likely to be more important than others. One way of coping with the infinite possibilities within human motivation is to pick out groups or areas of values and to consider which areas are likely to be important for school pupils. Amongst these are likely to be:

- involvement and interest;
- self-esteem and confidence;
- security of acceptance and collaboration;
- physical well-being and safety.

These tend to form a hierarchy in that the ones lower in the list usually require fulfilment before the upper ones come into play. This can vary between pupils and situations, but in particular circumstances a particular pupil is likely to have a priority of values, whether knowingly or unknowingly. Situations may be reacted to in function of the values *intrinsic* to them ('because I like it') or as an instrumental means to values *extrinsically* connected with them ('because of what it gets me') or, more usually, a mixture of many forms of intrinsic and extrinsic value.

Intrinsic motivation in the classroom depends on the stressors impinging on pupils. Realization of the various types of values listed above will clearly promote positive feelings and, other things equal, positive reactions, but involvement and interest also depend on an intermediate level of stressors like novelty and uncertainty. Too little, and there's boredom and the creating of distractions and other forms of stimulation. Too much, and it's anxiety-provoking, with avoidance reactions, which may involve 'flight' (withdrawal) or 'fight' (confrontation) or a mixture of the two (e.g. 'mucking around').

Extrinsic motivators may help to reinforce desired behaviours. If a pupil is intrinsically attracted by an activity he or she is likely to engage in it, but if not then one can use extrinsic motivation as a payoff. The traditional version of this is known as 'bribery', but the behaviourist version is called *reinforcement* and depends not so much on insights as on building an association between the action and some form of reward, such as social attention or praise. This sort of approach may have its limits, particularly with secondary school pupils, but the approach is worth including in one's repertoire.

Pupils' effort and task involvement is likely to depend on how they judge their own ability. Pupils' perspectives on classrooms and schooling in general are likely to influence their levels of commitment, though within situations their more important construals are likely to concern the ways they judge the difficulty and feasibility of tasks, and in particular their own abilities

Further detail section 6.1
Aspects of pupil motivation: behavioural and other approaches

Humanistic psychological perspectives and implications of skill approaches for ways in which human action is regulated have been introduced in previous chapters. Here, therefore, I want to add something on the influential behaviourist approach to the control of action and then to comment on its combination with other ideas on pupil motivation and behaviour.

The behavioural approach

This approach travels under various names, but springs from the behaviourist psychology of the late B.F. Skinner (Modgil and Modgil 1987), which has an external and simplifying view of action. It sees a person's action as governed by the *reinforcement* or rewarding experience that follows it very closely in time. Not a question of intention or insight, rather, if something we do is followed closely by a positively reinforcing event, then we shall become more likely to perform the same action in those circumstances. 'Become' is an important term here. Because reinforcement is said to work by association and not by deliberation or immediate insight, it's normally expected to do so only gradually. An action therefore tends to need reinforcing every time, especially in the early stages, to become an established tendency in that situation. *Positive reinforcers* may be thought of as *rewards*, as long as one remembers that different things may have a reinforcing effect on different pupils or in different contexts ('One pupil's welcome praise is another's kiss of death').

There's a good deal of evidence to suggest that positive reinforcement (following up with something nice) has more powerful and straightforward effects than punishment (following up with something nasty), perhaps partly because the experience of merely receiving attention from others appears to be valued by most of us, so since punishing tends to involve this, it can paradoxically be reinforcing as well as deterring.

The behavioural approach is very much to analyse the *reward contingencies* through the 'ABC' approach when considering behaviour one wishes either to promote or lessen. This means that we look at

A   The antecedents: in what circumstances does the behaviour tend to occur?

B   The behaviour: what is the actual type of overt behaviour in question?

C   The consequences: what tends to follow this behaviour, which may be maintaining its occurrence through reinforcing it?

To promote a particular behaviour, the behavioural approach recommends reinforcing it through immediate praise or whatever seems to function as reward. In particular, it favours a gradual approach called *'shaping'*. If we were to wait to reinforce the fully fledged behaviour we wish to establish, we might be waiting forever. Rather, in shaping the pupil is helped gradually to approximate and establish the desired behaviour tendency by at first being rewarded for doing parts or aspects of the desired type of behaviour, perhaps for very limited periods of time. As the tendency to do this becomes established, then they only get rewarded for adding something further, and so on until they're showing the full version desired in that setting. Those using the behavioural approach in the classroom are therefore on the lookout to 'catch them being good' in any way, so that they can reward and shape from there.

To remove a behaviour, this approach would ignore it as far as possible, but reward something else in the same circumstances. It might isolate the pupil if they were seriously disruptive (called 'time out from positive reinforcement' rather than punishment – the difference does appear to be important). The behavioural approach may be simple in some respects, though it has to be admitted that here I've only touched on the barest of its essentials. However, most of the many current books on class management cover it. It has had massive influence in special education and now features explicitly or implicitly in many education authority positive discipline resource schemes designed by local educational psychologists.

This approach tends to elicit all sorts of strong reactions. One gets the sense that some special education teachers have become converts because it's the only thing that seems to work at all with their pupils. Equally, others, including many student-teachers, seem to resist the line on the emotional basis of conflict with their own assumptions, or through misunderstanding the approach by seeing it in their own familiar terms (e.g. as simply bribery) rather than in its own. Such simplistic rejection sometimes converts into uncritical acceptance when once they give it half a chance.

Combining approaches for a repertoire of strategies

We don't have to 'buy or reject the whole story' from this or any approach. It may be, for instance, that the different sets of ideas are applicable to different instances of action at different times. It may also be that they're capable of describing different aspects of the same action. We can in any case try the techniques of any particular approach, perhaps reinterpreting and adapting them in the light of other ideas or combining them anyway. In earlier chapters, for instance, I introduced cognitive ideas about the nature of skilled action. Two of the main insights from this type of research are a) that human beings have certain sorts of limitations on how much information they can take into account and think about at a time, particularly at a conscious level, and b) that in both thought and action, we tend to become automatic and habitual at processes we do a lot.

A major point of the *cognitive approach*, for example, is that our actions depend generally on how we see our context and ourselves, including the possibilities open to us. Much recent work, for instance, has shown the importance of the causes to which pupils attribute their successes and failures, which may include themselves and their abilities or lack thereof, the ease or difficulty of the task, luck, and so forth. Their judgements here are likely to depend on many factors, not least the ways their own experience of success and failure as against the effort they've deployed. There is evidence in this respect, for instance, that boys tend to attribute success more to effort than do girls. Whatever the reason, it may leave them free to maintain an image of their own ability, whilst girls may conclude their ability is lacking, since they've failed in spite of trying their best. Such attributions also seem to be susceptible to 'definitions' by significant others, including not only their peers, but also their teachers.

This adds a dimension to the behavioural approach, without necessarily contradicting it. *Cognitive behaviourist approaches* now seek to combine the cognitive idea that humans may thoughtfully regulate their own actions with the behavioural emphasis on reward or felt payoff. So teachers may help pupils gradually regulate their own actions, without expecting too much at once.

Likewise, the cognitive idea of limits on the human capacity to deal with information fits well with the behavioural strategy of shaping and influencing behaviour gradually. Such insights also prompt the realization that even if the pupil does understand the message fully the first time (and that is doubtful in many cases), it's unlikely they can deploy it fully in totally changing their behaviour forthwith.

Perhaps the most important contribution of an intelligent combination of these various views is that a) they help student interns replace the relatively simplistic, rationalist assumptions they often bring to their concerns about discipline and b) they do suggest a variety of useful classroom strategies, which are covered in detail in the various further reading materials suggested at the end of the chapter.

and capacities for effort. These attributions have been shown to have considerable effect in recent years.

Managing with classroom strategies: DAM analysis

The DAM functional analysis introduced in Chapter 4 relates to interpersonal skill generally and should therefore apply to the classroom management of pupils. To recap the three functions:

- *Doing/defining* means giving out signals which define the situation and thereby direct the action by conveying to the pupil 'the nature of the game'.
- *Active awareness* means actively monitoring what's going on by way of pupil behaviour and feelings, including the effects of one's own defining.
- *Motivating* means attempting to satisfy pupil motives and values through the activities they engage in and the ways the teacher defines these and relates to them.

The motivating function permeates both of the other functions. Thus doing/defining might be relabelled relating to/influencing pupil motivation and behaviour. What I call active awareness has long been emphasized in the area of class management, in particular since the classic study by Jacob Kounin (1970), who referred to it as 'withitness'.

These functions need combining within multi-functional strategies, though particular functions may tend to predominate at certain times, for example, doing/definition by way of directions etc. may be particularly needed at transition points in lessons, especially the beginning. As skill theory might expect, Brown and McIntyre (1993) found that their effective teachers tended to go through constant small action cycles, in which they directed, then monitored, then adjusted further directions in the light of the feedback. Having already provided a progressive introduction to the concept mapping form of representing functional analysis for learning promotion, we can proceed to an intermediate detail version of the corresponding DAM analysis for management functions as shown in Figure 6.1.

You will notice that there are certain asymmetries and differences between this and the earlier learning function diagram, and also between aspects within each diagram. These have to do with the particular content of the functions and they again illustrate the point made earlier about task analysis for skill teaching; many such analyses are usually possible, as are many forms of representation.

Relating and influencing functions in pupil management

A more detailed version of the relating/influencing subfunctions from Figure 6.1 is shown in more expanded form below in Figure 6.2. It will be seen that the ways of relating to and influencing pupils, *how* these are deployed in managing them, are essentially identical to those already shown in the

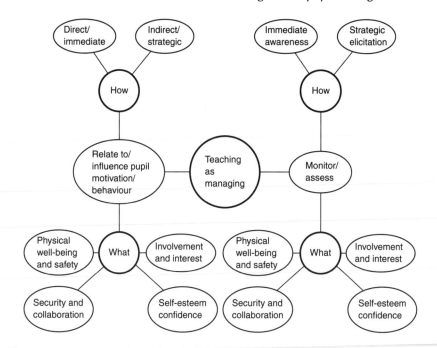

Figure 6.1 Intermediate detail concept map of management functions in teaching

case of the doing/defining aspect of the learning function. However, the targets under this pupil management function differ whilst overlapping to some extent.

Thus much of what the teacher does and communicates under the heading of 'actively relating and influencing' is targeted at pupils' *learning activities and understanding*. It's getting them to do and to see things so as to assist their learning. As such these were mentioned in the previous learning function analysis maps, under the heading of targets of *defining, assisting and influencing*. The management function concept map therefore leaves this notion implicit.

In the cases of the pupil well-being and motivation nodes, further specifications are offered as to experiences and provision likely to cater for that type of motive or concern. This is by way of at least mentioning these types of possibility, as the basis for an *aide-mémoire* for mentor monitoring, for example. It's not being implied, for instance, that motives and the ways of satisfying them can actually be lined up so neatly or exclusively. In reality particular classroom experiences will probably have very mixed impact on pupils and their reactions (the 'multi-functional' aspect of teaching strategies). Nevertheless, intern/teachers need to consider at least the following major areas of pupil motivation:

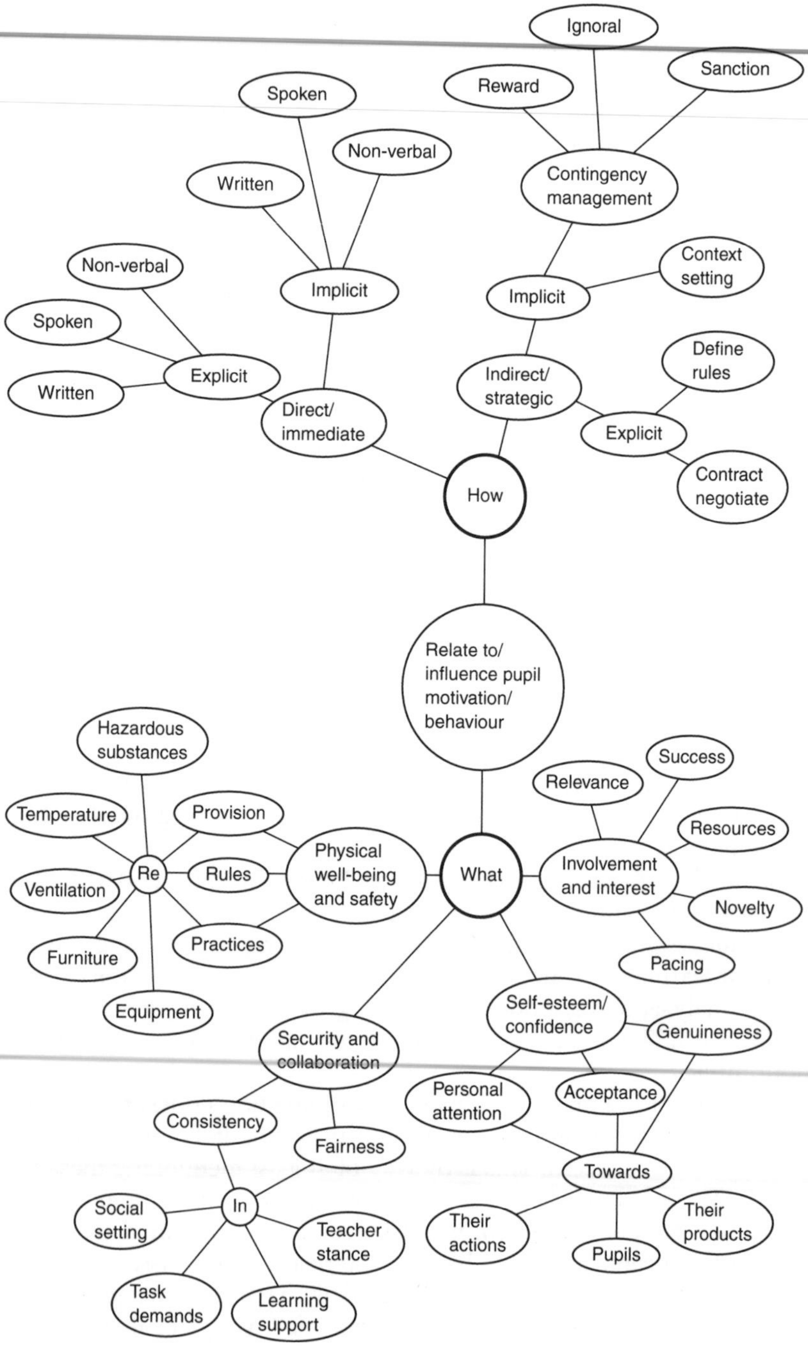

Ignoral

Sanction

Spoken

Reward

Non-verbal

Written

Contingency management

Context setting

Non-verbal

Implicit

Implicit

Spoken

Define rules

Explicit

Indirect/ strategic

Written

Direct/ immediate

Explicit

Contract negotiate

How

Relate to/ influence pupil motivation/ behaviour

Hazardous substances

Success

Relevance

Temperature

Provision

Resources

Physical well-being and safety

Re

Rules

What

Involvement and interest

Ventilation

Novelty

Furniture

Practices

Pacing

Equipment

Self-esteem/ confidence

Genuineness

Security and collaboration

Personal attention

Acceptance

Consistency

Fairness

Social setting

In

Towards

Their products

Teacher stance

Their actions

Pupils

Task demands

Learning support

Figure 6.2 Further detail concept map of relate/influence management functions

- *Involvement and interest:* these tend to be promoted by provision of the features shown in the further subbranches of this main branch, but remember that different individuals have different optimum levels when it comes to significance, novelty and pacing. By contrast, for pupil success it's probably safer to adopt Mae West's maxim that 'too much of a good thing can be wonderful'!
- *Self-esteem and confidence:* under this you may recognize the three 'core conditions' of counselling which have long been held to be central in facilitating personal involvement. These are relevant to dealing with pupils in classrooms, but they're likely to need some adaptation. As teachers we (genuinely) will not be able to tolerate certain sorts of pupil freedom, given the constraints of dealing with a whole class at a time and having to address a certain set of learning goals. It's also clear, for example, that although experience of success may be an important stimulator of interest and involvement, it's also central to the development of self-esteem and confidence.
- *Security and collaboration:* the somewhat obvious requirements here are consistency and fairness in the various indicated aspects of the intern/ teacher's dealings with pupils. Once again, it's clear that provision under this and other branch headings have their cross-effects.
- *Physical well-being and safety:* these are important at all times, though more obvious as issues in certain situations. Provision of resources, sharing of rules and adherence to practices regarding them are plainly relevant strategies which, once again, are likely to have wider effects on other aspects of pupil motivation and behaviour.

Monitoring and assessing functions in pupil management
Given the similarity of the forms and targets of the monitor and assessing functions in management to previously shown analyses, it does not seem worth reproducing it here. However, the importance of 'withitness' in classroom management and the tendency of so many past student teachers to neglect it are such that a number of points seem worth making.

- *Immediate awareness:* it may often need to be pointed out to student interns that awareness of many of the above target items is not really immediate, though it may feel like that. In most cases it's actually a matter of *inferring*, of reading the *signs indicating* the target item. Happiness isn't a smiling face any more than effort might be a matter of frowning; you can be happy without smiling or smile without being happy. We do tend to become automatic and unreflective in our everyday reliance on such signals, but as aspiring professionals who will deal systematically and effectively with such issues, student interns may well need to be alerted to a more careful type of appraisal of the above features in classroom situations; things are often less straightforward than common-sense approaches tend to assume. So given that intern/teachers always need to think about the *interpretation* of what they access, their main forms of direct awareness of the signs will be the following:

- *Looking: focused* attending on particular pupils comes relatively naturally, given the millions of one-to-one conversations any student intern will have held, but by the same token they find often visual *scanning* around the class difficult to engage in; doing this in normal conversations is something a socially skilled person normally avoids, but in the classroom situation it becomes an essential substrategy.
- *Listening:* whether focused or general, this is an equally obvious part of classroom monitoring, but is likewise often ignored as student-teachers anxiously orient towards what they can *do* to make things go as they want. A little more effort spent on reading the situation through such monitoring may pay dividends and at the same time calm them down through a bit of stepping back and acting cool.

- *Strategic elicitation:* the other, more 'active' and guided way of monitoring relevant features of classroom life involves engaging in deliberate actions which elicit the desired information. Given that much of this is about pupils' inner feelings and understanding, such strategic targeting is obviously of particular importance, as the traditional emphasis on some of the following subaspects indicates. I suggest a distinction into two major forms of strategic elicitation, namely *direct* and *indirect*. They involve various subforms.

  - *Direct:* here we have the use of more or less immediate interaction with pupils, in which the intern/teacher's inputs elicit pupil responses available to immediate awareness and interpretation. This type of approach may include:
    Questioning: 'if you want to find out, ask them' – but you have to be intelligent about what you ask, of whom, when, and how to interpret the response. The angles are legion and there is even a journal devoted entirely to the study of the use of questioning in teaching. Important forms of variation here include the open-closed distinction, meaning something slightly different from everyday use: *closed* questions are where one supplies a closed set of alternative responses (e.g. 'Which is the capital of France: Nice, Marseilles or Paris?'), *open* questions are where one leaves the alternative responses open to the respondent (e.g. 'What is the capital of France?'). Closed questions may be easier when they're about informational matters like the above examples, but they tend to be constraining and alienating when they're about personal reaction and motive (e.g. 'Did you help him because you were afraid of him or because I was looking?' versus 'Why did you help him?' or the more 'genuine' but implicit version: 'I'd be interested in knowing why you helped him').
    Discussion: a discussion obviously offers both obvious and implicit ways of getting at pupil response and reaction, though the setting and

participants will tend to have an important effect on what is or isn't disclosed.

Events and inputs: particular events and inputs to the situation may occasion pupil reactions of various sorts which may yield useful information, though these as always need intelligent interpretation.

• *Indirect:* here the teacher uses pupil products or records of activity and work as a basis for inferring aspects of pupil participation and motivation. *Classwork* and *homework* are mentioned in the earlier concept map, where one might possibly add *'information provided by other pupils'*. Obviously inferences made on the basis of the latter, even more than the former, may require careful thought and checking by other means.

The pupil and class management potential of classroom strategies

The above treatment of pupil management functions and subfunctions in teaching hopefully does provide a means of bringing out some of the important things that must be attended to in teaching and particularly in the process of learning to teach. However, it also shows us that like most concepts and distinctions, things aren't as clear at the boundaries as they might have seemed from the central instances. The last few pages, for instance, will perhaps have somewhat blurred the distinction between a teaching function and a classroom strategy, or at least a detailed substrategy. I have also thought it important to note and comment on some relatively specific behaviour management tactics which seem to flow directly from some of the psychological perspectives outlined earlier and which are currently recommended in various books on the subject. These are offered in Further detail section 6.2.

However, if we return to the broader levels of activity more generally associated with the phrase *teaching strategy* and involved in specific planning for teaching, then virtually all that was said in the previous chapter about the idea of learning potential applies, suitably adapted, to that of the pupil management potential of particular classroom strategies. In fact, this management aspect perhaps more clearly illustrates the notion of *negative* potential (i.e. some strategies may actually be worse than useless).

The pupil and class management potential of particular teaching strategies means the extent to which such activities enable effective management of pupil motivation and behaviour through operation of the DAM basic interpersonal functions: defining situations in ways that harness existing habitual action, gaining awareness of impacts and events, and in doing so catering for fulfilment of pupil motivation. This is putting it positively. The negative aspect refers to the extent to which particular strategies threaten or even hinder the operation of these DAM functions.

Thus the idea is that as well as examining possible teaching strategies for

Further detail section 6.2
Some modern pupil management tactics

Having done what might be called a top-down analysis from broad functions towards particular strategies, it seems appropriate to balance the picture by focusing on the specific end and considering some relatively concrete tactics which are widely recommended in current works on classroom management and discipline. First promoting the positive, then coping with the negative.

Promoting the positive

Establishing a good class atmosphere
Different teachers will probably have different ideas about what constitutes a 'good' atmosphere, but in terms of the DAM trio we might say it's mainly a matter of what and how you define and direct and what sort of motives are addressed by your style and the sort of action you promote (or allow). Good atmosphere would probably include addressing most of the positive motives listed earlier by being firm but also as positive and enthusiastic as possible, clear about basic rules but flexible and encouraging of pupil responsibility, fair and consistent. But these are rather broad features, which need filling out and further establishing through more detailed substrategies and tactics, such as the following.

Catch them being good (CBG)
This comes partly from the behaviourist line, but is consistent with other perspectives. It consists of the relatively specific tactic of being on the active lookout for pupils who are doing what you want them to be doing (or just beginning to do something related, so that you can reward them explicitly (e.g. verbal praise) or implicitly (e.g. smile, going over to talk about their work, etc.). This can be very hard for those who have a negative moralizing stance and who are inclined to take the positive for granted, but to react to the negative, even be obsessed by it. Perhaps this is why they can be astounded by the effect CBG can have if they do use it at all intelligently, particularly with children who haven't been used to being recognized or worse, who have been labelled negatively. Having said this, a single change on a particular day isn't likely to reverse the habits of a school lifetime, but you've got to start somewhere.

Negotiating rules with pupils
Not really feasible as a student-teacher and with the whole class, though

something it would be well worth student-teachers having the chance to observe. It may sound to some student-teachers like abdication, but of course the teacher is actually defining the situation quite heavily and in various ways (structuring and influence in explicit and implicit ways, for instance, raising issues of fairness and feasibility, setting boundaries). In so far as it can be done, it can be a considerable motivator, signalling respect for the pupils as responsible persons, defining them as responsible beings and hopefully thereby also influencing them towards being so. Of course, like any relatively extended tactic, it requires monitoring and awareness.

Dealing with problems

The stress so far has been upon positive classroom management through ways of defining and motivating pupils. Effective achievement in virtually all skills, from hitting tennis balls to class management, depends on strategic anticipation. This is in some contrast to 'commonsense' outlooks which seem not to think proactively about how to get what's wanted, perhaps particularly with regard to social interaction. Rather the tendency of student-teachers can be so often to worry themselves with the worst scenario, adopting a reactive, crisis management stance of 'what if they do x ?' or to take refuge in moralistic stances stressing how things ought to be. In the face of these tendencies, it's worth emphasizing that applying the above sorts of positive strategy is likely not only to prevent problems, but also to promote positive commitment. One of the great potential advantages of a school-based course is hopefully that students have more opportunity to see these positive strategies in action.

Nevertheless, no one can guarantee success in something so open as the management aspect of teaching, so one also needs to consider strategies for dealing with problems when a positive approach hasn't succeeded in cutting these problems out. The basic principles are very much the same as those already introduced, but with some specific adaptations to coping with trouble in the classroom.

Nip trouble in the bud

When one hasn't succeeded in preventing a problem, the next best thing is to deal with it early and prevent it snowballing. Most of us human beings seem to have something of a tendency to be drawn into unfortunate, somewhat uncontrolled reactions to problems; we get upset when we meet trouble. But *we* should be defining the situation, not being defined by it. For example, there may be good reason for public treatment of undesired behaviour in class (e.g. as an occasion for revisiting the rules – and even then with the possibility of perhaps 'defining' the situation as one in which the pupil has 'forgotten' the rule, rather than necessarily as a deliberate infringement justifying cross-examination and condemnation). At the very least, however, this stops the flow of things, perhaps for the whole class, when it needn't (particularly if the children are working in groups). More seriously, it can publicize evidence that the teacher is no longer running things, but reacting to the pupil initiative. Thus a generally desirable strategy to consider in the case of problems is 'privatization'.

'Privatization', define–ignore–reward, challenging and time out
Privatization means isolating the problem so as to prevent it having ripple effects across the class and thereby escalating into a bigger problem. This typically requires the teacher to get into the vicinity of the child in question (preferably without signalling that they are doing so deliberately in response to the child). The teacher then attempts to deal quietly and quickly with the issue (while still monitoring/scanning the class, of course). *Define–ignore–reward* is another useful if complex tactic. Perhaps we should call it 'redefine, ignore, reward', in that the teacher attempts to redirect the pupil's action and attention on to the desired task, by ignoring or 'not noticing' the lack of progress, looking for any aspect of task activity on which to build, rewarding the child for what has been done or could be said to have been done (often little). The ignoring of the lack of progress is part of defining the situation as 'potentially okay' and thereby opening up the possibility of getting the pupil back on task. Both as an introduction at the beginning of such an encounter and as a check before leaving the pupil it can be useful to get him or her to tell you what he or she is (supposed to be) doing now/next.

In such situations one may nevertheless judge that an explicit *challenging/confronting* of an infringement is required and/or that a public one cannot or ought not to be avoided. Here clear definition and direction needs to be given by the teacher. In these cases one still needs to remember that the ultimate purpose is to get the child back into useful activity and participating as a member of the class or group and to disrupt the rest of the class as little as possible whilst doing so.

The suggestion here is thus that one concentrates on the deviation/sin rather than on the child as deviant/sinner; that one express one's own negative feelings at the child's behaviour rather than piling on the moral prescriptions as to what s(h)e ought to be like, and perhaps most important, that one create a positive way out of the situation, a path on to which one can set the child. That is, one doesn't just focus on what's wrong, but helps him or her realize and do what's right. In this it's useful to remember that problems tend to arise perhaps most typically with children who are lacking in cognitive competence, or confidence and self-esteem, and often all of these, though it may not seem like this on the surface, when the only reaction they seem to know is an aggressive one.

When a child is indulging in problem behaviour which requires stopping, the use of the behaviourist tactic of *time out* from positive reinforcement can be useful. This is essentially a way of denying the child the rewards of interaction. It's not to be seen as a punishment inasmuch as the attention yielded by punishment, particularly public versions, also tends to act as reward and reinforcer. However, this strategy is difficult with older pupils and disruption on a scale not containable through the various other strategies and requiring time out needs to be seen in the context of whole-school arrangements, which student-teachers need to be made aware of relatively early. Again, one of the great benefits of being school-based is that the gradual, assisted transition into the teaching role means that student-teachers should not need to think in terms of such extreme possibilities.

The above strategies for dealing with behaviour problems are of course only strategies. They're not guaranteed effective unconditionally, but they should help deal with most situations. They need further extension in particular situations, of which no two are exactly the same.

their forms of learning potential, intern/teachers should also consider them for their pupil and class management potential. Here perhaps more than in the case of learning, experience will tend to count for more than formal research, since if there is any domain where 'there are more things in heaven and earth, Horatio, than are dreamt of in your philosophy', it has to be that of human conduct and motivation. Nevertheless, sometimes the problem, particularly visible with overstressed student-teachers, is that they fail to try approaches that don't spring from their intuition.

Here again, potential is only potential. In fact, this seems to apply particularly to the class management aspect, which seems more difficult to analyse in the first place than learning potential. This, I suggest, is because influencing pupils depends on many immediate features of teacher–pupil interaction and the ways the teacher 'defines the situation'.

The implication is that judging class management potential requires close consideration of the nitty-gritty of teacher strategies – the detailed ways in which they may be deployed. In addition, the particular flow of events and reactions throughout a teaching session can make a big difference. Thus one needs to consider not only the management potential of particular strategies and substrategies, but also of the sequence of strategies within the lesson and possibly beyond.

Illustrations of class management potential analyses

Table 6.1 offers three examples of class management potential analyses at the broad level of the DAM functions. These include one used in the previous learning potential analyses earlier in the previous chapter (namely 'pupil completion of worksheet') to illustrate that teaching/learning strategies also have their class management feasibility aspects. 'Giving instructions in a "no-nonsense, keep quiet whilst I'm talking" style' and 'Negotiating rules of behaviour with the class' represent strategies specifically designed for pupil behaviour management, but with differing degrees of complexity and somewhat contrasting orientations.

These examples again imply the need to combine specific strategies and the importance of knowing the context and pupils. The point may also be made again that it isn't enough for mentors just to use their considerable experience of local situations to derive intuitive recommendations as to what will or won't work. Rather, they need to try to articulate their reasons or at least indicate the sorts of considerations they think are influencing their views, so as to help initiate student interns into such processing for themselves.

Some pros and cons of functional analysis concept mapping

As I claimed in the previous chapter, this sort of functional analysis in progressively more detail can form one useful part of an explicit pedagogical framework for use in mentoring, even if it doesn't do everything. However, having seen its application to both the learning promotion side of teaching and its pupil and class management aspect, this may be a useful point at which to consider its pros and cons a bit more systematically. On the *positive* side, I think it may claim the following advantages.

Advantages
• *It reveals one aspect of the complexity of teaching.* It doesn't create this, even though experienced teachers who no longer have to think about the details very deliberately may have precisely this initial reaction. To the contrary, it will hopefully assist them to deal explicitly with such features when needing to do so in their mentor role.
• *It does some sort of justice to the hierarchically embedded nature of teaching activity.* It thereby allows us to distinguish major functions from less important details. The embedded subbranch format helps indicate that the details are important, in that major functions have eventually to be expressed

through particular sets of actions and subfunctions. But this sort of portrayal also helps us see where it's a matter of 'you need to deal with/ monitor all these subaspects' (e.g. the targets of the functions) as opposed to 'you'll need to involve at least one of these sublevel details' (e.g. one or other way of monitoring a particular type of target item).
• *It preserves awareness of the purposeful nature of teaching.* This is perhaps the major function of functional analyses. They help prevent us from getting lost in the action and bring us back to the issue of 'what is it for'. A hierarchical functional analysis such as the above reminds us that skilful actions aren't just a question of there being an overall purpose, but of letting 'blind technique' run its course in matters of detail. It rather shows that to will the whole is to will its parts and their integration.
• *The synoptic character of concept maps allows joint awareness of differentiation and integration of the aspects of teaching and thereby assists student-teacher development.* This is really a further aspect of the previous point, but concept maps, like visual representations generally, have particular potential to convey whole as well as part aspects of things. One of the major benefits for student-teachers should therefore be that such a framework should help them, in collaboration with their mentors, to plan and progress in their acquisition of aspects of teaching skill, which is hardly going to be learned all at once. It should thus help them diagnose and focus on relevant aspects of teaching function and strategy as necessary.
• *This sort of portrayal may be useful in the specification of teaching competence for assessment purposes.* As noted earlier, the UK government is now requiring the use of relatively precise competence statements in the assessment and development of student-teacher teaching capability. The above features may be one antidote to the sometimes simplistic and unmanageable forms of competence profiling seen in educational circles. This point will be taken up in the following chapter.
    However, there are as usual also *negative* aspects:

Disadvantages
• *Such representations still fragment teaching by failing to show the interplay and overlap of component functions.* Functional analyses do need to preserve the hierarchical nature of skilled action such as teaching and concept maps are particularly good at representing this. But there is still the problem of indicating the interplay and overlap of functions. To some extent the sort of portrayal offered here highlights this problem precisely by allowing clear reference to the different functions. One might, perhaps, draw more lines between nodes to cope with this feature, but that would threaten the clarity of what the approach does achieve. In any case, real actions and strategies just combine what is represented separately in such analysis (whether in this sort of representation or, say, just using word lists); when a teacher gives explicit instructions about a learning task, both *how* and *what* aspects are inherently involved.

Table 6.1 Class management potential analyses of selected strategies

Classroom strategy / Management function	Defining/doing (Relating/influencing)	Active awareness (Monitoring/assessing impact)	Motivating
Giving oral instructions in a 'no-nonsense, keep quiet whilst I'm talking' style	*Direct/immediate:* Explicit spoken directions can be very direct and effective, presuming clarity, non-overload, repetition. *Implicit* 'take this seriously' message of non-verbal aspects can be powerful, and this and sympathetic/open-minded side can be conveyed through voice modulation and adding of reasons.	*Immediate awareness:* a specific tactic geared to influencing, so as such little potential for monitoring pupil impact, except from broad non-verbal indicators of attention and reaction.	Clarity of expectation likely to enhance *security* and assist *involvement* by pupils, other things being equal; but *confidence, collaboration* and *interest* more dependent on content of task; setting, pupils; security and confidence of some pupils may be discouraged by implicit message of 'hardness' – giving of reasons as well as instructions may convey 'we treat each other as rational beings' definition of situation.
	Indirect/strategic: usable for later/ other tasks but may need later reminders or written directions.	*Strategic elicitation:* could be basis for further exploration of pupil reaction and viewpoint regarding content and other aspects of messages.	
Negotiating rules of behaviour with the class at the beginning of the year, whole-class setting	Will involve *direct/immediate* contributions and may require prior explanation of nature of exercise and conditions required from pupils or lead-up pair/small group work; *implicit* message of rationality and open-minded mutual respect may	Will involve both *immediate awareness* of pupil response and strategic elicitation of other possibilities as part of negotiation. Thus it allows possibility for public monitoring of reactions in	Considerable potential for enhancing *self-esteem*, *confidence, collaboration* and *involvement* of pupils, but only likely to promote *security* and *well-being* or to be feasible at all when

	need backing by indications (e.g. non-verbal) of firmness. *Indirect/strategic:* Its main function is indirect establishment of commitment to a framework.	whole-class discussion, but may require individual or group focus to get at reactions of pupils less willing to express before whole class, especially initially.	teacher has capability to manage these aspects in other ways and when class contains an insignificant number of really difficult children. Thus generally not a possibility or appropriate for interns to try, though useful for them to observe if available.
Pupil completion of worksheet task (following teacher input and with book and other resources available)	Needs setting up through clear spoken *direct/immediate* instructions and written ones with/on worksheet; clarity and difficulty levels need matching to pupils, with possible extensions/backup for early finishers etc. *Indirect/strategic:* way of getting pupils into independent work through initially more structured tasks, reinforcement and consolidation with practice	Is itself a way of *eliciting* evidence for diagnosis of various aspects of pupil knowledge and motivation, particularly through the active, immediate monitoring of all pupils' task grasp and progress it requires; also chance to monitor pupils' ongoing attempts at activity in question, but this deeper individual monitoring has to be achieved whilst retaining active awareness of rest of class too.	May be easier to sustain *pupil involvement* than for comparable period of teacher input; allows particular opportunity to *enhance pupil–teacher relationship* via pupil *security* and *collaboration*, by indicating your awareness of task demands, giving personal attention and assistance regarding problems, and by recognizing and rewarding achievements in relation to effort and ability.

We have, I think, simply to note that any particular strategy will be limited in what it can achieve. We therefore need both functional analyses and separate specifications of teaching strategies wherein functions can be jointly embodied and to which functional analyses apply.

• *The neatness of such analyses hides the messiness yet unity of teaching artistry.* It might and it can easily, but it needn't and shouldn't be allowed to as long as we remember the limitations on representation in general and this type in particular. Similar points to the previous one are relevant here. A functional analysis helps us check aspects of what a particular piece of teaching might be expected to achieve and where it may be strong or weak. It even helps us to see the different sides that a really good teacher is weaving together intuitively. It does not replace the actual teaching activity, however, which will always be messier and richer (for better or worse) than any representation of it, functional or otherwise.

Postscript: getting it all together

I recognize that this and the previous chapter may have taxed your concentration somewhat, since they have involved a lengthy attempt to unravel teaching complexities using approaches whose novelty may make them seem more daunting than they need be. On the other hand, we can safely say that the richness of teaching activity is such that a few tens of pages could be only poor in their capacity to represent it.

The intention, however, as indicated at the outset of the previous chapter, has been to derive a framework which can prompt critical and practical examination of potential teaching strategies and their rationales by student-teachers with their mentors. For reasons already rehearsed frequently in this book, it seems to me not an overstatement to suggest that whether or not teacher-mentors do generally succeed in adopting such a reflective approach will mean the making or breaking of quality professional teacher preparation under the new school-based arrangements.

I have needed to go into some detail in order to illustrate the approach put forward, indeed, perhaps I may have gone into *too little* detail to convince you of its realism. But if you look back over the chapters as a whole I hope you will see that the essential ideas are quite simple and straightforward, and that they are flexible and powerful enough to be taken up and applied individually by anyone thinking about aspects of teaching.

The central idea, namely, is that teaching is a purposeful activity, whose eventual purpose is always to promote learning and whose immediate function involves a teacher purposefully influencing learners to that end. The concrete activities that constitute classroom activities are therefore to be designed with the management of learning in mind and those strategies that are suggested should be seen as such and critically appraised for their potential to promote pupil involvement and learning. I have also sought in this chapter to extend this straightforward notion into a consideration of further subfunctions that need to be borne in mind as part of such appraisal and these various aspects very much need combining to do justice to any piece of teaching. As such, however, they should be able to inform not only discussion and planning of teaching between students and mentors, but also the assessment of their teaching. In the next chapter, therefore, some of these ideas will be taken up again in considering forms of competence profiling for the assessment and development of student-teacher progress.

Further reading

The 1980s saw the advent of an increasing number of good quality works on class management, amongst which I would recommend the following: Wheldall and Merrett (1984), Wragg (1984), Fontana (1985), Tattum (1986), McManus (1989), Montgomery (1989), Robertson (1989), Laslett and Smith (1993).

7

Teaching competence profiling for student assessment and development

Assessing what learning has occurred is an inherent part of any teaching or training. At the very least one wishes to gauge how well its purposes, that is, intended learning acquisitions, have been achieved. Also, as part of their self-development, reflective teachers will wish to monitor the outcomes of their teaching so as to feed this back into their thinking and future planning. These summative and formative uses of assessment are no less relevant to courses for the initial professional preparation of teachers and their broader social context. Here it's a question of assuring ourselves that we are in fact turning out newly qualified teachers who are able to teach effectively in the professional contexts they are about to enter.

Teaching competence formulations and their functions

The Department for Education has indicated that in school-based arrangements for teacher training it wishes to see a clear focus on the teaching capacities that such training should be aiming to produce. It now insists (DFE 1992, 1993a) that use be made of relatively specific *teaching competence statements* in assessing, recording and developing student-teachers' teaching capabilities. Its most recent proposals for the reform of teacher training (DFE 1993b) have clearly signalled a move to the use of profiles containing sets of such statements.

In promoting this move, the DFE's overt concern has been for increased accountability and consistency of assessment through precision of course aims. This includes making clear to students what they should be expecting of their courses. In principle, it does seem reasonable to think that for student-teachers, a clear idea of the aspects of teaching competence could give them:

- an overall view of the nature of the professional role to which they aspire;
- a reference point for judging the relevance of offered resources and experience;
- a basis for active planning and organization of their own learning as student-teachers.

These potential benefits may appear uncontentious, as I generally think they are. Indeed, there would be gains of similar sorts for mentors and others involved in providing school-based training. Nevertheless, the DFE's competence-based approach has been met with considerable suspicion (e.g. Warham 1993; Wilkin 1993) and some severe critiques. The latter seem to arise partly out of the fact that an American tradition of competence-based education (CBE) and teacher education (CBTE) has already existed and that some of its practices do appear to leave something to be desired. Many British teachers, for instance, will have felt some dissatisfaction with the 'million tick box' profiles they've come across in relation to such things as the *Certificate of Professional and Vocational Education* or *Records of Achievement*. The critiques have also been aimed at the scheme of National Vocational Qualifications (NVQs) and General National Vocational Qualifications (GNVQs) recently developed by the National Council for Vocational Qualifications (NCVQ). The NCVQ line represents an updated and significantly amended version of the earlier CBE approach.

My own view is that both the proponents of CBE/CBTE, particularly its traditional American version, and its opponents demonstrate some confusions. Moreover, there seem to have been some serious slips between what was intended by the designers of such approaches and the practices which actually got adopted in their name. However, if we bear in mind what we've been seeing about the nature of teaching as an example of skilled capability, then this gives a good basis for deciding which aspects of a competence-based approach are worth adopting, adapting or abandoning. So whilst Further detail section 7.1 offers a slightly fuller viewpoint on the traditional CBTE approach, the recent NCVQ ideas and their critics, here in the main text I want to consider lessons to be drawn from what we've seen so far for the specification and use of competence profiling in initial teacher preparation, including some main aspects of student-teacher assessment.

Principles for formulating and using teaching competence profiles

Given past confusions and controversies in the area of competence specification, it seems worth keeping in mind the following set of points which

Further detail section 7.1
Competence-based approaches in education and training

Although the competence (or competency) based movement in education can be traced back to the 1920s, it came strongly to the fore in the
context of American teacher education in the late 1960s (cf. Tuxworth
1989; Wolf 1994), though it has waned in influence in more recent
years due to a number of factors. The original focus was on specifying
the outcomes that courses were aiming at, so as to make those providing the courses more accountable for what they 'delivered' and the
assessment more valid.

From the outset, however, CBE tended to be framed in terms of
concepts coming from the behaviourist psychology predominant in
North America at the time. This meant that very soon the talk was not
so much of outcome capacities, as of the particular *behaviours* that
might exemplify them. Thus although traditionally we would say that
a person's performance flows from their competence, which is something broader (what they *can* do isn't necessarily exhausted or even
illustrated by what they *do* in fact do), CBE tended to reduce competence to performance. So, paradoxically, performance actually became
a synonym for competence, and CBE become known alternatively as
'performance-based education'. The focus was on the behaviours a
person could show after taking the course that they couldn't beforehand, but the confusion of terminology masked a basic error.

Similarly, the behaviourist emphasis tended to focus on very specific 'bits' of 'surface' behaviour. The CBE approach thus came to involve attempting to analyse a skill into a large number of component
behaviours. These 'atoms' of behaviour were seen not only as separately assessable, but also as capable of being taught in isolation and
then combined. The approach also became associated with certain other
themes, such as constant assessment and feedback to the learner during a training programme, the matching of instruction to individual
learner characteristics, e.g. existing strengths and weaknesses, learning styles, instructors modelling the attitudes and behaviours desired
of students.

Recently, an updated and amended version of the competence-based
approach has been heavily promoted by the UK government through
the National Council for Vocational Qualifications (NCVQ) and equivalent bodies, originally to rationalize the system of craft and professional
qualifications in the country. In principle, as promulgated by its main
'theoretician', Gilbert Jessup (1991), this approach has got rid of much
of the behaviourist baggage and concentrates on the specification of

job-related capacities as the intended outcomes of training. Thus it doesn't see itself as cutting a capability into separate bits, though it does try to specify the various functions that go to make up competence. In specifying a capacity, or *element* of competence, for instance, it requires a statement of what the (competent) person can do, together with a set of *performance criteria* which indicate aspects or subfunctions of what is involved. There is also specification of the *range* of applications or contexts required for such an element, as well as the degree of proficiency or standards of success.

The NVQ approach professes itself open as to the nature of the procedures which might fulfil these functions, since competences are capacities to produce outcomes of the sort in question and these may be achieved through different actions in different contexts. Similarly, this approach emphasizes the desirability of assessing competence as far as possible in the real context in which it will be applied, using real-life tasks which embody all the aspects, as opposed to specially designed part-tasks. It also says nothing about forms of training or instruction, since it sees its function only as the detailed specifying of the capabilities such courses ought to aim at.

Recent critics (e.g. Ashworth and Saxton 1990; Norris 1991; Hyland 1993) have attacked CBE for the failings of its underlying behaviourist psychology, in particular the fragmentation and 'atomism' associated with it, and its confusion of competence with performance. The latter point is a particularly basic one, in that not only is it a confusion which gets rid of the notion of capability on which the whole edifice had been founded, it also allows people to begin to talk about what are actually tendencies or values (e.g. commitments to particular goals or ways of doing things) as if they were capabilities. This may give the illusion of respecting human choice when one is actually prescribing particular stances. My view is therefore that in these respects, the critics of CBTE are quite right, particularly regarding its traditional forms. The more recent NCVQ approach seems less open to such basic criticisms, though there are recent indications that practices, even officially sanctioned ones in the further education sector, are once again not implementing all the principles of the Jessup approach (cf. Smithers 1993).

However, when some of them characterize the specification of *any* capacity as an intended outcome of a course of training or teaching as behaviourist, then the critics are surely reacting too strongly. Competence does traditionally mean capacity to achieve (cf. Carr 1993) and some form of this is what all teaching or training must aim to promote. Insisting that what counts in teaching or training is what the *learner* becomes able to do, not necessarily what the course has covered, is surely of great importance, because all teaching aims to promote learning, even if it doesn't always succeed. Such an insistence not only promotes accountability, it may also serve reflection by both teachers/trainers and learners, since they each have a relatively clear idea of the capabilities at which they're aiming.

Equally, clarity of purpose in training, whether for teaching or whatever, does not necessarily imply a behaviourist orientation towards the inculcation of particular behaviours, since different actions will be needed to achieve particular functions and outcomes in different contexts. These arguments are outlined in more detail in Tomlinson (1994).

emerge particularly from what we've seen about the nature of skilled capability.

• *In any teaching profile formulation, the pitfall of focusing on surface behaviours needs countering by embodying the idea of competence as capacity. Assessing competences therefore requires evidence of consistent, intelligent achievement.* CBTE behaviourism promoted a focus on learners' performance of behavioural procedures without reference to context and purpose. This can degenerate further into the noting of single acts, or even be totally misunderstood as a matter of ticking the competence statement when the item has been 'covered' in the course. But what it should actually be about is the learner's capability for intelligent action. This 'intelligent achievement capacity' notion of competence therefore needs to be promoted in various ways, including the following:

1 use of 'capacity language' in competence statements, involving such terminology as '*can*', 'is *able* to', 'does x or y *appropriately*', 'applies strategy x *effectively*';
2 requiring evidence of the intelligence of relevant actions and achievements and possibly also indication of this in competence formulations, signalling this through terminology such as 'with *understanding*', '*intelligently*', etc.;
3 inclusion of relevant areas of knowledge and understanding, e.g. aspects of pedagogy, within the overall competence profile as something the student-teacher should be able to articulate explicitly;
4 requiring consistency, i.e. some degree of reliable replication, in the forms of evidence relating to the two previous items. This should sooner or later include interjudge reliability and consistent moderation.

• *CBTE fragmentation of teaching at a single atomistic level should be replaced in competence profiles by portrayal of the multi-level, embedded nature of teaching functions and subfunctions.* We've seen that skill involves overall, integrated action, but also detailed subfunctions and subskills embedded within the whole. In analysing and specifying particular aspects of teaching competence, we therefore need to preserve and bring out its embedded nature. In other words, we don't rely totally on traditional, general formulations (like 'can teach effectively'), but nor do we think we've got the whole story when we've designed 'a thousand separate tick-boxes'. The hierarchical concept map approaches outlined in the previous chapter are one possibility here, but there are others.

• *The open-complex nature of teaching skill means that there can be a variety of valid formulations of teaching competence.* In keeping with what was said in the last chapter about the possibility of a range of consistent task analyses being possible for any given skill, it would be premature and unnecessarily constricting to insist on just one particular formulation for teaching competence profiling. Pluralism should prevail. So equally should modesty. It's unlikely that we're ever going to be able to capture *all* that is possible and useful within teaching. We don't in fact need to specify everything. We just need to come up with a framework that adequately assists communication, assessment and development with respect to teaching strategies and skill. It would nevertheless be useful and responsible to compare different teaching competence formulations to see whether particular versions appear to be missing anything.

• *Teaching competence profiles should reflect the distinction between teaching functions and teaching strategies by including reference to both.* Competence profiles are based generally on functional analysis, that is, analysis of the necessary constituent achievements and subgoals of an activity. However, we saw that in practice, skill requires the development of concrete strategies which tend to embody a number of functions at once. Teaching competence profiles should therefore include both teaching functions and teaching strategies.

• *Teaching competence profiling should reflect the open-complex nature of teaching skill through pluralism and a concern for development of a repertoire of teaching strategies and tactics.* Whilst multi-functional strategies make for economy of action and effort, there still tend to be different ways of doing the same thing, even in closed skills. Not only this, but particularly in open-complex skills like teaching, alternative strategies and tactics may actually be *required* by different circumstances. At any given level of teaching goal or subfunction, therefore, a competent teacher will be capable of a repertoire of strategies and will know how to select from them. Not only may a school-based system therefore profit from having a teaching competence profile which allows for the specification of a range of teaching strategies and tactics, but there may be particular emphases on certain types of teaching strategy within particular subject areas. However, representing functions and subfunctions, and having an awareness of the idea of learning potential are probably important. These would offset any tendency simply to inculcate 'what we do in this subject' ('good practice' without rationale), but would also promote the ongoing search for new teaching tactics and 'improved practice'.

• *Competence profiling should reflect the open-complex nature of teaching skill through pluralism regarding routes of student-teacher progress.* In similar vein, it's typically possible not only to teach the same thing in different ways, but also for student-teachers to gain teaching capability through a variety of routes. Narrative studies of teacher development bear witness to this in the case of teaching (cf. Elbaz 1983; Kelchtermans 1993). In contrast to the simplistic prescription associated with traditional CBTE, the more adequately a competence profile succeeded in articulating repertoires of teaching strategy capability, the *more* possibilities the mentor-teacher educator could envisage to adapt their approach to student-teacher and setting.

• *The above recommendations may cause initial problems in the use of teaching competence profiles by teacher-mentors, but this is in itself a new form of skill anyway.* As has been noted often, experienced practitioners typically find reflective analysis of their own skill difficult, unnatural and daunting. When this point is not realized by experienced teachers commencing mentoring, but nevertheless affects them along with their own need to appear capable, we have the ingredients for resistance to the sorts of recommendation I've been making above. One may even get a preference for the sort of 'tick-the-box-once-we've-covered-it' type of approach, since this at least allows a sort of clear set of procedures. It therefore seems important that teacher-mentors using any form of teaching competence profiling should be at ease with its approach and style. But like any complex skill, this requires that a) they understand the various aspects and issues at stake in the teaching such a profile is meant to characterize, and b) they realize that like any skill, at first it can feel difficult and therefore needs intelligent perseverance. In my experience, teachers who approach such a task thoughtfully soon feel at home, partly because if the system has any validity, it actually allows the application of their own tacit insights.

• *Competence profiling is only one aspect of teacher training, requiring deployment within a broader pedagogy of student-teacher learning and development which should itself be part of student-teachers' and mentors' shared reflective awareness.* This point extends the previous one; in a word, intelligent teacher education too requires a pedagogy (some would currently say 'andragogy' (Knowles 1980), but I'm using pedagogy in its general sense). Competence profiling is only part of teacher education, not any sort of replacement for it.

Developing a teaching competence profile

The DFE position

The UK government's new arrangements for initial teacher training in England and Wales have been outlined in two recent DFE circulars: circular

9/92 (DFE 1992) for secondary phase teaching and circular 14/93 (DFE 1993a) for the primary phase (so far the Northern Ireland equivalent is DENI 1993 and the Scottish version SOED 1993). The major features prescribed by the DFE for the new forms of initial teacher training (ITT) are that schools should play a much larger part than hitherto in ITT and that everyone concerned in such courses should focus on the teaching competences expected of newly qualified teachers. Each document provides its own (slightly differing) formulation of a set of such competences, but the secondary document makes clear that:

> The statements of the competences expected of newly qualified teachers do not purport to provide a complete syllabus for initial teacher training. They specify the issues on which the case for approval [of course] will be considered. It is recognised that institutions are developing their own competence-based approaches to the assessment of students.
>
> (DFE 1992, para. 11)

The indications are that this separate development will apply generally. Given the arguments I've been putting forward, the DFE's pluralism regarding teaching competence formulations is welcome in itself. Given also the strengths and weaknesses I see in the DFE competence statements (see Further detail section 7.2), it is also welcome as a licence to develop teaching competence profiles which embody the principles just suggested.

The LUSSP teaching competence profile materials and approach

In my own school of education's partnership arrangement with local secondary schools (the Leeds University Secondary School Partnership (LUSSP) an attempt has been made to embody the principles suggested above into the design of teaching competence profiling materials. These materials will hopefully become commercially available in the near future, following their review after a year's usage across some 45 schools. The LUSSP approach has a number of features.

Its analysis tries to reflect the multi-layered, embedded nature of teaching
The LUSSP approach analyses teaching functions into a *four-level hierarchy*, the first three of which are shown in Figure 7.1. Thus teaching as a whole is seen as consisting of a combination of five main areas of competence, and these are distinguished further into a total of 12 subareas.

The five main areas of teaching comprise the practical capacities to plan and prepare teaching (the preactive phase), to carry out teaching (the interactive phase), to fulfil wider professional roles and to engage in professional self-development. To these are added the explicit knowledge and understanding that is relevant to each of the other four areas.

Further detail section 7.2
The DFE teaching competence specifications

DFE circulars 9/92 and 14/93 each offer a formulation of teaching competence statements to guide initial training and these two sets differ discernibly. The secondary version is a two-level model with five general areas containing between them a total of 27 more specific competences, respectively: subject knowledge (3), subject application (7), class management (4), assessment and recording of pupils' progress (5) and further professional development (8). The primary phase formulation contains three levels. At its most general level are three main areas: curriculum content, planning and assessment; teaching strategies; further professional development. The first two of these are subdivided respectively into three and two intermediate levels and then further into the most specific level of competence statement, whilst the third main area subdivides straight into the specific level, giving a total of 33 specific level statements in the primary competence version. The Scottish version (SOED 1993) is similar but more reflective and the Northern Ireland version (DENI 1993) takes a much more integrated approach. The focus here is on the DFE version for England and Wales.

Strengths, weaknesses and implications

All in all, the DFE primary and secondary competence statements appear to embody a somewhat mixed model, with apparent elements of the CBTE approach, yet, if anything a preponderance of the original everyday view of competence as capacity. This somewhat ambiguous mix is reflected in a number of respects. There is reference to competences, of course, calling up the CBE tradition, but reference also to knowledge and understanding. There is specification of particular aspects of teaching, but this is within a framework with a degree of hierarchy which doesn't approach the 'tick-box atomism' of some profiles. Also, student-teachers are to show evidence of their competences, but the nature of such evidence is left open. Finally, it is recommended that 'progressive development of these competences should be monitored regularly during [initial] training', but the nature of that training is not pinned down beyond requirements concerning amount of course time to be spent in schools and broad recommendations, particularly in the primary phase document, concerning the need for variety of experience.

The strengths appear to be that the DFE competence model retains the notion of capacity as central, allows a welcome pluralism with respect to detail, but does urge attention to this within an implicitly hierarchical approach. On the other hand, although pedagogical understanding may be seen as implicitly required for the deployment of most of the competences listed, one could be forgiven for interpreting the documents, particularly the secondary one, as implying a dualist view of teaching skill, i.e. as a set of action-capacities devoid of any basis in understanding. But perhaps the strongest reason for seeking to develop an alternative formulation is the apparent mixture of levels within the various domains. This is not an issue on which total unanimity is ever likely, but, for example, at its most specific level the secondary document includes the following requirements under the (rather strange) heading of 'Subject application' in Annex A:

> 2.3 Newly qualified teachers should be able to:
> 2.3.4 employ a range of teaching strategies appropriate to the age, ability and attainment level of pupils;
> 2.3.5 present subject content in clear language and in a stimulating manner.

It might be considered that 2.3.5 is better seen as part of 2.3.4, rather than on a par with it. Likewise, under class management, newly qualified teachers are expected to be able to:

> 2.4.3 devise and use appropriate rewards and sanctions to maintain an effective learning environment;
> 2.4.4 maintain pupils' interest and motivation.

Here 2.4.3 is probably better seen as a substrategy within 2.4.4. This latter item also alerts us to another feature which is worthy of comment, though I hesitate to characterize it either as a strength or as a weakness.

Namely, there is an absence of any attempt to define explicitly the contexts and *levels of proficiency* required of newly qualified teachers' competences. On the one hand, this refusal to go with the NCVQ model might be seen as wise, in that one wonders where even to start in attempting to specify, for instance, the 'teachability' or 'manageability' of the sorts of classes in which newly qualified teachers should be able to succeed, still less to measure these. On the other hand, leaving the statement as bald as 2.4.4 may seem to imply that in order to achieve certification, newly qualified teachers should be able to maintain the interest and motivation of all and any pupils! Surely no one in their right mind would claim this, let alone beginning teachers.

The more substantial implication illustrated by this item, however, is that even if one did think it useful to be a bit more specific about pupil and resource contexts, we are never going to achieve a totally exhaustive and explicit formulation. Conversely, a degree of direct judgement and intuition will always be required in assessment. The standard response to this in 'competency' circles has been that this need not worry us, explicit justification of such judgements isn't needed, all that is necessary is independent agreement amongst the 'experts' who judge: 'they can achieve this in Olympic gymnastics and ice-skating, so why not in education?' This is of course counter to Jessup's (1991) claimed need for explicitness. Moreover, when I think of the 1994 Olympic ice-dancing finals, then I have to confess to not being filled with confidence regarding even ice-dancing assessment, let alone that of teaching! There does appear to be a basic issue of quality assurance here.

Two points are worth immediate comment. The first is that whilst articulating explicit knowledge and understanding as a major area of competence may help highlight its importance in student-teacher development, there are strong arguments for placing explicit understanding and practical capacity aspects *within* each substantive teaching function. This alternative approach is being taken in the primary phase competence specification we're currently designing.

The second is to note the view that whilst there is good reason to require particular commitments and values of teachers (such as respect for pupils, commitment to excellence and professional development), a profile specifying such items should therefore not simply be called a *competence* profile. Whatever terminology one does choose, the important point is that one is requiring not just capabilities, but also certain value commitments, and that these are slightly different matters. Perhaps better, then, to talk of something like a *teaching* profile.

Each of the main areas of teaching in the LUSSP framework is further analysed into component subareas, giving a total of 12 subareas of teaching capability, the groupings shown on the right of Figure 7.1 Thus, for instance, *planning and preparation* has two subareas (teaching goals and strategies), whilst *interactive teaching* involves four which you will recognize from the functional analyses of classroom teaching offered in the last two chapters (namely: influencing learning, monitoring learning progress, influencing behaviour and motivation, monitoring behaviour and reaction).

There is also a further level. Not shown in Figure 7.1 is the *further subaspects level* within each subarea. These are illustrated by the details provided in the concept-map analyses of Chapters 5 (see Figures 5.4, 5.5) and 6 (see

Overall level	Main areas	Subareas
Overall teaching competence	Explicit knowledge base	1 Subject knowledge and skills, curriculum resources 2 Pupils and pedagogy 3 Professional matters and commitment
	Planning and preparation	4 Clear learning goals appropriate for pupils, context, resources 5 Adequate range of learning activities and resources for pupils, goals and resources
	Interactive teaching	6 Intelligent and effective assistance for pupil learning, organization and resourcing 7 Effective assessment and monitoring of pupil learning activities and progress 8 Appropriate relating to and influencing pupils, their behaviour, motivation and well-being 9 Effective assessment and monitoring of pupil behaviour, motivation and well-being
	Wider professional roles	10 Wider educational role fulfilment through effective collaboration with various others
	Professional self-development	11 Development of explicit knowledge base of subject, pedagogy and professional matters 12 Improvement of professional capabilities through appropriate mentoring, reflection and change

Figure 7.1 The LUSSP teaching competence hierarchy: overall, main and subarea levels

Figures 6.1 and 6.2). In the case of the interactive teaching and the planning and preparation subareas, the further detail analysis includes a listing of teaching strategies and pupil activities and organization. These levels of detail are provided only as memory prompts by way of assistance in using the profile record.

The LUSSP profile record forms also embody the embedded nature of teaching
The record form provides a box for each of the 12 teaching subareas, large enough to write a summary relating to strengths and weaknesses in that area (there are never more than three such boxes on the A4 sized record sheets, as illustrated in Figure 7.2). In addition to this, there is the possibility of indicating levels of performance in each of the five main areas of teaching and of making an overall judgement of teaching competence. It is stressed in the guidelines for use of the LUSSP profile that although the order of the document goes from subareas to overall judgement, it is possible to go in either direction and that the overall judgement should not be seen simply as an aggregation of the more detailed levels (though certain minima are required in respect of the formal assessment aspects, as indicated below).

The approach attempts to embody pluralism and user-friendliness in various ways, but . . .
Although there may be many ways of analysing and specifying the aspects of teaching competence, nevertheless, within a single system such as a school–HEI (higher education institution) partnership like LUSSP, there is also a requirement for comparability and consistency which is even more unavoidably felt than that across the system of teacher training as a whole. LUSSP therefore adopts this one basic teaching analysis but also attempts to achieve pluralism within this and accessibility to different users in a number of ways. One is through having open-ended report 'boxes', as indicated, so that within the definitions constituted by the headings of the various subareas (see Figure 7.1) respondents are free to frame things in their own terms.

A further feature in this respect is that the 'further detail prompt materials' are provided in four equivalent versions: the *concept-map* version already illustrated in the previous chapter, the *tree-diagram* version, which is somewhat similar to the concept map, but having no 'bubbles', the *prose* version, in which the further detail aspects of subareas are portrayed, as the label suggests, in prose (as shown in Figure 7.2), and the *list* version, in which the items of the other versions are simply listed under each subheading. Subject-areas and schools have been offered the opportunity to choose between these different versions, which thus fall into two main types, the visual-hierarchical (concept map and tree-diagram) and verbal (the prose and list).

The profile record and further prompt material sheets are provided with standard hole-punching, so that different sets of prompt material may be intercalated in ring binders along with the particular profile record sheets to which they refer. Figure 7.2 shows an illustration of such a pair of facing pages, in this case subareas 6 and 7 of interactive teaching, with the prose version of the general prompt material on the left and the interim assessment profile record version on the right.

It is also made clear that the further prompt material may need amending or further addition, particularly in so far as different subject areas or age-ranges may involve particular teaching strategies and activities not envisaged in the general picture. Participants in the scheme, especially those within specific areas of subject teaching, are therefore encouraged to extend the further detail prompts as they wish, with review on an annual basis within the partnership as a whole.

In the early trials of the LUSSP profile prompt materials there was some indication that the visual versions were found daunting at first sight by teachers coming fresh to the profile material, perhaps because the complexity is particularly apparent in these portrayals. However, once they got into the swing of using the profiles, teachers actually showed some tendency towards preferring the visual types and in particular the concept map form.

This isn't entirely surprising and it has been borne out by further experience to date. It is to be expected that experienced practitioners will tend to be surprised at, even to deny the complexity of what they do, particularly when they have never had occasion to reflect thoroughly about it. There is also some indication that, as in the early trials, practice with profiling both allays the fears and allows teacher-mentors to bring their own craft knowledge into the frame.

However, it is my view that teacher-mentors stand here at a rather crucial choice-point in so far as they may be tempted to resist the articulation of detail and function of the teaching they are called upon to articulate to student-teachers. Failure to resist this temptation would not only threaten the quality of initial teacher training, it would also further the deprofessionalization of teachers the UK Conservative government has been accused of seeking through, amongst other things, its disconnecting of teacher preparation from the influence of higher education. If initial teacher preparation can benefit massively from being situated closer to practice (as I hope I have indicated to be my view), then it will nevertheless only achieve such benefit if schools and their teacher-mentors take on a thoughtful approach to the whole enterprise.

The LUSSP approach tries to serve the functions of both assessment and development
The profile record form comes in three colour coded versions. The two formal assessment versions (interim and final) contain tick-box rating scales comprising the following levels:

INTERACTIVE TEACHING

(6) Intelligently and effectively influences and assists pupil learning activities, their organisation and resource deployment through

Defining/influencing and assisting pupil learning goals, awareness and activities, their grouping and resource deployment through:

explicit and implicit means, including verbal and non-verbal, direct and indirect forms of communication and strategic action

In particular, direct teacher-based strategies such as explanation, information provision, demonstration/modelling, and directing in relation to individuals, groups and whole class, using oral and resource-media bases (e.g. chalkboard, flipchart, ohp) and oral means

and pupil activities such as information intake, analysis, application, problem-solving and production, utilising written, pictorial and information technology resources, as well as their combination in interactive strategies such as discussion, role-play and project work.

Specific learning/teaching activities/functions

Teacher: *Pupils:*

		Activities:		*Functions:*	
Directing	I - P- G - WC	Listening	I - P- G - WC	Information	
Information giving	I - P- G - WC	Reading	I - P- G - WC	finding	I - P- G - WC
Explaining	I - P- G - WC	Writing	I - P- G - WC	intake	I - P- G - WC
Eliciting/		Drawing/		recording	I - P- G - WC
questioning	I - P- G - WC	Designing	I - P- G - WC	Analysis	I - P- G - WC
Demonstrating	I - P- G - WC	Computer		Application	I - P- G - WC
		interaction	I - P- G - WC	Evaluation	I - P- G - WC
		Practicals/			
		Making	I - P- G - WC	Problem-solving	I - P- G - WC
		Performance/		Practising/	
Key		Role play	I - P- G - WC	consolidating	I - P- G - WC
I = individuals		Discussion	P- G - WC		
G = groups		Homework	I - P- G		
P = pairs					
WC = whole class					

---

(7) Monitoring/evaluating pupils' learning task awareness, activity and progress through:

Forms of immediate awareness and strategic elicitation, both direct and indirect.

Immediate forms of awareness will include looking and listening, both generally (scanning) and with particular focus.

Strategic elicitation may include relatively direct forms, such as questioning and discussion, and indirect forms, such as inferences from classroom events and pupil products by way of class- and homework.

Figure 7.2 Illustrative pages from the LUSSP interim assessment profile record with prose prompt further material
© 1993 School of Education University of Leeds

INTERACTIVE TEACHING (*Please refer to prompt material on opposite page left*)

(6) Intelligently and effectively influences and assists pupil learning activities, organisation and resource deployment *(please specify aspects and context where necessary)*

☐ Insufficient information ☐ Seriously weak ☐ Needs attention ☐ Satisfactory ☐ Strong ☐ Outstanding

Action plan:

(7) Effectively assesses and monitors pupil learning activities and progress *(please specify aspects and context where necessary)*

☐ Insufficient information ☐ Seriously weak ☐ Needs attention ☐ Satisfactory ☐ Strong ☐ Outstanding

Action plan:

Figure 7.2 Illustrative pages from the LUSSP interim assessment profile record with prose prompt further material
© 1993 School of Education University of Leeds

seriously weak – needs attention – satisfactory – strong – outstanding

(in the final assessment profile version 'needs attention' is replaced by 'unsatisfactory'). There is also a 'working profile' version, which has no such assessment scale, only an *action plan* heading, which it shares with the interim profile record shown in Figure 7.2. This working version is intended to be used informally at any and all times during the course, whether by tutors, teacher-mentors or students, alone or in consultation with each other.

Proficiency levels in the LUSSP approach are taken to be those
characterizing a newly qualified teacher with respect to average classes
Two important, but difficult issues arise with regard to the meaning and assessment of teaching proficiency levels.

Final outcome versus developmental anchoring: the dilemma regarding the use of the above sort of rating scale to record assessment of teaching proficiency level is between anchoring one's judgements in the intended/required end-of-course level, on the one hand, or using a notion of 'reasonable progress' as the baseline for one's judgements.

Using the former has the arguable advantage of being simpler, in that it requires 'only' a consistent idea to be shared by assessors of the levels of teaching proficiency being aimed at as appropriate for a newly qualified teacher as they enter the profession. It also means there is constant reference to where one wants students to get by way of teaching skill. Its major disadvantage appears to be that one therefore can't sound as positive as with the alternative approach. In the early part of the course, for instance, it wouldn't be surprising when using the LUSSP-type rating scale, to be generally indicating 'needs attention'.

Using the latter, the developmental baseline approach, has the advantage of being able to say that the student is 'doing well' for that stage of the course, even though in end-of-course terms they may need to improve somewhat. However, this approach appears to require assessors within a scheme to have not only a notion of appropriate end of course levels of proficiency, but also a mapping of a normal course of progress, which would presumably have to be assumed applicable to all students. Even though this is to me a more complicated and less plausible assumption, a developmental approach may nevertheless be somewhat embedded within many people's approaches. This would certainly help explain indications from research on Articled Teacher schemes that mentors can be uncomfortable about challenging students over needed improvements (cf. Elliott and Calderhead 1993), which can in turn then 'catch up with them' when the final assessment chips are down.

The LUSSP approach has therefore been to take the DFE circular rather literally and go for the intended course outcome level, but it remains to be seen how well this actually works in practice. What does seem indisputable, nevertheless, is that whichever of the two approaches one does adopt within a particular course scheme, it must be clearly shared and consistently deployed by all concerned.

The relevance of teaching context, pupils and resources: although the use of competence-based approaches is supposedly in order to make things tight and 'tough', as Circular 14/93 puts it, the DFE guidelines nicely side-step the issue of trying to define the actual nature of the proficiency level to be required of beginning qualified teachers. When it comes to *proficiency* and contextual *range* (centrally including pupil variation, resources availability, etc.), which are two of the elements which the NVQ approach (Jessup 1991) rightly considers central to the specification of competence, things are less than clear. These two are inextricable in particular cases, but they each vary across teaching instances. For instance, the nature of the pupils can obviously make a considerable difference to the outcome of the teaching process, that is, to its proficiency.

The only way the DFE circulars specify this interlinked pair of aspects is to urge in somewhat circular fashion that 'attainment [of the competences] at a level appropriate to newly qualified teachers should be the objective of every student' and to phrase competences in completely general terms, with no indication as to pupil range (Annex A, para. 2.1 of each document). The apparent implication that newly qualified teachers ought to be able to teach *any and all* pupils effectively might seem a far-fetched alternative, but this interpretation is supported, for instance, by the specific DFE requirement simply that 'newly qualified teachers should be able to maintain pupils' interest and motivation'.

As indicated earlier, I believe there are some rather intractable issues here. However, some reference to context and pupil variation seems in order and necessary. The LUSSP approach has therefore been that since newly qualified teachers are expected to be capable of taking sole responsibility for managing the learning of at least an average class in terms of teachability and manageability, then the outcome proficiency levels in an ITT profiling approach should take this as its baseline. This is perhaps a step forward, but the immediately encountered issue is then how to judge such qualities and to ensure that 'average' means 'for the system as a whole' rather than, say, just the school in question.

Suffice it to say that this places considerable demand on the quality assurance side of the new arrangements. Previously we had an HEI-dominated situation in which, although teachers might claim that HEI assessment of student-teachers' teaching was based on inadequate access, the wide-ranging involvement of college tutors across schools in a particular area was backed up by an external examiner system which moderated across areas and regions to some extent. Now, to the extent that arrangements become school-based within HEI-school partnerships and even more in the case of entirely 'school-centred schemes', assessment will tend to be devolved to local teacher mentors who are more restricted in their awareness of pupil and other relevant variations. It may well be that there will be gains from their closer and more extensive involvement, though there are also grave doubts as to how and whether the available resourcing will actually enable this. The new arrangements therefore pose considerable challenges on the quality and consistency front, especially in the early phases.

Student-teacher assessment and development

As indicated at the outset of the chapter, assessment within teacher preparation courses needs to be both:

- *summative:* seeing where student-teachers have got in their teaching competence development at particular points in the course, and
- *formative:* yielding information for use in further mentoring and student development.

Given that a number of aspects and areas of teaching are at stake and that it is likely that a number of teachers within a school or department will be involved in mentoring, whether 'officially' or 'unofficially' (but see also the final chapter), then a combination of personal contributions and types of procedure is likely to be required. The sort of teaching competence profile required by the DFE and discussed above in the LUSSP illustration may function as a way of summarizing things, but would not be useful for all purposes. In particular, the process of recording and reflecting on particular pieces of teaching seems to require something rather different. In this section I propose first to discuss this and then to return to the broader picture of combining assessment resources for formative and summative purposes.

Assessing interactive teaching

I suggested above that teaching competence profiles should include mention of a repertoire of particular teaching strategies and their constituent pupil activities, organizations and functions. Nevertheless, this doesn't reflect the nature of concrete teaching activity sufficiently to make such a document useful as a vehicle for lesson observation and recording. There is for example a need to characterize the actual sequence of events that have taken place. However, teaching is a purposeful activity and a piece of teaching can certainly only be assessed by reference to its particular aims. The assessment of teaching therefore clearly needs to take into account the student-teacher's lesson plan, including their aims. Not only this, but since planning and preparation can be seen as relatively independent aspects of teaching in their own right (as illustrated, for instance, by their designation as a main area in the LUSSP profile analysis), it also makes sense to have some sort of documentary form in which student-teachers express their planning. Since a lesson or interactive teaching record would usefully build from such a planning document, let me consider lesson planning documentation first.

Lesson planning records
Any approach to lesson planning needs to consider a variety of factors, including the nature of the pupils, the broader context of the syllabus coverage over the shorter and longer term, the resources available, and so forth. However, by way of minimum, a lesson plan needs to indicate both the *aims* and the *intended activities*. Since lessons take place in real time, adequate planning needs to consider the *timing*, including both the duration and sequence of class activities, as well as the nature of the transitions involved between them.

The overall aims of the lesson will include intended learning outcomes, with reference where appropriate to the relevant parts of the latest version of the national curriculum for that area. The different activities of the lesson will also have their particular aims by way of task achievement ('What do I want them to do/come up with?') and learning outcome ('Why this activity, to what learning does it have the potential to contribute?').

However, to recall Chapter 5, the planning of each specific classroom activity requires not just an indication of aims, but also of the form of *pupil organization* involved (whole class, pairs, etc.), the *resources* to be deployed, what the *pupils* will be doing and what the *teacher* will be doing, and not least, an indication of the time-points envisaged.

Thus at the broad level a completed lesson plan would show the lesson aims plus sequential activities within something like Figure 7.3. One might argue whether the opening and closing of the lesson ought to be seen as transitions or activity phases, given their importance from the class management viewpoint, but the overall picture would look much the same. Equally, a transition is often seen as arising out of a particular activity. The point of labelling transitions separately, however, is to help student-teachers think explicitly about the managerial issues and potential at stake.

I should perhaps make clear that here I am not suggesting any sort of rigidly formatted document with labelled boxes for particular items. It may be possible and even useful to embody certain features on a general form, such as having an area at the top for logging details of class, subject etc., then lesson aims, and perhaps a left margin for time indications, but at least the remainder of the form needs to be somewhat open-ended, since different lesson periods will have different numbers of activities and transitions.

The same applies at the more detailed level of each *constituent activity*, where there needs to be some sort of recording of the various aspects indicated earlier, though not necessarily through items appearing on a printed pro forma, as long as the format is made clear in notes of guidance on lesson planning. In the LUSSP scheme, for instance, it is proposed that each

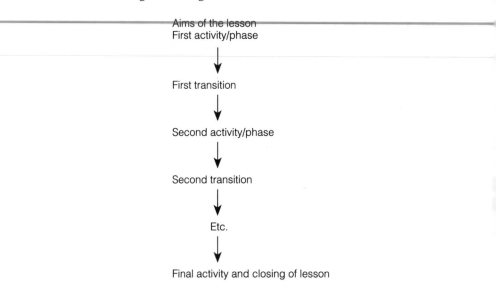

Figure 7.3　Broad outline of lesson plan format

activity outlined in a lesson plan should include the various aspects indicated in Figure 7.4.

Transitions likewise need to show what the teacher and pupils will be doing. In both transitions and activities, the pupil and teacher activities might usefully be portrayed in two columns, with specific or rough timings shown on the left. Once again, it's not the particular form of such a portrayal that counts (though clarity and consistency can help considerably), rather that certain aspects are important and need to be dealt with explicitly, one way or another. A teaching profile analysis, such as that of the LUSSP model, can act at the planning stage as a memory prompt to assist completeness of planning.

The level of detail needed in planning/preparation cannot be legislated in general and must depend on the judgement of student intern and mentor in particular contexts. In the early stages it's likely to be particularly important to consider things at the most concrete level of detail, though this in turn will depend on the overall programme and the extent to which student interns have been let into actual teaching through the sorts of sequences suggested in Chapter 9.

Lesson observation
Lesson observation and assessment clearly need to start with a consideration of the aims, planning and preparation of the lesson. A copy of the lesson plan can provide a recording of much of this, but the mentor will

Activity/phase: Label for activity

Time: From: To:

(1)   [Aim/Function: *what learning this activity/phase is intended to achieve*]
(2)   [Pupil organization/layout: *how pupils will be grouped, e.g. I-P-G-WC*]
(3)   [Resources/deployment: *what resources will be involved and how distributed*]
(4)   [Constituent activities]

[a]   [Teacher activity]   [b]   [Pupil activity]

[What *you as teacher will do* by way of defining/assisting/relating to pupils' planned activities and possible backup tasks – (see LUSSP competence subareas (5), (6), (8) including Specific Activities/Strategies lists) and by way of monitoring/assessing pupil activity, progress and motivation – see LUSSP competence subareas (5), (7), (9)]

[What *task goals pupils should be attempting and what activities they should be engaging in* (see Specific Activities/Strategies lists in LUSSP competence subareas (5) and (7), including possible alternative back-up contingency activities)]

Figure 7.4   Detailed aspects of specific activities in a lesson plan

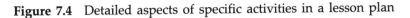

usually wish to record notes regarding them in a first part of their lesson record. The suggestion, corresponding to that given above for planning, is then that lesson observation be recorded in the natural sequence in which things occur, noting the nature of major activity and transition phases, with relevant time-points.

The temptation in observing and assessing lessons is perhaps to react passively, only noting anything unusual, in particular anything negative. This may not be totally disastrous, in that an experienced teacher's tacit knowledge will tend to alert them to relevant features. But at best it isn't likely to help them very much in articulating their views and in explaining their rationales to student interns, let alone celebrating the positive achievements and displaying the warmth student-teachers tend to prefer in their mentors. In this connection it may therefore be useful, if not to have explicit headings on a lesson observation form, then at least to use aspects of a teaching competence analysis such as the LUSSP one to guide one's attention whilst observing. As Figure 7.5 shows, the LUSSP lesson observation record provides for noting lesson phase activities and their timings in a narrow left-hand column. The user fills these in as necessary, going on to further sheets if needed. The form then orients the user towards noting instructional or learning promotion aspects of the teaching in a main central column and class management aspect in the right-hand column. In each case, the two major functions of the relevant LUSSP profile subareas are indicated, namely the doing/defining/influencing and the monitoring/assessing functions.

Thus a teaching profile record is typically not of much use on its own for recording and assessing actual teaching. Nevertheless, when its categories

LESSON OBSERVATION RECORD Student _____ Class _____ Subject _____		
Lesson phase	Teaching/learning aspects Assisting and monitoring	Class management aspects Influencing and monitoring
Planning preparation		
(Time) Opening phase Main activity 1 Transition 1 Main activity 2 Transition 2 Etc.		

Figure 7.5   The LUSSP lesson observation record form (top part)

are brought into or even indicated within a specific record form, a functional and strategic analysis can help the observer/assessor to focus on relevant aspects. These potentially include use of teaching activity and strategy lists to record which parts of a repertoire are building up. Such an approach does of course also help in providing a basis for feedback discussion and the presentation of rationales for mentors' views in relation to the competence profile they happen to be using. It also gives a common framework which should assist complementarity of 'coverage' by different mentors, as well as reliability across their assessment of specific aspects of students' teaching.

A broad assessment approach

Even if school-based teacher preparation were only interested in summative assessment of student progress and outcome in school-based teacher preparation, the complexity and variation involved in teaching competence, the effects of differing pupils and contexts, and the variety of people likely to be involved in official and unofficial mentoring roles would make a quite broad-ranging assessment strategy necessary. When we add the formative function of monitoring and assessment, plus the need to involve student-teachers as fully as possible in this as a basis for their own reflective learning and professional development, then the picture gets even more complicated.

Validity and reliability

Both for summative and formative purposes, judgements about student-teachers' teaching competence need to be valid and reliable, each in a number of respects.

Validity: The two major aspects of validity of particular relevance here are known technically as construct and content validity. *Construct validity* concerns the obvious requirement that evidence used to indicate something should actually indicate it and not something else. In seeking to assess explicit understanding, for instance, it would hardly suffice to use the fact that a topic had been 'covered in the course', for example that it had been the subject of a lecture or printed handout, or that it had been discussed in a tutorial. One of the healthier emphases of competence-based approaches is that they make it very clear that it's the learner's competence we're talking about – in this case the student-teacher's. Student essays may thus be a better guide as to their explicit understanding, though even these do require certain assumptions (e.g. that they did write the essay themselves), so may performances in seminar and tutorial discussion, and equally, informal conversations. A combination of these would doubtless be even better. But these particular means shouldn't count much as indicators of (in LUSSP terms) interactive teaching competence, or even of the capacity to plan and prepare teaching.

On the other hand, seeking to assess and monitor interactive teaching capability simply by looking at student-teaching behaviour and outcomes, whilst an essential part, is hardly sufficient in itself. As I pointed out earlier, it means assessing intelligent skilfulness. In interactive teaching, for instance, we therefore need to relate what we witness student-teachers doing to the aims they have set for themselves and to gain some idea of how and why they did what they did do and didn't do what we thought they'd omitted. We need, in a word, to access the *intelligence* and the *effectiveness* of their actions.

This can be harder than it sounds. The issue of effectiveness is fraught with difficulties; should we require, for instance, that pupils make certain minimum gains through the student teaching in question? The openness of teaching skill and the dependence of its success on the cooperation of other human beings, pupils in particular, makes this far from straightforward. Here the issue of context and pupil 'teachability' will doubtless play a part, though pinning down whether pupils did actually achieve learning gains and whether it was from the student in question that they gained them is hardly straightforward. Mentors will nevertheless want to see what sort of effect a student seems actually to achieve in her or his management strategies, as well as in what ways she or he is apparently 'getting through' to pupils in terms of learning.

In turn, this sort of limitation places more importance on the intelligence with which students are making teaching attempts. That is, are they at least taking into account the sorts of factor that need taking into account (pupil feedback, etc.)? Are they trying to apply otherwise appropriate strategies whose rationales and learning potential they show they understand? Are they actually deploying such strategies in an efficient manner likely to realize their learning and management potential (even if on a particular occasion, they don't actually work that well)?

To access the perspectives and insights that are actually generating student-teacher action in the classroom, mentors will obviously discuss teaching plans in advance and lessons in retrospect. These obviously do not access 'thought-in-action' directly, they get at intentions or memories, and there is always some issue as to their validity in this respect. The closer one can get to the action as it occurs, of course, the more valid the student's commentary is likely to be and the better we can gauge whether they're engaging in intelligently-based action. All of this can raise all sorts of further issues, but such access is potentially one of the major advantages in school-based arrangements, especially through the arrangement I earlier referred to as progressively collaborative teaching or PCT.

Content validity refers to the need to gain sufficient evidence to cover all important aspects of the type of thing we're after. The sorts of teaching competence analyses now required and illustrated here by the LUSSP example may help clarify things in one sense, but in another they begin to show the complexity of what is at stake. Not that all the various aspects of teaching competence need separate performances as their evidence. The opposite, in fact, as was pointed out earlier; we're looking for the integration of these various facets. A specific piece of teaching is therefore likely to provide evidence concerning very many of the functional and subfunctional aspects of teaching competence, though for the different types of teaching strategy thought important for the repertoire in a particular subject area, one is likely to involve a number of different sessions. This overlaps with the issue of reliability of assessment.

Reliability: reliability is a matter of consistency in assessing student-teacher competence. One needs consistent evidence of intelligent ability and, where appropriate, commitment. Such consistency needs to apply to various aspects of the likely evidence.

A first aspect is that of *occasions* and *contexts*. Seeing 'one bit of good intelligent teaching' hardly suffices as a basis for certification, for instance, one needs to have repeated evidence over a number of occasions of intelligently effective teaching, each involving a realistic time period, minimally a lesson period. The situation is of course complicated by its fluidity, in which one is expecting to see changes over the duration of the course, but the less consistent the evidence, also in the everyday sense of the word, the less reliable.

A second facet of reliability concerns consistency across different *assessors*. Although certain factors are capable of bringing about a spurious level of agreement (e.g. student reputation, stereotyping, etc.), the range of perspectives held by those fulfilling mentoring roles and the variations in the teaching contexts in which they see particular student teachers is perhaps more likely to produce variations of impression and judgement. In this respect a good profiling system which has been thoroughly discussed by different mentors is an obvious advantage. Equally, the more opportunity mentors can take to record the nature and contexts of the evidence on which they are basing profile entries, the better, though the collation of different viewpoints and preferably face to face discussion of each student seems important as a general rule in school-based courses, and not only in cases where mentors appear to have a disagreement.

Promoting student development in and through assessment
Having dwelled on assessment aspects for a while, perhaps this is a useful point to remind ourselves that there is much more to mentoring than just assessing, as we have seen and will be seeing again in the next chapter. But not only is assessment central to any systematic educational process, it is an aspect which can be recruited in the service of the learning the educator intends to promote. This is the explicit recommendation of the DFE in requiring the use of competence statements in ITT and I hope you will agree that this and the previous chapters have shown how central aspects of classroom pedagogy can be portrayed through functional and strategy-based competence analyses. Such material does not suffice on its own, of course, but it does give a common reference point from which to think about and investigate rationales for what might be contemplated by way of classroom teaching strategy. Thus a teaching profile gives the student-teacher one basis for their own active involvement in reflective learning, helping them to discern different possibilities for focus. Three more specific possibilities exist here.
    Linking aspects of formal and informal assessment: having a common reference base for both formal summative and informal formative assessment has various advantages. It should make the assessment experience less arbitrary and more authentic. Because it's more extended, the student gets used to it and hopefully, with assistance, internalizes both the pedagogical possibilities and the practice of self-monitoring and reflection. But this does imply, I think, that students need to be enabled to use their own forms of self-monitoring which link with a profile analysis of teaching.
    These forms should include reflective notes on their own teaching, including *lesson reviews* (see next chapter). Personal logs and diaries may be of use, as long as they do seriously reflect on teaching specifics and do not degenerate into producing wordage. For all of these functions it appears necessary to make available some version of the profile analysis and linked record which can be used informally, like the LUSSP working profile. However, there is also a further need.

Involving student-teachers in the formal assessment process: the practice of having the student-teacher participate in the *compilation of their own formal assessment* record has a number of advantages, even if it also brings potential challenges. It remains true that the power of assessment and thus certification lies with the qualified professionals on the course team and, in my view, correctly so. There is no question of kidding the student in any sense. However, involving the student so centrally ought to help their commitment to learning teaching generally and in particular to becoming skilfully reflective and articulate in reviewing their own teaching, so that they can at worst 'defend their corner' in the final negotiation. It should help prepare them for reflective self-development and teacher appraisal as newly qualified professionals on exit from the course.

From the mentor's point of view, the blessings of such involvement are likely to be a little more mixed. On the one hand, I can say from experience of doing the same thing in traditional course settings that having to compile or at least agree a relatively detailed assessment report with a student-teacher face-to-face can tend to make negative judgements harder to express. On the other hand, this generally also highlights the requirement for a mentor or tutor to be able to make their case clearly, which in turn pushes them towards clearer thinking and articulation of evidence and rationale.

Another way of involving the student in the formal process whilst also promoting informal reflection is to have them compile an *assessment folder* or *portfolio*. This will include all the assessable products of the course, including essays, reviews, teaching materials and lesson review materials by mentors and other teachers and tutors, or by the student themselves if they wished. It would include any formally completed teaching profiles. Not all documentation need necessarily feature in the assessment portfolio and it is probably important that some should not: for example, the student's own diary or some of their lesson notes, or the informal working profile records he or she may have used for private reflection at certain points. The same may be true of some of the mentor's own notes and working profiles on the student. But what does accrue in the assessment portfolio will be a major part, if not the whole documentary basis for the formal assessments using the teaching profile. As indicated above, the student will normally participate in such sessions and be a cosignatory to the formal document.

Sequence and timing in assessment processes
The considerable variation in the ways that HEI–school partnerships are likely to fulfil the requirement for the DFE's requisite number of days to be spent in school during ITT courses makes generalizations about suitable frequency and timing of assessment activities difficult. This is particularly true of informal events and opportunities, which in any case mix in with the formal aspects by providing contributions to the overall evidence base via the assessment portfolio or whatever other means are used.

Nevertheless, if only given the general DFE requirement and the limits on human memory, there probably needs to be some *regularity* of feedback and discussion by mentors and a *weekly basis* providing feedback or discussion on at least one substantial item would appear necessary. In the early days (see the programme suggestions in the next chapter) this might relate only to lesson observations, but would involve feedback and discussion of the student's own teaching as soon as this commenced.

The same caveats are applicable to formal points of progressive summative assessment. That is, it appears sensible to have a series of points at which formal interim and eventually a final formal assessment are made of student progress, using the relevant teaching profile. But again, course variations make recommendations concerning these problematic. In so far as a BEd or PGCE course still contains periods of more concentrated teaching, then an obvious procedure is to have such assessments at the end of such blocks. On the other hand, in so far as there is gradual involvement within schools before the beginning of any blocks of school-based work, then there seems little point in a fully fledged assessment event.

In my own school of education's secondary partnership PGCE arrangement, for instance, the first term involves two days per week in school, the second term spent entirely in school, and their third term back to the two days in school pattern. At the end of the first term there is a formal *preliminary assessment* in the mode of a *nihil obstat*. That is, it is presumed, other things equal, that the student intern will proceed into the block practice of the second term, but in case basic doubts about ability to complete the course successfully or suitability for the profession have arisen during the first term, the preliminary assessment form allows the institution of a review of that student's situation. At the middle of the block practice term there is a formal *interim assessment* and at the end of it a *final assessment*, each using the appropriate version of the full LUSSP profile record.

Putting Humpty together again: issues of aggregation in profiling
There is a basic issue which eventually arises when a capacity is analysed into aspects as in competence profile analyses. The issue is how to relate the part-aspects to the whole when making an overall assessment. There is no problem as long as one is thinking only in development terms, since one simply focuses on those aspects which appear to need improvement. However, if we're talking about assessment in the service of a single judgement, namely whether or not to award qualified teacher status, then the issue remains: how to put Humpty together again – and the more parts, the more difficult the reassembly.

If a teaching profile were thought to be based on an essential functional analysis, i.e. an analysis yielding the essential achievement capability aspects of teaching, then it would follow that minimum proficiency in all aspects should be required. The DFE position seems to be somewhat uncertain in this respect, as indicated on the one hand by its bothering to specify 27 competence statements, each set prefaced by 'newly qualified teachers should be able to' or equivalent, yet on the other by its envisaging alternative possible profile schemes and by the fact that when it gets down to conditions for the award of qualified teacher status (QTS), these are framed only in terms of:

demonstrating in the classroom

* the ability to teach effectively and to secure effective learning;
* the ability to manage pupil behaviour.

(DFE 1992, Annex A, para. 3.4.1)

Apart from wondering in passing what else teaching might be apart from the securing of effective learning, we may therefore note that this is consistent with a general interpretation that the DFE is not pushing a traditional CBTE fragmentation and aggregation model. Nevertheless, having made a serious attempt to conduct a valid functional and strategic analysis of teaching, surely this should make some difference to the way we arrive at our ultimate assessment decisions regarding QTS.

Here, once again, the hierarchically embedded nature of skilled capability seems relevant to teaching and a number of points need to be made in relation to it. A first is that functional analysis is only that, namely an attempt to discern what goes on in a successful activity. The activity itself has sooner or later to be seen in its own terms. In at least one sense, the whole of the activity is a unity in itself. It is more than the sum of its parts or aspects, though not in the sense of being some other part in addition to them (as some talk about parts and wholes seems to imply). A house does include its rooms, hall, stairs and other parts. The whole is the structure of parts or better, the structured parts.

The assessment implication here appears to be that we ought not to think we could assess teaching adequately by aggregating judgements about separate aspects from separate actions, rather we have also at some point to consider the whole activity as such. But we do also still need to consider the part-aspects, and we shall be in less danger of making invalid judgements based on them if we have in the first place considered those precisely as aspects of a natural, total performance, rather than, say, by trying to assess different functions separately (for example one task to assess monitoring in class management, another to assess positive action and influence, and so on).

This leads to the idea of some sort of qualified combination of judgements about different levels of a hierarchical competence profile of teaching, such that one weights the part-aspects and subfunctions, but to some extent allows the emergence of corrective impressions at more general levels.

In the LUSSP approach, for instance, the onus is placed on the *overall teaching competence* rating, which must be at least *satisfactory* to allow the award of QTS. This is not seen *just* as an aggregate of main area ratings, any more than these are seen as aggregates of subarea ratings, but a final overall satisfactory judgement does require certain minima, namely:

* no occurrence of a *seriously weak* rating in *any subarea* at all;
* at least a *satisfactory* rating in the *main teaching areas* of *explicit knowledge base, planning and preparation* and *interactive teaching.*

Where there is a less than satisfactory overall rating or where there is disagreement involving such a rating, further consultation and decision making procedures are invoked.

It must be admitted that this does have the potential to lead to some very messy complexities. However, I would hold that this is actually evidence in favour of its validity. Any system which offered to clean up decision making about teaching so as to once and for all get rid of the perennial messiness of its concerns would in my view merit treating with some suspicion of reductionism and oversimplification. Whether the particular arrangements just outlined above actually do result in more valid assessment and effective teacher preparation cannot yet be said, nor is it easily established. What does seem clear, however, is that either a totally global approach or a fully fragmented one will have less validity in principle.

Further reading

Background and recent developments in competence-based approaches are usefully covered in Alison Wolf's 1994 book and the collection edited by Burke (1989) and the bible for recent NCVQ work is Gilbert Jessup's (1991) book. A fuller treatment of the critiques and counter-critiques relating to competence profiling, with particular reference to teacher preparation, will be found in Tomlinson (1994).

8

Mentoring in practice: coaching tactics

In these final two chapters I want to pull together strands and implications from previous material to consider some concrete details of school-based mentoring. The present chapter focuses on the individual mentor level by building particularly on Chapters 2 and 3 for a somewhat more detailed treatment of coaching assistance. This is placed within the basic forms of student-teacher learning activity distinguished earlier.

I have already presented a rationale for considering learning promotion and interpersonal facilitation aspects of mentoring in Chapters 3 and 4, which also proposed four main forms of student-teacher learning activity in school-based courses, namely:

- learning from others teaching;
- learning through their own teaching;
- learning through progressively collaborative teaching (PCT);
- exploring central ideas and broader issues.

We also saw that mentoring assistance, particularly in the first three of these, involves a number of basic coaching functions relating to the plan–attempt–monitor–reflect phases of the teaching skill cycle. These need not only separate focus, but also integration, particularly as regards students' awareness of specific aspects and phases of teaching; to help remember this latter point, Chapter 3 proposed the letters PAMR as a mnemonic. Chapter 4 urged the view that all these functions have a vitally important interpersonal, motivational side and proposed a functional analysis of its facilitation. This stressed the importance of the way mentors *define* and act on the situation, their *active awareness* of student feeling and reaction, and the constant aim of gearing all this to the *motivation* and involvement of the student-teacher. These interpersonal influence functions were encapsulated in another acronym, DAM.

Although Chapters 3 and 4 did venture towards specific detail and example, they did not proceed to the specifics in a systematic way. How far a book like the present one should actually attempt to do so by dealing in concrete examples and recommendations is, however, a matter for some conjecture. On the one hand, there are always going to be at least some readers who find a particular item a totally obvious matter of common sense (common sense being whatever *we* take for granted). The more concrete the point, the more so, though it will concern different items for different people. On the other hand, I believe that in the past, a failure to address specifics has sometimes been a shortcoming in traditional teacher education. The remedy isn't just to offer isolated tips, but to offer concrete guidance which is an expression of the informing principles, whose utility and application should thereby be promoted. The first part of this chapter will therefore offer some specific recommendations concerning coaching assistance and interpersonal facilitation within the major forms of school-based student-teacher learning activity. Given that PCT involves the combination of the first two types of student learning activity, the bulk of the treatment will be achieved in relation to those.

I should point out that given the detailed nature of the focus here and the existence of some general principles with wide application, a sense of repetition is perhaps inevitable as you encounter the same ideas applied to similar phases in different activities. But as you'll see, there are differences of detail, on which the chapter attempts to focus. I must also make clear that these recommendations can, of course, only be recommendations 'in principle'. That is, I think them desirable and worth applying if possible. Issues of time, resources and actual feasibility obviously cannot be ignored, but to use whatever opportunity one does end up having, it's necessary at least to have worked out what one wishes to try.

Assisting students to learn from others teaching

(a) *Unpacking the planning and promoting student enquiry*

When students have the opportunity to learn by examining other people's teaching, whether directly observed or indirectly accessed via video recordings, there usually needs to be some advance indication of the planning aspects listed below, with provision of opportunity for the intern to explore and grasp what is involved. The teacher or mentor whose teaching is involved may or may not have formally documented lesson plans, but some sort of communication is needed and teaching competence analysis documentation (such as the LUSSP prompt materials sections 4 and 5) can help the focus here. It will include:

- *teaching goals for the lesson or teaching segment in question:* ideally including the *rationale* for choosing these goals now in relation to the subject syllabus, pupils and current teaching topic sequence. Also any *differentiation* and *pupil matching* envisaged.
- *intended strategies for the management of learning:* including *teaching/ learning activities, resource deployment, pupil organization* and *lesson phase sequencing*, with *rationales* for these in relation to learning and pupil management potential in the light of intended learning outcomes, pupil characteristics and any other intervening factors. Specific *behaviour management strategies* with corresponding *rationales*. Ideally, *resource materials* would be available in advance for discussion.
- *intended forms of monitoring own teaching action and its effects*: including ways of *assessing* the achievement of task and learning progress.

The *degree of detail* useful in the explanation of planning will depend on the intern's background and progress by the point at which it occurs, their familiarity with this area of the subject, with teaching and management strategies, and so on. Relatively detailed expansion may be needed in the early stages (e.g. 'Understanding X, by which I include knowing about aspects a, b and c and their interrelationship'), but too much at once may simply *overload* the student. As usual with explanation, it's a matter of taking account of where they start from, concentrating on main ideas, and helping them get to grips and make sense. Prior explanation need not be exhaustive, precisely because the observing student-teacher will have the chance to see more of what is meant as the lesson unfolds. Since *time* is likely to be restricted anyway, mentors may find it useful to use the major general headings in the competence prompt materials, particularly the concept map and tree diagram versions, as starting points.

Effective mentoring, in this phase as in all others, depends not only on the content coverage just indicated, but also on the way one relates to the student. This isn't just a question of the motivation side, but also of helping the student get into the skills and stances needed. Both aspects are intertwined. It's therefore important to do the following.

- *Check your general deployment of DAM strategies and core conditions of helping*. Do this routinely anyway in your encounters with interns. The way we would like them to develop and function needs also to be lived and exemplified, not just stated. In other words, we probably only define the situation effectively if we act in it the way we intend. At the most concrete levels, voice-tone and other non-verbal signs of positiveness and warmth make all the difference to one's relationship with the student-teacher and to what they get out of it. Other than these defining and motivating aspects of the DAM triad, we also need to remember active awareness, as well as the alternative core conditions of acceptance, empathy and genuineness.

- *Try to ensure that a reflective approach continues to be realized both by practising it and by explicitly referring to it.* Deploying a reflective, open-complex skill approach means *exploring* what particular teaching goals actually consist in, *examining* the rationale and workings of particular strategies for aspects of teaching, *considering* alternatives and possible indications of their appropriateness. The idea is to do this as a matter of course, through various sorts of prompt. But it also needs to be made quite clear that the underlying perspective is that whilst we're assuming some things are more worthwhile than others and will pursue this, we're dealing with open-complex, not closed-simple skill, so that there may for instance be many plausible goals, right answers, strategies.

Such a 'second-order' or underlying perspective is of course likely to be confusing and alienating if invoked too frequently, the earlier in the proceedings the moreso. But one doesn't want to be seen resorting to it only when one is uncertain or when interns witness disagreement or inconsistency of practice. If a reflective approach is proactively stated and adhered to, it's also likely to be a major factor in preventing interns becoming defensive. Apart from this, it would of course also be providing a model of the sort of purposeful openness appropriate to a profession. The expression of such a reflective stance will tend to include the following subcomponents:

- *Facilitating interns' active, open-minded exploration of your perspectives:* helping them actively gain access to your knowledge and thinking doesn't preclude informing and explaining to them directly, in fact far from it. But it does require you to define the situation in ways that encourage and convey acceptance of such exploration. This is likely to include invitations to interrogate and such explicit prompts as 'What's your first reaction to this?' or 'Is there anything you'd like to query me about regarding this?', 'Can you think of other ways I might have tried to do this?' and so on. But it will also as always require continuing implicit definition, including the usual 'non-verbals' indicating openness. In this connection, a particularly basic and powerful definer of possibilities is of course the appropriate and adequate allocation of *time* and *situational resources*, such as which room, etc.;
- *Referring to alternatives:* 'there are various ways of doing this'; 'I thought about trying x or y, but ...';
- *Providing rationales:* 'I might have tried x or y, but I didn't because in my experience ...', 'another possibility might have been z, which would have had the likely advantage of a, but the disadvantage of b'.

- *Acknowledge difficulty levels in relation to teacher development.* As well as explaining in whatever detail is needed, giving some idea of the likely difficulty of a particular strategy is likely to promote interns' sense of realism and therefore comfort. Whilst striking a balance between this and encouraging them to be adventurous is often a matter of fine judgement, it may help for the mentor to combine *comments* on what they consider the relative ease/difficulty of a strategy with a little *self-disclosure* to put things into developmental perspective (e.g.: 'As a student-teacher I saw this method being used very effectively, but I found I couldn't make it work until I realized that . . .' or 'I now think this particular approach requires the teacher to be very much on their toes, so I think I'd only try it once I'd got *very* familiar with that part of the syllabus').

• *Avoid the shackles of 'implicit perfectionism' by acknowledging the nature of teaching skill realistically.* To the extent that interns (or teachers for that matter) entertain the crude technical view of skill as all-or-nothing, magical capability against all odds, they burden the observed teacher-model with the expectation of perfect performance. This not only feeds any defensive avoidance tendencies the student intern may possess, it also threatens the teacher, who is after all only human. Mentors helping interns to learn from others teaching (whether their own or other teachers') therefore need to define the situation and its assumptions in terms of a more adequate and subtle view of skilfulness, such as has been offered in these pages. This may be attempted through tactics such as:

• reference during planning and other discussion to the *impossibility of total certainty* in most things human, in particular teaching (e.g. 'I'm pretty confident this will work with this class, but it depends on so many factors you can't predict with certainty');
• reference to specific *factors that may influence success*: (e.g. 'It's a great strategy, but it does depend on x'; or 'I'll see how it goes with this class before I decide whether to bring in that particular bit');
• *self-disclosure* regarding one's own perceived capability, preference and confidence with respect to the aspect in question ('This approach is something I've been trying out a bit recently. I'm getting it together, but it still has some way to go, so I'll be interested in your comments on x and y aspects'; 'I don't particularly like this topic, so I make myself use a tighter approach than I'd otherwise do', etc.).

These tactics for avoiding 'implicit perfectionism' may perhaps sound as if they're sailing close to the wind of 'defensive excusing in advance', which we certainly don't want to be encouraging in our interns. In reality though, it's a subtle matter of degree of emphasis and therefore specific dos and don'ts are dangerous here. The important thing to remember is the nature of the basic viewpoint we're trying to promote and demonstrate. This is inherently tied up with an adequate conception of skill and self-development, but from the interpersonal motivation angle the desirable stance is surely something like: 'No one can be a perfect teacher, rather we're seeking insights and skilful strategies. Some of us are a bit further along this road and wish to share our perceived gains particularly with those of you who are just starting out. This means there's likely to be mutual learning, even if it takes slightly different forms in each of us, intern and mentor'.

(b) Observing the action

Even when placed directly in a working classroom for a couple of weeks, there is evidence that beginning students don't tend to learn much from the experience as such. It just is difficult for any novice to see what a skilled performer is doing, to distinguish the various components of the action. At a global level, the nature of the activity may seem relatively obvious, but it may take a lot of close, guided attending to see *how* the action is actually being done. We also need *time* to register perceptions in memory, but teaching events are complex and fleeting. It will also be difficult to hear what's going on in the many important conversations held with individuals and groups beyond the observer's earshot, and what we do actually manage to register tends to be limited and selective. With time our memories of them fade still more selectively.

These problems of access may be assisted through various means, though some of these do pose their own difficulties. There seem to be three major requirements which merge into each other:

- *Providing guidance regarding how and what to observe:* this may be given *in advance*, for instance through the sort of planning explanation indicated above, or it may be *'on-line'* in the form of ongoing commentary/discussion between student and mentor if they are able to observe teaching together, though this may require exceptional resourcing in the case of live teaching. In either case, it may be very helpful to make use of observation records and detailed teaching strategy prompt materials comparable to the LUSSP ones described earlier. Once again, it's important though often difficult to remember the likely limitations on what student-teachers can track and note in the detail of classroom activity, especially at first.

- *Giving as full access to the action as possible:* if, as traditionally, the student takes up a particular position in a classroom, many of the teacher's inputs and communications other than those addressing the whole class *won't be accessible*. The student may therefore need to follow the teacher around or at least move into their vicinity, but this needs to be unobtrusive or it will create problems. This is in fact one of the reasons for promoting collaborative teaching. An alternative would be to have the teacher wearing a radio-microphone which transmits to a receiver heard by the student-teacher (see the Appendix). Although the somewhat staid traditions of teaching practice supervision perhaps make this sound inappropriate and obtrusive, it's interesting to note that the wearing of such microphones is now recognized as essential in the production of classroom video recordings of teaching.

The interpersonal aspects of this side of student-teacher learning relate perhaps more to the teacher doing the teaching that is being observed than to the student. Initially at least, some teachers may find it threatening to have interns observing them at all, let alone listening to their every word or videoing their every action and gesture! However, the importance of assisted observation is considerable, and not just as something that occurs in the early stages. What was said above under 'avoiding the shackles of implicit perfectionism' seems particularly relevant here too.

- *Providing for some sort of record*: there is a need for a record of events. Open-ended notes by the student or their use of specific observation record forms such as the LUSSP example can provide the basis for a written record for subsequent discussion. Such records will of course be highly selective. Much richer and in some senses more objective (though still in some senses selective and subjective) would be a video recording of the teaching. The obvious advantage of a concrete record such as a video recording is the potential it offers for repeated analysis and discussion (more of this in the Appendix).

(c) Promoting monitoring

To benefit from the 'by proxy skill cycle' offered by studying others teaching, a student needs not only to see the actions that are taking place, but what is happening through them. Telling whether something was actually the outcome of this or that action, or would have occurred anyway due to some other factor, can be a problem even in principle, but in the first place the student needs help *to monitor outcomes of lessons and broader teaching segments* as well as *to explore what goes on by way of local actions and their mini-effects*. The latter will occur at varying levels of detail in the fine grain of ongoing teaching ('What actually happened when he gave directions about the experiment?'). In both of the above respects, students may be assisted to focus their attention on two types of effect:

- outcomes *intended* by the previously accessed planning, in consultation with their mentor, and
- outcomes *noticed* anyway by the student and/or mentor. Here again LUSSP-type profile documentation may be of assistance and the mentor may assist through discussion of lesson outcomes or commentary/discussion during the lesson on the mini-effects within it (e.g. with reference to class management subskills).

Students are also likely to need assistance to *demonstrate monitoring*. If having your teaching observed can be daunting, then also encouraging the observer to monitor its effectiveness is really asking something by way of resilience and openness on the part of the observed teacher. I suggested above that all sorts of unfortunate expectations abound. Nevertheless, monitoring effects is crucial by way of gaining feedback in learning any skill (in this case effects of teaching). Not only this, however, for established teachers and mentors have here a particularly strong opportunity to get rid of 'perfectionist' assumptions and to define the student-teacher into a professional, learning stance precisely by demonstrating it themselves.

On the whole, student-teachers will appreciate and learn fast from such unravelling of teaching effects. It will allow teacher-mentors to let their openness and limitations be seen and it should make it easier for the students themselves to accept and engage in such monitoring of their own efforts. It has nevertheless to be recognized that there is always some probability of encountering students who are indeed so concrete in their thinking that they persist in seeing skill as all or nothing and teacher imperfections as entirely avoidable. Not only do such attitudes not promote the student's own learning, they obviously also make mentor openness more difficult. In itself, of course, this sort of stance could be a useful indicator of their potential (or rather, lack of it) as entrants to the profession, relevant to the heading of *professional self-development*.

In addition, the following specifics should help promote open-minded neutral analysis by the student, which in turn should help the mentor/teacher open up more positively:

• *agree a focus in advance:* many writers suggest that this should be *specific, analytical and evidence oriented*: what exactly occurred, how and why do we think it occurred, what particular information do we have in relation to these views and interpretations? Whilst thoroughly underlining the analytical and evidence orientation aspects, a student may surely need to look not only at relatively specific features, but also at *broader* and *longer term processes* such as how a lesson developed, how the atmosphere seemed to shift and why, what factors gradually built up as the actual causes of a particular decisive event, and so on. A focus of *some* sort is usually useful, though it shouldn't be used to outlaw other issues which may have arisen unpredictably during the teaching.

• *agree to focus on both positive and negative points*: we seem to be prone to picking up the negative when witnessing purposeful action and this may have something to do both with our implicitly perfectionist views of skill and our learned (offensive) defences. In the face of this, some writers recommend that in monitoring lessons, one should stick to *objective* matters. I agree with this in so far as it means the accepting, analytical and evidence oriented stance we recommended above. However, avoiding the value aspects seems a rather unhealthy and defensive sort of approach and hardly possible anyway when what's being considered is a *purposeful* activity; our interns are trying to learn how to achieve certain teaching *goals*.

The *interpersonal* impact of these sorts of matters depends a lot on what we do with them by way of reflection and discussion (see next subsection) and this issue is doubtless more crucial in the case of monitoring interns' own teaching attempts, but as far as their monitoring of other teachers' teaching goes, I therefore suggest that any evaluative focuses ought to be balanced between the positive and the negative, with the positive focus occurring first. Thus one might agree to look at, say, three aspects that seemed to go well than anything that didn't seem to go so well (and in each case, to anticipate the reflection subsection: *why* do we think they did and *what evidence* do we have?). The firm placing of the positive aspects first is designed to counter the human negative judgemental tendency, though it's also likely that the social roles are such that interns will not generally criticize (as they see it) their mentors too readily.

Fill in the feedback gaps
In spite of the above procedures, there are going to be things interns aren't able to spot for themselves. As we saw, this is a typical part of being a novice. Whether considering their own or other teachers' teaching, mentors are therefore likely to have to help the student intern gain access to these aspects. Some suggestions for ways of doing this include:

* *prompting interns towards available pieces of information:* this obvious strategy includes both open-ended and leading questions, and can be particularly effective when an independent record such as an audio or video recording is available or when the mentor and intern are teaching together in the same PCT setting, so that the mentor can alert the intern to developing events not already noticed.
* *providing the information directly:* often it's not possible to get the intern to obtain the information, as when, for instance, only the mentor has recorded the relevant items in their written notes. Given the difficulties of later recall from within the flow of teaching action, one may just have to provide the information oneself.

(d) Modelling analysis and reflection

It's nowadays firmly established amongst the specialists (philosophers of science and psychological researchers on perception and judgement) that even our basic observations of the world around us are influenced by our existing ideas and terms of reference, our perceptions and understanding are partly *constructions*. At the very least, our existing ideas sensitize us and help frame what we pick up through our perceptions. In judging people and social activities like teaching, we can't get by without *interpreting* matters, even though we may be doing so unconsciously. Add to this the sheer complexity and subtlety of the events occurring in the average classroom, and one realizes that analysing and pinning down 'why it happened like that' in classrooms, 'what this or that action led to', 'how it ended up like that', tends always to be somewhat open and problematic.

This is something which can *threaten and deskill* people setting out in a mentoring role, but it can also *stimulate and revitalize* them as educational professionals if they cope with it thoughtfully and resiliently. The dangers come perhaps from the fact that as experienced teachers, new mentors may have been subject to the typical time pressures in teaching and perhaps even ridiculed for attempts to stand back and analyse their teaching. When they're now given even a little time to observe or even just to think about teaching processes – their own or that of others – they may be disturbed to find that they begin noticing things they didn't ever have time to pick up before, but can't now ignore. This can raise pretty basic uncertainties ('have I/has X really been teaching all these years without realizing this?'). Like the person driving home on the familiar route, they catch themselves not paying full conscious attention to the driving and wondering whether they've just been completely lucky not to crash. This can in itself prompt defensiveness of various sorts.

Actually, like such drivers, what we've *probably* been doing is processing the expected information in an intuitive and largely unconscious way. We've probably been teaching skilfully. But this 'jolt' rightly draws attention to two forms of uncertainty which need recognizing and coping with, not ignoring, if mentors are going to be successful in their mentoring.

• *As mentors we can be guided by our intuitions and initial assumptions, but mustn't take them totally for granted. We need to help students question us by being willing to explore the teaching they witness, whether ours or that of others.* It doubtless is impossible to take conscious account of all that goes on in a classroom and as experienced teachers part of our skill *is* our ability to read a lot of classroom cues simultaneously yet unconsciously (we noted this as one of the skill paradoxes in Chapter 2). But by the same token, like the distracted driver, we therefore *cannot be sure* what we were actually processing (we *may* just have been lucky). By definition, intuition isn't open to explicit checking, but as mentors we can't just drive on and forget it, like the driver going home. Mentors are in a position of being charged with helping students make sense of the teaching they've observed and monitored (whether that of the mentor or someone else). Realizing this may help us to try to test our assumptions and it should also help us appreciate the very different approach our students may bring to an understanding of the action.

We will then also realize that *we need as mentors to help students examine teaching actions and their effects in a systematic and analytical way, partly by illustrating such an approach ourselves.* Basic sorts of stance in doing this might therefore be expressed as: 'Looking at things so far, it seems to me that maybe x is happening, so let's see what evidence there is that's consistent or inconsistent with that' or 'This and this seem to suggest that both x and y may be occurring, but do we have any other confirming or disconfirming indicators?' When mentors go in for this sort of 'detective work' on their own or others' teaching activities and outcomes, it may achieve three kinds of relevant gain:

- First, by looking carefully at the teaching and checking up on their hunches as to what was influencing what, by standing back and looking for evidence of alternative possibilities, mentors are more likely to arrive at insights that *are* explicit and thus capable of being articulated in response to students' queries and uncertainties. When they're having difficulties seeing what's going on, or when they're plumping for surface trends, mentors will hopefully be in a position to offer useful interpretations together with evidence for the validity of these interpretations. They're more likely to be able to do this than students can, because although the problem is that mentors' own teaching experience may have 'only' given them intuitive capabilities, these intuitive capabilities will actually be at play in guiding the detective work. So like any detective, mentors need to listen to their hunches, but also to follow them up with sound investigation, so that they have a good case to make.
- Second, by articulating our thinking processes out loud, rather than just telling the student what we end up deciding is correct, we can as mentors be both arriving at insights *and* illustrating to students how they may go about doing so for themselves. We will be indicating such things as: what sorts of things to look for, the need to suspend judgement until things become clear and the evidence checked, the need to investigate different possibilities, the possibility that different processes and explanations may all apply to different aspects of the same classroom events. In a word, as mentors we will be *modelling* reflection and analysis. If we can draw our students into the investigation, rather than just doing it for them, so much the better.
- Third, at the same time, by reflecting out loud we'll also be indicating something at the 'meta-level' of basic assumption, about the underlying nature both of *being an intelligently professional teacher* and of *learning to become such a professional*. Namely, we'll be illustrating Donald Schön's point that from the start, effective professionals are those who engage in *reflective practice*. Such people thereby tend to carry on improving, not only because they repeat and automatize their strategies, but because they're also intelligently examining things all along.

- *We may well need to deal with the basic assumption level explicitly and point out implications of the openness of the activity of teaching.* As I suggested briefly above, the complexities and human subtleties involved in teaching situations mean that simple clear certainties are probably only enjoyed by those not really examining the evidence. We may need as mentors to point out this 'meta-perspective'. However, we can also be clear that if students bother at this point to be analytical and systematic in reflecting on teaching events, it's likely to pay dividends. It tends to lead to increasingly intuitive skill at telling what's going on and at acting accordingly.

Much of what I've been saying here amounts to suggesting that by going about *open-minded reflection in a cool, yet committed way*, the mentor/teacher is codefining an approach that the intern may hopefully switch into. Nevertheless, even bearing all the above in mind, this reflection phase has to be recognized as posing perhaps even more psychological threat to the mentor than the monitoring function discussed just previously. For they may experience a pressure to fulfil their mentoring role to the optimum, yet also feel a risk that openness and scrutiny may reveal failings they would be embarrassed to reveal, particularly as teachers deemed worthy of a tutoring role. After all, to say the least, here they're doing something very few teachers have had the time to do. Even if they appreciate the likelihood of learning something for themselves about (their own) teaching, however, there's clearly some danger of defensive withdrawal and nothing being gained (except temporary safety) because nothing is ventured. Hopefully, given all the arguments and using present suggestions, mentors will feel able to take the high ground.

Assisting students to learn from their own teaching

Many of the points and suggestions from the previous subsection apply to this one, nevertheless, the emphasis and issues shift decisively when it comes to students learning from their own attempts at teaching. Once more, the PAMR emphasis on relating all aspects of the teaching cycle, planning–attempt–monitoring–reflection on feedback, is of considerable importance, but let us proceed through these phases one by one.

Assisting planning

Anyone attempting action has to have *some* idea of what they're doing and students will have been acquiring their ideas from experiences such as subject teaching method courses and previous study and observation of their mentors and others teaching. Clearly the mentor needs to discuss the student's planning and preparation in advance of the teaching. Here again, systematic competence prompt materials may be useful. The broad headings requiring attention are:

- *teaching/learning goals for the lesson or teaching segment in question:* this should include the *rationale* for choosing these goals now in relation to the subject syllabus, pupils and current teaching topic sequence, also any *differentiation* and *pupil matching* envisaged;
- *intended strategies for the management of learning:* including *teaching/learning activities, resource deployment, pupil organization* and *lesson phase sequencing,* with potential back-up possibilities and *rationales* for all these in relation to learning and pupil management potential in the light of intended learning outcomes, pupil characteristics and any other intervening

factors. Specific *behaviour management strategies* with corresponding rationales should be dealt with and, ideally, *resource materials* would be available in advance for discussion. These and the learning goals should be indicated explicitly in writing using any relevant documentation and conventions, such as the lesson planning sheet suggestions outlined earlier from the LUSSP scheme;

- *intended forms of monitoring own teaching action and its effects:* including ways of *assessing* the achievement of task and learning progress.

In so far as here it's the *student's action* that is being facilitated, the *mentor's major functions* appear to be to:

- *Explore the student's ideas and intentions:* the mentor does the listening, letting the student do the talking and explaining. The mentor prompts the student as necessary to explain *what* they intend and *why, how* they see it working, what they see as *alternatives,* etc. The mentor is on the lookout to check that:

  - what the student intends is *pedagogically appropriate* as regards learning goals, teaching and management strategies;
  - what they intend is *realistic* for the pupils, context and resources in question;
  - the student *understands things in enough detail* that the plans can be translated into action. Here it may help actually to descend to the level of precise wording, particularly if one has reason for doubt ('What sort of thing do you think you'll actually say to them at this point?'; 'How do you think you'll put that?'). As experienced teachers, mentors are likely to find various things just crop up intuitively. The point, however, is that they should always check on the sorts of basics listed just above, and they should be willing to check the student's grasp and preparation for such aspects beforehand;
  - the student appears *capable* in practice of executing the planned strategies in that particular context of pupils and resources.

- *Keep the discussion proactive, avoiding a reactive 'crisis management' stance:* where, as is desirable, student interns are given the initiative in consulting their mentors regarding their planned teaching, this nevertheless runs the considerable risk of them sliding into the familiar 'what if they . . .?' type of approach. This is unfortunate in so far as it detracts from essential features of skilful teaching, which include being proactive and anticipatory to a considerable extent. Even worse, it threatens instead to redefine teaching implicitly as a series of crisis-managing reactions.

Of course, major or minor classroom crises *will* sooner or later occur, in spite of the best laid teaching plans and the most anticipatory strategies. So it's clearly appropriate to consider strategies to adopt if and when such situations arise. But better than cure is prevention, and better still is harnessing of positive potential. Various substrategies are available to avoid endorsement of the crisis management stance whilst still promoting active consultation by interns, including mentors:

- *pointing out the power of a positive stance to define the classroom situation;*
- *pointing out that the bottom line is that support is available if the worse comes to the worst.* Find out their 'worst nightmare', but try not to get drawn into a 'what if it's got three heads and swears?' type of escalation; relate things, for example, to the school's behaviour management/disciplinary policy. Don't be too ready to take the line 'It simply could not happen' since the only true certainties are matters of logic and people feeling anxious sense this! Rather, an open stance is also a more credible one; a finite possibility exists, but given everything, it's very low. The strategies for avoiding it are x, for containing it they're y and the mentor is in the classroom and the school behaviour management policy is such and such for escalating situations. Student anxiety runs the danger of defining the situation so negatively that its worst fears are in fact realized.

- *Alert, explain and challenge if necessary:* where the mentor has reason to think there are problems in one or other of the above aspects, the student needs alerting to this, with explanation as to why. Mentors will need to remember that in doing this they're supposed to be *modelling a systematic and thoughtful approach,* as well as hopefully facilitating students' creativity. As in teaching, so in mentoring: in the early days especially, it may be hard to contain one's astonishment at what one considers out of the question (the 'No way – 10f won't wear that!' type of response), but even if the mentor did go on to give their reasons, a closed climate of authority-reference and non-exploration may have been established through the certainty of the dismissal. A more measured approach is thus desirable, but this doesn't of course mean that anything goes.

Challenging and resisting is something some prospective mentors worry about, perhaps because of 'implicit perfectionism', or because of anxiety or shyness about being seen as negative and confrontational. It may help them to remember that there have been surveys amongst Articled Teacher participants indicating that teacher trainees are concerned about their mentors' avoiding difficult issues. However, they also want them to be warm and helpful, so there does seem to be a potential difficulty if problems appear in students' plans or other aspects of their stances.

Problems with challenge and disagreement are obviously less likely to occur to the extent that mentors are already exploring the intern's planning in an open and supportive way, mainly doing the listening as they probe for various aspects of the intern's planning and rationale, trying as far as time allows to get a sense of the whole picture before deciding which aspects may need challenging. This way any sudden impasse is hardly likely.

If the mentor does decide that particular aspects of the planned teaching are in need of revision, then a whole range of specific forms of response are open to them, depending on the time available. A counselling style 'offering back of the issues' to the student is perhaps most desirable as regards positiveness and student learning opportunity (e.g. 'I wonder about fitting all that in: can we just see in a bit more detail how much time each activity is going to take?' or 'Okay, now what would happen if they've forgotten the instructions you gave them at the beginning?'). But sooner or later it may be necessary to challenge directly ('In spite of what you've said, I don't really think you will have time for all this, because I think activity a will need x minutes to set up, then . . .'). Sometimes the issue is one that is a matter of judgement where the mentor just does feel he or she has knowledge the student does not ('In my experience, 8E aren't capable of getting through that activity in that time'), though this sort of possibility would be lessened if the student has had a good chance to observe the particular class or, even better, to engage in PCT with the mentor in that class. There is also clearly a balance to be struck between the offering of guidance in advance and the need for student-teachers to be allowed to learn from their own experience, possibly including mistakes, with the welfare and learning of the pupils being an important factor here.

- *Negotiate, suggest and inform:* in the case where the student's planning/ understanding turns out to reveals gaps or they're having trouble deciding between alternatives, then it may be for the mentor to *suggest specific possibilities with informing rationales*: 'You might think of doing x, which would tend to be good for this and this, though perhaps more difficult for that, because in my experience y tends to happen.' It may come to a need for closure which the mentor has to assist by proposing clearly, 'All in all, I'd suggest you try x this time and we'll see how it goes.'

In all this the question of *appropriate level of detail* remains a difficult one. It's very easy to overload novices who are unfamiliar with a domain and its terminology. Mentors and students will have their preferred styles, but I'm inclined to suggest a generally 'top-down' approach in the sense of dealing with the bigger chunks first, then the details as needed. More specifically, start from the *major activities/phases planned for the lesson*, using available planning documentation, then perhaps consult further teaching analysis details of interactive aspects of teaching (e.g. as in the LUSSP prompt material). It is clear that the amount of time available for such functions is of the utmost importance, but at present it doesn't appear that this commodity will be in too great supply. This is at least one reason for considering below the possibility of specifying some sort of minimum programme of activities and experiences to which students ought to be entitled and obliged.

Supporting the teaching activity

This is perhaps the prime example of a coaching function highlighted by current understanding of the nature of skill learning, but which has not featured much at all in traditional forms of teacher education and teaching practice supervision. The idea has tended to be that of discussing the planning, then simply observing as the student conducts the lesson, followed by feedback and discussion (given resource limitations, the reality has tended to be still less ambitious). Perhaps this was because of yet another commonsense theory of (teaching) skill acquisition, the 'crude experiential' or 'chuck 'em in the deep end' approach. Of course, modern skill insights also emphasize the point of 'letting the student have a go', do it on their own or at least without active support, whether for a whole lesson period or something shorter. In that case and for the period of teaching in question, we shall wish to just observe the teaching, which is dealt with under the next subsection, 'Assisting monitoring and feedback'.

However, the skill cycle approach and its associated insights also suggest that having been assisted with their planning, student-teachers making their actual attempt to teach pupils would be assisted in the learning by active mentor support.

Active support for ongoing teaching

Various forms of support for the actual teaching seem to be effective, including:

- *simply having a supportive mentor-figure present:* the function that person is perceived as fulfilling tends to make quite a bit of difference, but even if it's only the traditional 'observation and crit' function of supervising tutors, their presence has typically been seen as a safety net;
- *receiving important information* about the situation which the student is as yet too unskilled or overloaded to have gathered (certain pupils are getting left out of the discussion; the quiet child in the middle/back is writing something else, etc.). This might well include *feedback* by the mentor following their monitoring of student action and its consequences ('I think you'll find that x is occurring as a result of . . .'). Problems of overload do of course need bearing in mind, though work with radio-assisted practice (see Appendix) suggests that this can be less of a problem than many people assume;
- *being reminded/prompted to carry out planned strategies and tactics of the teaching,* perhaps at subskill detail level, which seem to have been forgotten (perhaps because the novice has everything to do just to keep tabs on the topic and the front row). Such prompts might of course include suggestions that the student herself or himself gathers the information and feedback that the mentor was thinking of providing ('Have you checked what's

happening as a result of . . .?'), but again, overload needs watching. Within a systematic programme, it may be useful to agree to focus on particular aspects of the teaching diagnosed previously as needing attention. The present range of points would then apply to support with such a focus;

- *receiving on-the-spot guidance and suggestions* for tactics to respond to unforeseen contingencies arising ('What about doing x or y to take care of that?');
- *receiving encouragement and positive feedback* during the action. Any teacher who has seen the effects of positive praise on pupils won't be surprised at its power to encourage student-teachers and increase their sense of security.

This brings us to the interpersonal facilitation side of teaching support. In general, mentors need constantly to *check general deployment of DAM strategies and core conditions of helping*. The situation definition aspect can have many forms of expression, as Chapter 3 tried to show in some detail. In the case of mentors and student-teachers, the following items appear important.

- *Be sensitive to how you define the intern's situation to pupils:* hearing a teacher introduce a student-teacher to their potentially difficult class by telling them what will happen if they don't 'behave themselves for young Mr/Ms X who is a student' has been understandable in the traditional teaching practice situation, but also seen as a 'kiss of death' by not a few Mr/Ms Xs! Not surprising, perhaps, in that it appears to be an implicit definition of the situation, communicating negative expectancies from the outset. One of the things interns like about school-based courses appears to be the recognition they get as beginning *teachers*, as opposed to students; indeed, in many schemes the title 'intern' has been chosen partly because of this. Remembering that defining/influencing involves such explicit aspects but also implicit ones suggest the *use of explicit terminology and appropriate titles*, including terms like *intern*. 'Ms X will be spending some time teaching you this year. We will sometimes teach together, sometimes separately.'

  Behave consistently with this definition. If the student-teacher is doing the teaching, try, other things being equal, to resist having the pupils 'redefine' you into being 'the teacher', as they will tend to do if only out of habit. Avoiding eye contact and simply ignoring pupils may suffice, but it may also be necessary to explicitly redirect pupils towards the student-teacher. Of course, there is potentially some degree of tension between this and the idea of overt assistance and guidance for the intern in the classroom. A mentor may thus have to be careful in choosing moments for 'a quick word', but this often has to be too quick and it's still relatively public, which is why the use of radio-microphones may seem worthy of consideration.

- *Encourage the intern by complimenting positive aspects and conveying an atmosphere of positive expectation:* as well as providing the sorts of prompts, information and on-the-spot guidance that will help the intern put their plans into action, it bears repeating that in-class support should include the important functions of recognizing and praising positive achievements. Given (rather negative) British cultural practices in this area, it's probably worth pointing out that one doesn't need to wait for unusual or surprising achievements before communicating confirmatory feedback and combining it with positive approval. The obvious principle is surely to target those aspects and subaspects that have been singled out for attention in previous discussion. But any aspect or partial success is a worthy candidate for such treatment, particularly if the intern is at all lacking in confidence or is self-critical.
- *Gradually increase the scope and difficulty of teaching activity:* constant reference here to the 'chucking them into the deep end' tradition alerts us to a major potential strategy in school-based courses, namely, to require only limited teaching attempts at first and then to increase the demand gradually. Since this is hard to accomplish with student-teachers in isolation and is a major defining feature of PCT, I will deal with it later under that heading.

Supporting the ongoing teaching can be a powerful and positive influence. It's clear that such support requires the mentor to be able to *monitor the situation* in the light of the previous lesson planning, so as to *diagnose* any need to assist the student to achieve agreed purposes in practice. It's therefore clear that in relation to seeing what's going on, but perhaps even more for providing the above types of guidance and support during ongoing teaching, there's a *problem of access*.

Teaching is itself a communicative activity and so any further overt communication by the mentor with the sole teacher (student) in charge of the class would tend to interrupt and disrupt the teaching. The same problem characterizes many human interactions in which we might wish to provide ongoing assistance, so doing anything about this is likely to require something rather novel. During 1993, for example, viewers of BBC television were impressed by a programme showing family therapists using radio-microphones to communicate coaching guidance, in this case to parents attempting to manage a very difficult preschool child. Such an approach had in fact previously been tried with considerable success in coaching teaching, under the label of *radio-assisted practice* or *RAP* (Smith and Tomlinson 1984). The advent of school-based teacher preparation and in particular collaborative teaching between mentors and students may well remove the need for such a technique. On the other hand, they may precisely be a useful ground for specific uses of it, which is why it is briefly introduced in this book's appendix.

Assisting monitoring and feedback

It's worth drawing attention to the precise title of this function. Mentors clearly need to monitor and record student's teaching for a variety of purposes, but prime amongst these is to *get the student-teacher to realize what's going on*, since it's the student's skill learning we're trying to promote. Even if, as under traditional arrangements, we stay out of the action and just observe, there remains the task of getting our insights through to the student's awareness. In the light of this, then, there is here a further set of access problems which need to borne in mind.

- *Selectivity of awareness*: an immense amount goes on even during brief teaching encounters, let alone whole lessons. We humans are highly selective in that we can and do pick up only limited amounts of information from our surroundings – especially when we're hard-pressed novices very new to classrooms. Experienced teachers, as research has shown (cf. Kagan 1992), are likely not only to take account of more, but to have become intuitive at this. So as I've suggested previously, mentors can let their natural inclinations guide their observation and monitoring, but they also need to be vigilant in an explicit way, for instance, by reference to the functions and strategies discussed in planning and other sessions. Mentors will also need to remember that, like all of us, students may not only miss certain things, they may assume they did or didn't occur, often to fit in with what they *did* see.
- *Limitations of memory:* even if it was picked up by the mentor-observer, the student-teacher may well have difficulty in recalling it. One can use what are grandly known as 'stimulated recall' techniques (e.g. 'Remember that bit when you were telling Jason about the essay and Jessica shouted out?'), but people tend only to recall consciously what they *consciously attended* to in the first place – and often what we want them to become aware of is precisely what they weren't seeing (see Yinger 1986). By the end of the lesson, much of what they did see earlier may be difficult to recall or already unconsciously reinterpreted to fit the main/preferred bits (research on eyewitness testimony is pretty revealing in this respect!).
- *Lesson observation should generally use at least a written note form of record:* the obvious need for some sort of *record* of the events is thus strongly confirmed by the above considerations. Even for the relatively short periods of teaching they observe, a mentor needs at least to make a written note recording the events and outcomes in and of the teaching, which can be the basis for discussion with the student at the reflection stage. A lesson record sheet used in conjunction with a teaching competence analysis may be of assistance here, particularly when a specific set of focuses has been agreed upon for mentor monitoring.
- *The poverty of words and the credibility of their writers:* however, when it comes to the kind of record, note-taking has the advantage of being

economical, but can convey very little in concrete terms to the student-teacher who really needs to witness what actually happened. If a thousand words is a mild estimate of what's required in place of a picture, how much is required for a set of classroom activities lasting half an hour and more (not to mention the subtle but often importantly different shades of meaning people attach to the same words)? Even if the student-teacher understood exactly what the mentor meant, the more important and challenging revelations may take some believing; students have their values, preferences, selective perceptions and memories. They can rightly say to themselves that this was another human being judging and may tell themselves a suitable story to resist the judgement offered ('I don't think he really liked my sort of approach', etc.).

The above sorts of consideration tend to push towards the use of technology such as audio or video recording, which would in many respects provide a much fuller and potentially less biased form of access, particularly for students to their own teaching and its actual effects in the short term. However, the use of such powerful means of recording tends for various reasons to be experienced as very threatening by many people, student-teachers included. Since on the other hand the potential benefits can be very great, it's worth considering strategies for removing the threat from such approaches, as well as from the general experience of being monitored.

Points made previously about the facilitation of student involvement and positive commitment apply here also, perhaps with particular relevance, since here it's the student who feels 'on the line'. The general points need only summarizing here: *Check general deployment of DAM strategies and core conditions of helping.* This refers to personal actions as well as general arrangements, including specifics such as: *Defining monitoring as normal and positive can be greatly influenced by the mentors' own example.*

Through having their own teaching observed and recorded by interns, mentors will lead the way by expecting interns to make use of lesson observation records and profile materials. To this implicit defining of such methods as normal and non-threatening, they'll hopefully add explicit statements which link them with the conceptions of teaching skill and professional learning being discussed in other contexts.

- *Agree a focus in advance:* this should help to keep things specific, analytical and evidence-oriented. It should not, however, be maintained to the extent of excluding any notice of important teaching events outside of the agreed focus.
- *Picking up positive effects and outcomes:* I argued earlier that since teaching is purposeful, we as mentors do need to confront goals and values. We need not only to pick up the negatives, to which we tend to be drawn anyway, but also to see what worked and how. Students need to know what to do, as much if not more than they need to know what to avoid,

since there tend to be less ways of getting it right and many ways of getting it wrong. Apart from this informational learning point, *positive feedback* obviously also encourages.

- *Gradual introduction and extension of useful forms of monitoring:* not only is it possible to have a systematic and gradual increase in the difficulty and extent of intern involvement, the same applies to what one monitors, whether using video recording or not. Furthermore, it may be useful to record small, successful excerpts initially, so as to build up confidence and relaxation concerning being monitored and recorded. See the section on PCT below for more on this.
- *Sensitivity in the introduction and use of video and/or audio recording:* video and audio recordings provide a basis for more powerful self-monitoring, both over longer periods of teaching and for detailed analysis of smaller segments, but the threat with which they're typically perceived urges caution and sensitivity. If one leaves it entirely open to students, then some of those who need it most will be the most likely to decline it. A reasonable approach may be to 'define' the use of these forms of recording as normal on the course, which will be greatly enhanced if teacher-mentors themselves set the example by letting students videotape parts of teacher-taught lessons and by engaging in the sort of open and positive discussions of these recommended earlier. The use of these approaches may also be introduced progressively, as suggested in the previous point.

Assisting analysis and reflection

Much of what's just been said about access to monitoring and feedback is also relevant to the further activity of analysing and reflecting, since both involve the need for some sort of access to the actual events that occurred. The quality and fullness of that record tends to place a limit on useful discussion. This said, the mentor's functions are to:

- *Prompt the student to analyse and reflect on their teaching and its aims.*
- *Provide hypotheses, information, alternatives and especially evidence and rationales:* these are to complement, extend, even correct the student's own reasoning. Once again, the best basic stance appears to be, what seems to have led to what appears to have occurred and what are the forms of evidence for any particular account we consider? The point is that it's the *student's* reflection we're assisting as mentors. This doesn't preclude our offering particular views, 'telling them what we think', but this should be with reasons and our giving them should certainly not be all that goes on. If we tell the student something, this doesn't guarantee they hear it. The mentor's job, like that of any teacher, is to try to ensure that the student 'processes it meaningfully' – so that even if they don't happen to agree, they are encouraged to offer evidence and rationales themselves.
- *Particularly with some students, mentors may need to deal with the 'meta-level' explicitly:* that is, they may need to re-establish that reflection is designed

to help them gain insights. This will be all the more credible if as mentors we've alerted them to positive effects in our monitoring record. We can then apply the next point for the reasons persistently rehearsed here.

- *Analyse and reflect on the positive achievements just as much if not more than the negatives.*
- *Remember the limits of articulation and reflection:* Articulation, analysis and reflection are vitally important, but they're not the whole thing. It's by no means always possible to say it all and *sometimes* the key thing is to do with something that's best demonstrated rather than discussed. Analysis and reflection *can* be overplayed on particular occasions, overloading the student, with negative effects. Given the amount of time they take, however, this is perhaps not a major risk.
- *Promote a proactive approach by assisting the intern to plan for further development:* without saying that every single reflection on any piece of teaching should give rise to an action plan for the intern, nevertheless, it is useful to think of positive ways forward. These build on the discussion and apply the insights gained, or at least they turn attention to the issues and tasks revealed. In keeping with the teaching skill cycle and current approaches to helping, the idea in reflective discussion isn't just to mourn the negatives and celebrate the positives, it's also to follow these by devising strategies to continue the learning effectively. For this reason it will be useful if teaching competence profile records contain prompts for the indicating of action plans.
- *Deal with any defences and denials, particularly when reviewing intern teaching activities:* if a mentor follows the sorts of strategies and informing principles discussed here, this should minimize the likelihood of serious blockages and resistance from students. Nevertheless, one is always going to encounter varying degrees of resistance, denial and other defences amongst student-teachers. These perhaps tend mainly to involve relatively specific items, but then many of the specifics in teaching can play quite powerful roles. As has been seen, novices just do not tend to notice as much relevant information as experts, nor can they digest it so readily. If they don't realize or truly believe this – and even when they do – they can be quite resistant about taking on board those things they don't so far acknowledge. The sorts of strategy listed above are likely to be helpful even in rescuing such a situation (that's what the core counselling conditions were designed for anyway), but a couple of further strategies for relatively persisting denial and defence are worth considering.
- *Test whether and how far it is actually a case of denial or defence; look at the pattern and consult others:* if, for instance, on raising a potentially negative feature of a student's teaching the mentor gets as response a brisk 'Yes, I noticed that' in a voice tone that seems also to convey 'so we needn't dwell on it', then of course there's not much she or he could immediately conclude. It may just be the intern's normal tone (which we ought to be able to tell), or it might indicate their impatience/embarrassment at not

having noticed it themselves, or perhaps their wish to get on with what they see as more urgent aspects, as well as their possibly being slightly defensive. If they 'couldn't remember that', then similar ambiguities abound. If they appeared to be remembering most comparable events (and remember how difficult it can be to pull out the details after a 40 minute period), but said they couldn't remember this one, the mentor perhaps ought to begin to wonder. If they said they were sure it hadn't happened, when the mentor was sure with the aid of their notes that it had, then she or he would really want to start treating this as a form of resistance, but would want to check in any way he or she could.

The point is that solitary events aren't often reliably interpretable on their own. Rather, we need some sort of *pattern* – either of other events surrounding it or of repetition of that type of event, or both. The better one knows the intern and the class involved, the easier it may be, but still perhaps not very straightforward. This applies to all our interpretations, but we need to remember it particularly in the case of negative possibilities like the various types of psychological defence outlined earlier in Chapter 4. Thus it would be appropriate, to the extent that one is dealing with anything of basic or major importance, to *consult other opinions*. These would for instance include other teachers the intern has worked with and in particular those in coordinating roles within the school.

- *Pursue defence and denial using the same interpersonal facilitation strategies and assumptions, possibly indirectly and after some delay:* Where the intern seems to be persistently avoiding or denying some negative feature ('not owning it' as the counselling tradition puts it), then when we decide it needs to be dealt with, the same general strategies and principles are appropriate and useful within this sort of focus. As a function of this point, *oblique* or *delayed attention* to such an issue, rather than immediate confrontation, may help keep things as open and honest as possible. At some point, however, the mentor may need to discuss the issue openly, when she or he will want to maintain the core counselling conditions and define the situation as a helpful search for learning and improvement, using the evidence available. The involvement of relevant colleagues may become desirable in so far as the issue seems basic. Intuitive judgement and gut feeling will tend to be called into play here, and should not be simply dismissed. But deliberate thought and discussion of the nature and importance of what's at stake will also be needed. In this respect, once more, a good hierarchical analysis of teaching aspects may be of considerable use.

Progressively collaborative teaching (PCT)

To recall, by *progressively collaborative teaching* I mean an arrangement where the student engages in teaching with another, usually more experienced/

mentor teacher, initially staying very much within the mentor's framework and undertaking limited aspects with support, but progressively trying out and taking on a wider range of more extensive aspects of the teaching. PCT can involve more than one student working with the same teacher-mentor and there are some clear benefits to purely student–student collaboration, without mentors, which it can include at any point. PCT appears to offer more than just the sum of the advantages of learning from other teachers and from one's own efforts. Amongst its general advantages are that:

- It involves repeated collaboration and assisted learning at all points in the teaching skill cycle: planning, carrying out the teaching, monitoring and reflecting.
- It acknowledges and builds on typical phases of teaching skill acquisition by allowing gradual but flexible *'scaffolding'*; that is, support that can be removed as the learner becomes independently capable.
- It allows the student to learn from their own teaching in a real situation, yet *without the full task demands* which make the early phase of teaching skill acquisition so difficult, stressful and inefficient. Thus it allows the embodiment of one of the suggestions made above under *students learning from their own teaching*.
- At the same time it gives the student a better reason and basis for learning from another teacher, because he or she *shares teaching goals and investment of effort* with that teacher.
- This should help build a *close professional relationship* between mentor and student which should in turn be advantageous to both in many respects.
- It's *economical* in that it allows the mentor to assist students, potentially more than one at a time, during their own teaching time, thus leaving the mentor's 'dedicated time' to activities which cannot be achieved in their own classroom. It also allows a much richer and more flexible set of learning activities for pupils in the classroom through the presence of more than one adult.
- It can help the mentor in their own professional development, through giving time for reflection in their own classroom, during their own teaching and thus with an exceptional opportunity to reflect in and on their action.

Nevertheless

- PCT requires varying kinds of *explicit planning* to be achieved in organized, economical and profitable ways. This takes time, though like most things, the first occasion is the most taxing.
- The *mentoring function* of PCT may need *safeguarding* against the economic advantages of 'extra hands'. The school teaching profession and the DFE may care to learn here from the experience of the nursing profession, where being used merely as 'a pair of hands' under traditional

nurse training arrangements is now credited with all manner of negative effects and has helped generate changes of considerable magnitude.

- In so far as PCT may be a powerful way of 'letting students into existing teaching strategies and styles' they ought probably to engage in PCT with two or more teachers with contrasting styles.
- For the same reason, there do need to be opportunities for students to engage in *independent development* of ideas and teaching. These are likely to occur outside a PCT arrangement, perhaps once the student is into a block practice following PCT in an earlier phase.
- PCT may pose a learning opportunity for teacher-mentors, but by the same token it also offers *challenges* to their openness and flexibility, because of the factors discussed above under *student learning from others teaching*. This can also be the case for some students.

More specific aspects of opportunity and challenge will emerge as we now consider the ways in which the various skill cycle functions may be assisted in PCT.

Progressive joint planning

Since what teachers are charged with teaching is generally now prescribed relatively fully by the national curriculum, it seems obvious that mentoring teachers should let students into their planning and performance of teaching. A number of points are worth making about this aspect.

- With respect to *teacher-mentors conveying their general planning*, the points made earlier under learning from others teaching apply.
- In so far as teachers offer students chances to *design sections of teaching* within the overall programme, then the points made earlier about assisting student planning apply.
- The involvement of both teacher and student contributions within a common teaching programme for pupils should add a number of elements, including:
  - *motivation* by each to see both of their contributions complement each other and succeed;
  - a *common reference framework* for both parties, with continuing development and contribution by both meaning that mentor and student are likely to penetrate more fully into each others' ideas and thinking.

Progressive aspects of joint planning and implementation of PCT
The following represents a suggested sequence based on relatively obvious considerations. It might thus be a basis for the development of specific programmes of experience within subject teaching during school experience, which will be taken up in the following chapter.

1 The earliest phases of PCT will tend to involve mentor and students discussing the relevant portions of the national curriculum and the mentor introducing their *longer term planning* for the current term or half-term. They will then narrow down to their *planning for the lessons immediately ahead*, some of which students would then systematically observe and monitor.

2 In a next phase the student might carry out *restricted aspects of the teaching* designed and resourced by the mentor as part of their teaching, for example work with individual pupils, taking responsibility for one amongst a number of groups in class or laboratory, or the same for a number of pairs doing pairwork, or perhaps provide a short whole-class explanation or introduction. All of these would typically be with the *mentor continuing to be present* as main teacher for other aspects. This and following phases could involve single students or students working in pairs or more.

3 The student(s) and mentor might next select specific strategies or focus on particular demands (e.g. differentiation), already observed and used by the student, and the student(s) would *plan and prepare the teaching and resourcing of certain aspects* (concepts, principles, topics) in the subject using them, then *discuss and revise this planning* as necessary, prior to *carrying out the teaching* themselves within collaborative settings.

4 This type of activity would be *repeated* using different teaching/learning strategies and their combinations.

5 This type of activity would then be extended to *non-collaborative* settings in which the student(s) teaches alone or is simply observed by the mentor (which of course includes discussion of planning and outcome).

6 Students would then begin to plan and prepare for *increasingly larger chunks of collaborative teaching* within the overall year and term framework of topics.

7 At the same time, students should be engaging in an increasing amount of planning and preparation and teaching on their own.

The timing and extent of such a general development would depend on many features, not least length of course. In a one-year PGCE, for example, the above progression might be expected to commence early in the first term and to proceed into the second term without major discontinuity. The nature and rates of sequences may also depend on subject area, for instance as a function of range of essentials such as safety in laboratory and practical work. In practice such arrangements would also require differentiation and adaptation to the needs of individual students and their actual progress.

Teaching as a learning team

PCT requires planning not just for separate items of teaching, but for collaboration and meshing of activities within the classroom. It isn't a matter of scripting things down to who says which words in which sentence (though on occasion, particular details may require such precision). As in all teaching, however well planned, a relaxed flexibility and adaptability to arising circumstance is a basic requirement for smooth and flowing classroom interaction. Nevertheless, perhaps particularly so as to avoid pupil confusion about roles and authority, the following aspects of collaborative classroom teaching are important enough to merit attention during both the classroom period and in planning beforehand.

- *Who is 'in charge', taking the lead in any particular segment/activity?* The possibilities here are likely to alter over time and in some senses the mentor always retains underlying responsibility and control. Nevertheless, at the level of who directs the action as far as the pupils are concerned, it is important in various respects that the intern sooner or later be seen to be leading particular segments (such respects would for instance include class management efficiency, establishing professional status and respect for the student intern). In the case of pairs of interns working in a class, with or without a mentor, the same principle applies.
- *What are both teachers, mentor and intern(s), supposed to be doing at any particular time?* The possibilities here are enormous and depend to a considerable extent on the chosen teaching strategies. They may include anything from 'strength in numbers' doing the *same thing* (e.g. all teacher figures separately check the small groups' progress during a particular phase), through to different people carrying out *different but complementary functions* (e.g. the student-teacher is explaining, the teacher-mentor is circulating, checking, etc). This aspect also leads immediately into the teaching skill function of monitoring, given that PCT is being used as a learning mode. However, within the ongoing action, support also needs to be established for the student.
- *In what ways can the mentor support the intern's teaching?* Being together in the same room allows close access to what's going on and should therefore allow diagnosis and support as needed. This is perhaps the most notable of all the strengths of PCT, though the brevity of time available during the action means that many issues will only be noted for later discussion.

Mutual monitoring

Another major advantage of collaborative teaching is that it enables close observation and monitoring by both student intern and mentor of each other, during the teaching, as well as following it. The need is thus for:

- *Opportunity* for mentor and student-intern(s) each to *observe each other* carrying out teaching functions.

- *Recording* of such observations using notes or perhaps commentaries on audio-cassette whilst they're being carried out, or very soon thereafter. Video recording remains a possibility, but a very remote one, given the numbers in the classroom and the need for closely coordinated teaching.
- Systematic *planning* for both of the above.

Joint analysis and reflection

PCT has the further advantage of allowing and giving particular point to joint, assisted analysis and reflection during the action. One needs therefore to think in terms of:

- opportunities not just for observation/monitoring during the teaching, but also for *thinking and reflection*;
- opportunities for *mini-discussions* at points during the teaching (e.g. during transitions, during unproblematic pupil activities, etc.);
- the usual opportunity for overall reflection and analysis *after* the completion of teaching periods.

During all of this, the interpersonal aspect of course never disappears, however, the combination of close collaborative planning for externally established teaching goals and focus on joint action tend to help keep a functional concern. As such, they constitute a further advantage of PCT, the possibility of which seems to me to be perhaps the greatest advantage of the switch to school-based ITT. Its potential will only be realized, nevertheless, if a reflective stance is maintained, so that by the same token, the practicality orientation of PCT is itself a possible threat to the realization of its learning potential for student-teachers. This is also a reason why it needs combining with their other forms of learning activity.

Exploring basic and background issues

The last form of student-teacher learning activity, introduced at the end of Chapter 3, was the exploration of basic and background issues. I suggested that this could include direct experience and researching of wider aspects of the teaching context, such as tracking pupils and staff colleagues, investigating pastoral and special needs provision, having some experience of staff meetings and governors' view, INSET and so on. It would also include reading and other inputs, plus their organized discussion in seminars and tutorials, concerning basic educational ideas and pedagogy, historical and political aspects, and the legal and financial framework of teaching.

The general principles and concrete tactics for these active forms of investigation will hopefully be familiar to teachers and therefore not in need of treatment here. Suffice it to say that it's not a question of either one tells them or one lets them find out totally on their own. It is much more a matter of:

- *suggesting some specific focuses whilst still allowing openness to notice things for themselves;* for example, when tracking a randomly chosen pupil for a day, what difficulties does he or she encounter? How does he or she react and cope? What situational features seem to bring out his or her positive side? What does he or she seem to be actually gaining by way of learning in each lesson? What else do you notice that seems worthy of discussion?
- *requiring some sort of record of insights and issues experienced;* for example, make notes on the above aspects of pupil-tracking or of background reading, etc.;
- *setting aside time for structured discussion of such issues;* by 'structured' I mean that mentors or others involved in the scheme facilitate a balance between dealing with the specific area on an agenda and exploring personal perspectives and broader implications arising from its consideration. The usual teaching skills of guiding the focus, promoting systematic coverage whilst recognizing individual angles and interests, bringing shy members in, and so forth, will need to be brought into play;
- *linking such investigation and discussion to deeper and lengthier treatments,* for example, in essays and seminar papers for formal assessment within the course, under the heading of explicit knowledge and understanding.

The comments in this chapter have already touched at various points on issues of general provision and organization. Basic aspects of these will be considered next in the final chapter.

Further reading

Sound and detailed suggestions on practical aspects of school-based mentoring are offered in publications by Hagger *et al.* (1993) and Watkins and Whalley (1993), based respectively on the secondary partnership schemes at Oxford University and the London University Institute of Education respectively.

9

Mentoring in practice: student programmes and organizational issues

This book has addressed itself mainly to mentoring strategies and the background ideas and principles informing them, but concern for practical relevance requires some attention to detail. The previous chapter therefore looked more closely at coaching tactics within mentoring. The book would be incomplete, however, if it didn't include at least brief coverage of applications with respect to the sorts of learning programmes which might be organized for student-teachers and some mention of the organizational and whole school issues which are likely to need addressing within any programme. Although it is my view that higher education institution (HEI)–school partnerships provide the best basis for school-based initial teacher training (ITT), nevertheless, virtually the whole of the book so far could apply not only to such situations, but also to *school-centred* arrangements in which schools take the whole responsibility for setting up and organizing ITT courses. Some indication of the basic requirements and themes would probably be of particular value in such cases. The student activity programmes and basic organizational aspects which form the topic of this final chapter are nevertheless framed largely within the persepctive of HEI–school partnerships.

Systematic programmes for student-teacher learning

Given the great variety in ITT course lengths, age-phase specifics, local possibilities, and so on, offering a systematic treatment of possible school-based provision would clearly take another book in itself. I hope that it will therefore suffice to offer some general comments and relatively detailed illustration of one possibility in relation to school-based student learning programmes.

An entitlement programme for student-teachers?

What I've been offering in this book has been generally concerned with possibilities through which students may be assisted by reflective coaching in their learning through the cycle of teaching skill. Earlier in Chapters 2 and 3 I reviewed functions and phases of the skill cycle through which students may be assisted to learn to teach with the help of reflective coaching. I proposed four major types of assisted activity for student-teacher learning and the previous chapter looked at some of the concrete tactics involved in fulfilling the associated mentoring functions.

The issue sooner or later arises of what actual programme of experiences and activities to build into any particular course of school-based initial teacher training. One way of looking at this is to take the systematic line of the competence-based approach now urged on teacher education and ask what sort of provision would appear plausible as a basis for developing the kind of teaching competence student interns are going to be required to demonstrate in order to achieve qualified teacher status (QTS).

Students, this line would say, are entitled to be offered at least that much; courses should include a programme of *student entitlement*. In my view, there are pros and cons to such a view. We should *not*, for instance, see this in a mechanistic sort of way which expects any particular framework of provision necessarily to 'deliver' the learning goals of teacher preparation. On the other hand, there would be something wrong somewhere if courses systematically underprovided useful learning opportunity and assistance. Traditionally, for instance, many educationists have held the view that one year for a Postgraduate Certificate of Education route to QTS is not enough. Whilst the new arrangements perhaps do offer possibilities with considerably improved potential for the acquisition of intelligent teaching skill, nevertheless PGCE courses are still only a year in length and nowadays there is increasing prescription especially concerning the amount of subject discipline study to be provided.

Such issues are of considerable importance and hopefully as experience is gained in the new school-based arrangements, there will be reflection, debate and improvement. One suspects, for instance, that present overall resourcing may be inadequate. If so, hopefully the plea will be for better means to put good programmes into practice, rather than complaints about difficulties under present resources being used as an excuse for a cheaper model which is so much less ambitious that it's actually inferior (as many would say has occurred with aspects of national curriculum assessment).

However, it is not within my present scope to explore these possibilities here nor, given the range of potential course and partnership arrangements, to go in for anything like a review of possible programme types, necessary though this will be at some point. More realistic and in keeping with the general thrust of the book is to start from the circumstances facing us and at least to offer and exemplify the sort of considerations that might enter into programme design. I shall do this only for the case of one-year PGCE courses and then against only one particular example of what seems to be a minimum programme.

Basic considerations and an example

Basic principles which seem necessary in the designing of school-based programmes include the following:

- *All four of the basic types of student learning activity should be involved, but if anything, progressively collaborative teaching (PCT) deserves priority.* I hope the case has already been accepted for all four types of student-teacher learning activity introduced earlier. My basic reason for claiming some priority for PCT is that it not only combines awareness of someone else's teaching with the student's own gradually graded attempts, but it also has the other advantages argued for earlier.
- *Time needs setting aside particularly for discussion of planning and reflection on teaching.* The indications are that although increased time spent in classrooms may have some benefit, this largely depends on suitable guidance and subsequent discussion to fulfil the coaching functions. These need protected teacher-mentor and student time.
- *The student learning activities should be interconnected and sequenced for cross-fertilization and progression.* Generally speaking, observation needs to precede actual teaching attempts and this applies most naturally within PCT, but not forgetting that for the majority of the time and especially in the beginning, observation generally needs to be guided and focused within an awareness of the teaching goals and strategy rationales in question ('what and why'). Whether pedagogy and broader issues are studied within an integrated approach to subject teaching or involve separate course components, there is obvious advantage if such coverage can dovetail with experiences in teaching and student 'research activities' such as pupil tracking. Observation of other teaching should not, however, cease once the student-teacher gets into their own teaching attempts. Rather, own teaching attempts serve to sensitize and alert observation. This is a good reason for getting into teaching attempts relatively early within PCT, but this should indeed be gradual and progressive as a general rule.
- *Student interns should have access to a variety of mentors within each type of activity.* The DFE requires students to have experience of at least two

schools, but as interns have suggested to me, it's if anything more important to ensure that they work with a number of different teachers. On this argument, PCT should preferably be engaged in with at least two different teacher-mentors. The same is surely desirable for seminars and tutorial discussions, at least through having some overlaps in the subjects discussed in different contexts, if not the actual alternation and combination of staff within particular components.

- *Teacher-mentors should be involved in more than one type of student learning activity.* By a similar argument, teacher-mentors should not be restricted to one type of activity, such as having their teaching observed, or discussing planning. Mentors need to have a sense of the whole course as well as the specific parts with which they're most concerned.

- *In HEI–school partnerships openness, cross-institutional resourcing and collaborative working are to be encouraged.* The latter point extends in the case of HEI–school partnerships to urge full sharing of resources and awareness across and within institutions, so that, for example, mentors in school know not only when particular topics are being covered in college-based elements, but what is being offered by way of resource and input content. Even better if teacher-mentors can become involved in course seminars and tutorials, and this will be the more possible if these are held in the school setting. In the ongoing reflection and redesign of such courses, the DFE injunction to achieve a balanced partnership similarly urges two-way communication and joint discussion of all facets.

An example of a minimum student programme

Table 9.1 outlines one possible programme of school-based activities and experiences within a one-year PGCE course, many but by no means all of its features coming from a programme devised for the LUSSP secondary age-range scheme at the University of Leeds. It assumes, for instance, that two days per week are spent in school during the first term and a block teaching period in the major part of the second school/university term in which there is virtually no university-based work. Other programme structures would clearly need adaptation of this model.

It is presented in general terms, but would be situated within particular subject and/or age range specialisms, where more specific details would be decided. Thus, for example, it proposes common forms of varied experience such as that student interns should study other teachers using *at least* three forms of teaching strategy, with precise forms of variation to be decided within subject teaching groups (in this case, *which* teaching strategies to sample).

The general principle that certain sorts of experience are needed before more demanding ones is seen, for example, in the tendency of the first three columns to show more entries as one goes down through time and across towards more independence. So although specific time points are suggested for the commencement of particular types of activity, these have been based on an estimate of how long it would take for the intern to have got into the sorts of experience designated under a given activity type/column. They would thus need changing in particular cases in line with the professional judgements of those involved.

Various details in the programme need comment:

- *Week numbers* in the far left column may be treated as approximate, but assume a *start close to the beginning of the school year*. It appears to me particularly important for student-teachers to gain access to teachers dealing with classes at the beginning of a year. Here they can be guided to observe the deployment of strategies, particularly for class management, which may no longer be used at the later points at which students have traditionally accessed classrooms (and by which time atmospheres and ways of working tend to have been set, so that teacher strategies are even more difficult to discern).
- *Learning from others teaching:* the second column activities may begin to focus on the teacher/mentor who will be working with the intern in PCT as well as on other teachers. This is why the third column (PCT) refers only to the intern teaching activity parts of PCT.
- PAMR stands for *plan–attempt–monitor–reflect,* a memory prompt to reflect the need to consider whatever is observed in the light of all parts of the teaching cycle, in particular learning goals, and for students to be guided in their observation and monitoring.
- *Observation of teaching later in the course*: the rationale for having further PAMR observation extending well into the course is that student interns tend to become much more sensitive to specific issues as a result of their teaching and reflection. Opportunity to observe and participate in further PCT could be very profitable indeed. Note also the suggestion that guided observation of *primary school teaching* may be conducted *after* the major period of student intern teaching, which is based on the same principle and on Calderhead's (1988) finding that preliminary observations conducted before ITT courses appear to achieve little apart from confirmation of stereotypes. Observation in a further secondary school, laid down in the DFE requirements, may take place on a student-partner basis within same subject.
- In going from *learning from others teaching* in column two to *PCT* in column three another general principle has been that a student needs to observe something *at least twice* to learn much from it and that interns ought to be exposed to *at least three major types of teaching strategy* in their subject teaching area. The definition of these strategies is hardly unproblematic and three is only defensible as a minimum if one is thinking of relatively broad and inclusive strategies (e.g. group work practicals versus whole class inputs and discussion). Different subject areas will have typically

Table 9.1 Example of a minimum secondary-school-based student learning programme

Student learning activity	Learning from others teaching (including PCT observation)	Progressively collaborative teaching (active aspect)	Learning from intern's own teaching	Other activities
Week 1–2	PAMR observations of early 'settling in' Year 7–8 (i.e. younger) classes General/class management orientation			Initial meetings with tutors and mentors Discussion of planning then of observation of observed classes
Week 3–4	PAMR observations of early 'settling in' Year 10–12 (i.e. older) classes General/class management orientation			Discussion of planning and observation in relation to observed classes
Week 4–5	PAMR observations of teaching of Year 7–8 (i.e. younger) class lesson General/class management orientation			Commencement of tutorial discussion and course inputs. Introduction to school and departmental resources including initial training
Week 6	PAMR observations of teaching of Year 9–10 (i.e. older) class lesson General/class management	Discussion of part of national curriculum being covered by teacher(s) with whom PCT will be carried out		Tracking a class for a whole day, taking notes on 'pupil' experience: enjoyment, boredom, stress, difficulty, teacher variation

Week 7	PAMR observations of teaching using *Teaching Strategy 1* Teaching/learning process focus		Tracking and interviewing a teacher in own teaching subject over a half day
Week 8	PAMR observations of teaching using *Teaching Strategy 2* Teaching/learning process focus	*Teaching of limited portion of PCT mentor's planned/resourced teaching using Teaching Strategy 1*	Tracking a specific pupil over a half-morning session with notes/interviewing for perspectives, motives, reactions, difficulties
Week 9	PAMR observations of teaching using *Teaching Strategy 3* Teaching/learning process focus	*Teaching of limited portion of PCT mentor's planned/resourced teaching using Teaching Strategy 2*	Tracking and interviewing a pupil with special needs over two lessons – specific input from special needs coordinator
Week 10	Continuing PAMR observation with focus on learning processes and class management aspects	*Teaching of limited portion of PCT mentor's planned/resourced teaching using Teaching Strategy 3*	
Week 11	Continuing PAMR observation with focus on learning processes and class management aspects	*Planning, preparation and teaching of limited topic within PCT mentor's intended coverage using strategies 1/2/3*	

Table 9.1 (Continued)

Student learning activity	Learning from others teaching (including PCT observation)	Progressively collaborative teaching (active aspect)	Learning from intern's own teaching	Other activities
Week 12	Continuing PAMR observation with focus on learning processes and class management aspects	Planning, preparation and teaching of limited topic within PCT mentor's intended coverage using strategies 1/2/3	From week 12 →	Ongoing follow-up tutorial discussion of topics covered in course (educational and method studies)
Week 13	Continuing PAMR observation with focus on learning processes and class management aspects	Planning, preparation and teaching of occasional whole lesson as part of existing teaching sequence		Session/discussion on appraisal and staff development with member of management team
Week 14		Planning, preparation and teaching of occasional whole lesson as part of existing teaching sequence		
Approx. week 15			From week 15 (Block practice) →	

		Increasing amount of full teaching (planning, preparation, performance, monitoring) assisted by mentor	
Block practice →	Further opportunities for PAMR observations with specific purpose/focus		*Interview/discussion with other secondary school staff concerning methods and assumptions*
Week 26 approx. onwards	PAMR observation in another secondary school: learning processes and class management aspects focus		*Tracking primary school class for day, notes on 'pupil' experience and teaching/management strategies*
	PAMR observations in primary school: learning processes and class management aspects focus		
	Further opportunity for PAMR observation with specific purpose/focus		*Interview/discussion with primary school staff concerning methods and assumptions*

rather different though overlapping ranges of preferred classroom strategies. Thus the suggestion here is that students should achieve at least two observations of a type of teaching before trying it themselves in collaborative situations and similarly in the case of whole lesson teaching on their own. There may be gaps to fill or alterations to make in particular cases.
• *Other activity* timing is thought of somewhat more loosely. The far right column mentions some of the types of activity which may take place within the school setting, possibly including the holding of weekly general tutorial discussion of educational studies inputs. Other aspects of a course are not included in the table, but the need to dovetail them with school-based activities is obviously of great importance.

Organizational matters

Basic government requirements of initial teacher training courses are currently set out for England and Wales in DFE circulars 9/92 and 14/93 with guidance from the Council for the Accreditation of Teacher Education (CATE) in two corresponding notes (CATE 1992, 1993), for Northern Ireland in DENI (1993) and for Scotland in SOED (1993). More specific criteria for school-centred schemes are contained in the appendix to the DFE SCITT letter of September 1993 (DFE 1993c).

Basic provision

These documents generally rely on an outcomes model of training, rather than focusing on course content, but they do, particularly in the primary and SCITT documents, deal especially with the development of subject knowledge. There is also reference to curriculum studies, in spite of criticisms that the DFE has listened to right-wing lobby groups and gone for an inadequate, mechanistic view of teaching skill.

All in all, therefore, an ITT course is going to have to offer provision for:

• curriculum and broader educational studies, studying pedagogy and broader issues;
• subject method studies making provision for specialist subject knowledge and teaching;
• opportunities for the development of intelligent teaching skill through reflective practice and coaching.

The last category is largely school-based and thus corresponds very much to what I have attempted to cover in this book, with the first two categories corresponding to major elements in traditional higher education institution provision. However, if the lessons of that era and the issues discussed so far in this book show anything, it is surely the need for integration of the various facets. A number of comments seem relevant.

First, the most urgent yet most difficult aspect to aim for is the integration of understanding and action (in traditional terms 'theory and practice', but remembering that theory refers here to any thinking and awareness). I have been arguing that in principle school-based arrangements offer considerable advantages for this and virtually all of what has preceded in the book may be seen as geared towards the realization of that learning potential. The student learning activity programme considered in the first part of this chapter is, for instance, intended precisely as an illustration of this concern to 'get it together' in this sense.

Second, there is a need to integrate pedagogical insights into the ways student-teachers think about and teach their subjects. The traditional problem has been that although it may have been more economical to provide curriculum and educational studies separately from courses on specific subject teaching, this was almost bound to result in their perception by students as less relevant. The potential of much of what was conveyed or brought in from, say psychology, in the heyday of the educational disciplines (history, philosophy, psychology, sociology) was in any case limited to say the least (cf. Tomlinson 1992). As I hope this book has indicated, however, by the time educationists had begun to 'turn off' from such sources and replace the traditional disciplines with more integrated 'educational studies', psychology and pedagogy had in fact progressed towards considerably more relevant insights which were in danger of being missed. Since one can hardly expect school subject specialists to keep up with such other fields, the danger is that in the new dispensation, we may decline into a dark age in which we simply recycle a dominant conception of 'good practice', without critique or justification. The government's promotion of school-centred schemes and its public disavowals of 'educational theory' perhaps threaten this even more.

My view is that the new school-based partnership schemes nevertheless have the potential to combine a variety of contributions and contributors in powerful ways. The perceived relevance for student-teachers of school involvement is surely assured. Whilst it would be desirable if teachers in general had more time and support for reflection and updating on pedagogical matters, hopefully those engaged as mentors in such schemes will have at least an incentive and some support for this from the demands of their roles: curious students asking for reasons will hopefully make reflection and articulation of craft-based assumptions unavoidable. From the other side, the involvement of schools and a heavy school-based component in ITT should mean that the educationists, pedagogues and psychologists in the higher education institutions will have the incentive to offer new perspectives effectively enough for their relevance to be perceived, which will certainly include translating general pedagogical ideas into the contexts of specific subject and age-range teaching.

Roles and functions in school-based schemes

In the HEI–school partnerships schemes now being developed across Great Britain, the models, roles, and certainly the nomenclature varies considerably. Apart from the student-teachers who are the clients of ITT provision and not forgetting the school pupils who are the clients of the other sort of institution in such partnerships, we need to consider what appear to be the basic roles and functions. There are arguably four basic types of role. The allocation of functions may be carved up in a considerable variety of ways, so that the particular distribution mentioned in what follows should be seen as only one possibility. Amongst other things, it is at least a way of listing the overall sorts of functions which do need catering for in any scheme.

School coordinator

Alternative titles include: *school organizer, school mentor, ITT coordinator*. This would probably be a designated senior member of the school staff with whole-school responsibilities who accepts an agreed coordinating responsibility for the full group of interns within the school. The duties of such a role with a partnership scheme might include:

- organizing the framework of ITT within the partner school;
- communicating information about the scheme to the whole school community – such as headteacher, teachers, parents, governor, ancillary staff;
- monitoring the progress of the scheme within the school;
- induction of subject departments and teachers into ITT arrangements;
- coordinating and supporting the work of teacher tutors;
- induction of interns into the context of the school;
- implementation of 'other activities' including follow-up to curriculum studies sessions in conjunction with the link tutor;
- monitoring and co-assessing the acquisition of teaching competences by interns.

Link tutor

Alternative titles include: *college/university tutor, college/university mentor, general tutor*. This is a member of the HE institution staff who is responsible, in consultation with the appropriate school coordinator, for coordinating the work of a group of interns working within a particular school and for ensuring that the interns receive their entitlement to a coherent course. The duties of this role would probably include:

- maintaining regular links between the partner school and the HE institution, including necessary administrative functions;
- implementation of the follow-up to the curriculum studies component in conjunction with the school coordinator;

- ensuring, through liaison with the school coordinator, that non-subject-specific aspects of the teaching role are covered;
- coordinating the assessment process, counselling, target setting and offering guidance;
- comonitoring the acquisition of competences by interns;
- undertaking an administrative and pastoral role for the group of interns.

Teacher tutor
Alternative titles include: *mentor, teacher-mentor, subject mentor*. The teacher tutor is an established teacher who takes an agreed responsibility over a particular duration (e.g. for a one-year course) for a limited number (probably a maximum of two) of student interns in their subject area of the curriculum. Responsibilities might include:

- contributing to provision of a suitable programme of classroom experiences in the subject area;
- discussion and coaching of student-teacher learning in the teaching of the specialist subject, through observation, own teaching and progressively collaborative teaching;
- coassessing the acquisition of competencies by interns;
- counselling and target setting;
- liaising with other key personnel.

Method tutor
Alternative titles include: *university/college subject tutor, subject tutor*. The method tutor is a member of the HE staff specializing within a defined subject area of the curriculum, providing student interns with access to models of teaching and learning in the subject area beyond their school-specific experiences. Responsibilities might include:

- interns' introduction to pedagogy and practice relevant to the teaching of the subject, including: principles, research and practice in the teaching of the subject, including catering for common learning difficulties, class management, assessment and recording pupils' progress, applications to the 'world of work', safety issues, professional support networks;
- linking with and contextualizing any other course inputs, for example educational studies programmes dealing with issues of learning and class management;
- coassessing the acquisition of competences by interns;
- initiating, coordinating and reviewing the work of teacher tutors in the curriculum area;
- liaising with other key personnel.

It is clear that certain sorts of functions will require some sort of combination or teamwork amongst such personnel, for instance, subject departments

within schools will need to introduce the student-teachers in that area to
their departmental staff, resources and ways of working.

However a range of issues remain. An obvious one with respect to teaching
experience and capability is who should be eligible to act in a mentoring role.
There is a tendency to think in terms of a considerable amount of teaching
experience as a minimum necessity, but on the other hand, teachers who
have qualified relatively recently may be closer to the perspectives, worries
and aspirations of student-teachers. They are perhaps less likely to suffer
from the 'skill paradox' described earlier, of automatization and intuition.
In any reasonably sized school or subject department there is actually no
need to choose between these two poles, of course. One could have relatively experienced as well as more recently qualified teachers taking on
mentoring roles, combining in assistance for particular student-teachers, for
example in PCT.

Another basic issue concerns who is to be regarded as a mentor. At the
level of labels, having for present purposes defined mentoring as any sort
of direct assistance for student-teacher learning of teaching, I would have
to call all of the above role-holders 'mentors'. However, it is also clear that
it's the *teacher tutors* who are perhaps likely to be charged with the bulk of
such assistance and who most of us now naturally tend to think of under
the heading of *mentor*. Most of the references to mentors in the book so far
have in fact been to teacher holders of that role.

However, there arises another issue in this connection, which could have
a considerable variety of possible implications, managerially and organiza-
tionally within schools. This is the issue of who gets designated as an 'official' teacher tutor, to use the role-labels suggested above. It is clear that on
the views expressed here, within any subject area it is preferable if more
than one teacher tutor can be involved.

At one extreme, it might be possible to designate a very limited number
of individual teachers to act as 'official' mentors. However, apart from under
using what are probably other capable talents within a staff, this set-up
would be asking for 'them and us' types of division, especially if allied with
payments and allowances. That would threaten not only the quality of ITT,
but also the broader ethos and effectiveness of the staff and school as a
whole.

The other, surely more preferable option would be to involve as many
teachers in mentoring as possible. Not only does one want to use as many
staff members as possible, but, for instance, areas such as special needs and
pastoral care need systematic treatment for the student interns, so the list
of involved staff members does tend to spread quite wide anyway. This
option might require more by way of their development and training, but
the benefits to the unity, vigour and intelligence with which the whole
school goes about its tasks, both teaching and teacher preparation, stand to
be very great (cf. Shaw 1992). The issue of how this or any other version of

staff involvement is resourced is another thorny matter into which I do not intend to go. Let me say only that when one compares the approach and funding characterizing school-based systems in certain other countries,[1] then whatever the potential of the new UK system (and I hope to have indicated that in principle it's considerable), accusations that it was borne out of government disdain for higher education involvement and desire to save money do not seem that far-fetched.

The need for liaison and communication structures
It will be clear that even within a school, there is going to be a need for good communication between mentors involved with student-teachers. This is important enough to warrant a coordinating role to be set up within any given school, as suggested above, but there will probably also need to be coordination between mentors at subject department level.

If within-school communication is important, then no less is HEI-school communication within partnership arrangements. The more interpenetration of activity and personnel, the less likely that any sort of division or devaluation will occur. In this connection, perhaps the most important aspect in which one stands to lose or gain is in the promotion of intelligently effective teaching through the bringing together of reflection and action. I hope to have indicated here how at the very least, reflectiveness in the form of flexible thinking about how teaching strategies work (or do not) is important for the development of intelligent teaching skill. However, since school-based courses will likely involve the sorts of component suggested above and the range of participants indicated, there is need for attention to a unity of involvement in these respects too. It will help, namely, if school teacher tutors can be involved together with link tutors and HEI method staff as far as possible, for instance in discussion seminars and tutorials so that the HE staff are not seen as the sole 'theoreticians'. In this connection, it has been interesting to find partner schools in the LUSSP scheme welcoming the fact that link tutors make at least weekly visits to schools to conduct tutorials there with the set of interns in the school. Not only does this appear to strengthen the links and enhance the communication, but it also allows joint participation of HEI and school staff in such seminars.

This last point alerts us to another important matter in maintaining constantly good communication, which is that as in any organized activity with a human purpose, one needs to watch the tendency for individuals to form 'coalitions' with or without realizing it. This can be simply a function of particular individuals tending to focus on slightly different matters in different company. But in school-based ITT, unless all channels are kept truly open, it may be particularly likely that particular coalitions emerge, for instance between the student and the teacher tutor against the HE method tutor, or the student and the HE mentor against the school, not to mention the student–method tutor coalition against educational studies specialist, which is not unknown in the HEI tradition. The involvement of a number of personnel from both institutions in a partnership, as well as of different individuals from different parts of each, is likely to counter this. It is also a reason why, although there are very good arguments for having some mentors who are involved with students without having an assessment role in relation to them (especially that it promotes honesty and openness), all who have been involved in any mentoring function with respect to a student should have an input to their formal assessments and not just their learning assistance. If one did have non-assessing mentor roles, then clearly this distinction ought not to correlate with HEI or school affiliation.

The above clearly does not exhaust the possibilities which will need consideration at the level of concrete organization if school-based forms of ITT are to bring the improvement in teacher preparation I believe they are capable of in principle. As I said earlier, this topic would require a further book of its own to do it any justice. The point of the present one, however, is that whilst resources and concrete arrangements are needed to make something work, not everything does, but in human affairs many alternative paths and arrangements may suffice. If they do it will be because they embody a range of factors which have a central influence on the process in question. The first task is therefore to understand what we would like to do and why. In this book my hope has therefore been to make a contribution to such understanding in the case of school-based teacher mentoring.

Further reading

Aspects of student provision and relationships within school-based programmes are also covered by the sources cited as further reading for the previous chapter, namely Hagger *et al.* (1993) and Watkins and Whalley (1993).

Note

1 I am indebted to Professor R. Fischer of the University of Zurich for his description of the enviable arrangements in Switzerland.

Appendix: notes on audio recording, video recording and radio-microphones in mentoring

One of the difficulties in the way of applying skill acquisition insights to learning to teach is the problem of gaining access to the actual process of teaching in order to carry out the various reflective coaching functions. This problem appears to spring from two main sources.

A first reason is the actual nature of teaching itself. For a start, as a human enterprise involving purpose, concentration and communication, it isn't easy to influence or gain information about the actual process of teaching without disrupting and denaturing it. Again, given the sheer complexity of what has gone on at different levels of detail even in a short teaching segment, recall can be difficult and biased by a variety of factors. In any case, as we've seen, much of the action we would like to examine has been carried out intuitively and is thus not directly accessible to conscious recall (Yinger 1986).

A second factor is human motivation. People generally tend to experience discomfort and threat when explicit attention is focused on their attempts to perform actions in which they have values invested; student teachers are no exception. Such motives notably include the self-esteem related types we saw in Chapters 4 and 6 and doubtless relate to the 'implicit perfectionism' aspect of persisting inadequate views of skill. There are of course individual differences in this as in all other things human, but such defensive feelings and reactions not only tend to get in the way of access to the teaching a mentor would like to assist, they may also lead to unfortunate, closed stances fuelled by the student's own inner conflicts between feeling defensive and wanting assistance and support. 'I don't really need this, you get better anyway with experience' would be an unfortunate professional stance to take into one's teaching career, but one suspects it hasn't been unknown in the past.

One of the benefits of audio-visual (AV) technology is that it can help with the first difficulty by giving relatively unobtrusive and rich access to the teaching process. The problem, which is hardly surprising, is that this tends to trade off with the second difficulty. Namely, such improved access is often felt to be even more threatening. This is particularly frustrating for anyone who has seen the benefits of audio-visual resources and heard the comments of student-teachers who have had anything like successful experiences with them. Indeed, given the nature of teaching, it is hard to see how certain central forms of monitoring and feedback can be gained except by such means.

If AV resources are going to be used in mentoring, as I believe they should, then the lesson seems clear; not only do mentors need to master the technical specifics of the equipment (which is increasingly easy with today's products), they also need particularly to:

- make sure they use them in the service of skill learning functions;
- do so with sensitivity to students' motivations and feelings.

Strategies for achieving these desirable aspirations are, as always, debatable. On the one hand, one wants no coercion. On the other hand, given the above discussion of anxiety and negative expectations in this area, it's perhaps more realistic to

- establish the general definition/expectation that such methods are normal, for instance by saying so and suggesting that students use audio-visual means to record portions of mentors' teaching. But one should give opportunity for students to indicate their reactions, so that any extreme cases of anxiety or discomfort can be picked up and plans amended accordingly;
- agree and plan a focus that is appropriate for the particular kind of AV method involved;
- have mentors demonstrate a cool, open-minded reflectivity in the analysis of recordings of their own teaching;
- promote a supportive, positive approach by recognizing the positive and not just reacting to the negative;
- define the use of AV equipment as 'normal' to pupils in the classes concerned (which it will become with practice anyway) by saying, for instance, that you're investigating different ways of teaching, by being willing to discuss these with them at some point but not now, and then carrying on with 'teaching as normal'.

Audio recording

Functions

Audio recording is useful for access to a range of aspects of classroom communication, but in particular for individual inputs, since without specialist equipment, unselective pickup of noise tends to make for a meaningless cacophony. It therefore seems well suited for examining student-teachers'

- clarity, coherence, adequacy, pacing of explanations and directions or requests;
- communicative features such as voice-tone, volume, modulation, which tend to define relationships and affect the motivational reactions of recipients;
- turn-taking in conversations and lengths of pauses in questioning, etc.

Equipment and deployment

The most obvious and unobtrusive form of audio recording apparatus to use is the small *hand-holdable cassette tape recorder*, whether the standard size taking up to c-120 cassettes or the microcassette version which can often be used at the slower of two available speeds to allow recording of more than an hour per side. These small machines are particularly useful in that they can be worn in a pocket, with an extension microphone being attached to clothing such as a buttonhole or lapel so that it picks up the student-teacher's speech and voice-tone.

Reflection and debriefing

I have found the following approach useful in promoting supportive reflection of audio and video recordings, especially in small group contexts where all members of the group expect to have recordings of them discussed. It may obviously need amending for particular purposes.

- *Define the 'rules of procedure' (i.e. announce the following steps).*
- *Play the relevant segment through twice without any comment.* This is both to allow a decent degree of assimilation of the material to occur and to allow thoughts to develop about it. Most segments, even very short ones, can do with many repeated playings, but at this point more than twice can be frustrating and one can come back to the material in pursuing particular aspects later. It may be useful to remind listeners that they should be careful about judging noise levels, since tape-recorders un-selectively pick-up background noise which human hearing would naturally filter out.

The question arises of what length limit to set on such segments. This will depend on what one wishes to get at, but the amount of information available in recordings is such that it is difficult to 'pull out' items by memory with segments of more than a few minutes. In more extended sessions of analysing AV material, a useful tactic may thus be to have those involved make notes on specific aspects within lengthier segments, after these have been played through once to get a general impression of the whole.

- *Invite the person featuring in the recording to point out at least two positive features.* This is in order to establish the positive, supportive function of the whole activity and in particular to counteract the widespread tendency people have to be negatively judgemental about human performances, their own included. It may well be necessary to be strategically insistent here, since students often find it very difficult to come up with *anything* positive. Thus the mentor may have to cut off such moves gently but firmly as they become apparent, saying that we don't want anything negative yet. It may even be necessary for the mentor to provide positive points or to invite other members of the group to do so, remaining vigilant that such inputs do target the positive.

  To make a credible impact such points may need to be backed up with some explanation or rationale. Thus, for example, 'I thought you were coming over as quite confident, which is part of defining the situation. How did you actually feel?' to which the response is often that they hadn't *felt* confident, raising in turn the possibility that they've interpreted things on the basis of their inner feeling, rather than looking and seeing or listening and hearing the actual evidence. Again, 'Your pronunciation and diction I found very clear, and I have to tell you that doesn't always occur, so it's worth pointing out'. Such tactics are of course not only attempting to help the student's ease and confidence, but also to draw attention to functional rather than dysfunctional aspects of classroom teaching behaviour.

- *Invite the student-teacher featuring in the recording to indicate some points needing attention.* Remaining vigilant about preventing the student from playing the social game *'ain't it awful'* (Berne 1964), the mentor invites the recorded student-teacher to indicate any points he or she feels might need attention and why. No other group members yet enter the conversation. The mentor attempts to make sure the student considers not only any negative features from the recording, but also positive strategies for their improvement and thoughts about where to begin with these.

- *Open the conversation to other members of the group.* Here, as usual, the mentor has the task of encouraging full exploration, whilst nevertheless ensuring relevant focus and positive atmosphere using the tactics just suggested.

- *Round off with a balanced summary of points and conclusions.* This might be done by the student whose recording has been the focus of that part of the discussion, but the mentor will wish to try and ensure that participants end up with a balanced set of insights and may need to make their own concluding remarks.

Video recording

Functions

Video-recording can be used to get at much more of what is going on in a classroom, but still has problems of selectivity and access, with a range of obvious trade-offs. Wide-angle focuses show more global and thereby less detailed information in which, for instance, aspects of facial expression may be lost. There is therefore very much a need to decide on the functions and purposes before thinking about the equipment and approach. Video recording can thus cover the student-teacher related functions suggested above under audio recording, but it could also be used to get more of a sense of the overall action.

Equipment and deployment

Currently the range of camcorders using standard and smaller-size tapes is considerable, with numerous useful functions being available; many schools will already have their own versions of these and they are quite sufficient for informal training purposes. Although many modern camcorders are very light, nevertheless when contemplating recording a half-hour or more, it is worth thinking about the use of a tripod, situated in a suitable place in the classroom.

The issue of audio pickup remains somewhat problematic, however, directional microphones still tend to pick up much background noise, so that particular speech inputs may easily be lost. Apart from the use of sophisticated boom microphone systems, an obvious and now widely-adopted remedy (though not for *all* functions) lies in the wearing of radio-microphones by 'target persons'. In mentoring, this will largely mean the student-teacher. A radio-microphone worn on the lapel transmits back to the camcorder or video recorder not just the student-teacher's speech, but the speech of nearby pupils in noisy situations and most others in relatively quiet whole-class teaching.

Reflection and debriefing

The subsection above on this aspect of audio-recording also applies to video-recording. A rich source on the use of video in teacher preparation is Verloop (1989).

Radio-assisted practice

Radio-assisted practice (RAP) involves the use of miniaturized radio equipment to provide direct but unobtrusive guidance for student-teachers during their actual teaching. Smith and Tomlinson presented this idea formally in 1984 and have followed it up with trials in secondary as well as primary settings and recently it has been used with success in coaching parents of difficult-to-control children at the Maudsley Institute of Psychiatry, London.

In RAP the tutor has a small radio transmitter unit and microphone which allows her or him to send messages to the student-teacher, who receives these via a similarly small earpiece and radio receiver unit. Usually in this context, simultaneous two-way equipment is used with pocket units containing transmitters and receivers. Hence the student also wears a small microphone wired to their radio unit which transmits back eventually to the supervisor's earphone. The supervisor can also hear the student-teacher and those around her or him, even when the student is not addressing the whole class. Tutors may thus 'RAP' student teachers during ongoing classroom teaching; that is, the covert radio link allows them to send messages to the student without interrupting the lesson or disrupting the student's flow.

The main functions of RAP inputs are guiding/cueing/suggesting, giving information and evaluating, with the first two of these tending to dominate, since it's designed mainly as a form of direct support. The central idea is to take account of the difficulties of the early phase of skill acquisition (see Chapters 2 and 3) and support the student-teacher in bringing into the action the strategies he or she has discussed previously, but which tend to get lost in the stress and information overload of the classroom. The supportive nature of RAP can also be considerable, as a recent research project at Leeds indicated. How far RAP might be useful or appropriate in assisting the development of all student-teachers is open to question; the use of PCT, for instance, would obviate much of its point by making mentor–student-teacher interaction a natural thing in the training classroom. However, particularly in cases needing 'remediation', it may have a particularly useful role.

On first coming across the RAP idea, many people see it in terms of the crude dualist theory of skill I dealt with in the early chapters and therefore react to it negatively as a simplistic and controlling approach. Although RAP is actually far less disruptive than everyday assumptions tend to assume, in the face of this sort of reaction, it needs emphasizing that RAP is actually based on a more developed view of skilled action and values the development of sensitive autonomy on the part of student-teachers. Its deployment therefore requires intelligent application of a range of principles coming from the work summarized earlier in the present book, including the need to discuss things in advance, the need to respect student-teacher autonomy, to mesh in with their actions, and so on. Rather than give the impression of a quick-fix hand-me-down, therefore, I refer any interested reader to an unpublished guide *How to RAP* (1991), which I will be happy to supply if contacted at the School of Education, University of Leeds, Leeds LS2 9JT.

References

Anderson, J.A. (1990) *Cognitive Psychology and its Implications*. 3rd edn. New York: Freeman.

Ausubel, D.P., Novak, J.D. and Hanesian, H. (1978) *Educational Psychology: A Cognitive View*. 2nd Edn. New York: Holt, Rinehart and Winston.

Argyris, C. and Schön, D.A. (1974) *Theory into Practice: Increasing Professional Effectiveness*. San Francisco: Jossey-Bass.

Ashton, P., Peacock, A. and Henderson, E. (1989) *Teacher Education through Classroom Evaluation: The Principles and Practice of IT-INSET*. London: Routledge.

Ashworth, P.D. and Saxton, J. (1990) On competence, *Journal of Further and Higher Education*, **14** (1), 3–25.

Benner, P. (1984) *From Novice to Expert: Excellence and Power in Clinical Nursing Practice*. Menlo Park, CA: Addison-Wesley.

Bereiter, C. and Scardamalia, M. (1993) *Surpassing Ourselves: An Inquiry into the Nature and Implications of Expertise*. Chicago and La Salle, IL: Open Court.

Berliner, D.C. (1986) In pursuit of the expert pedagogue. *Educational Researcher*, **15**, 5–13.

Berne, E. (1964) *Games People Play*. London: Penguin Books.

Bridges, D. and Kerry, T. (Eds) (1993) *Developing Teachers Professionally: Reflections for Initial and In-service Trainers*. London: Routledge.

Brown, A.L., Bransford, J.D., Ferrara, R.A. and Campione, J.C. (1983) Learning, remembering and understanding, in J.H. Flavell and E.M. Markman (Eds) *Handbook of Child Psychology*, vol. 3, *Cognitive Development*. New York: Wiley.

Brown, S. and McIntyre, D. (1993) *Making Sense of Teaching*. Buckingham: Open University Press.

Burke, J.W. (Ed.) (1989) *Competency-based Education and Training*. London: Falmer Press.

Burn, K. (1992) Collaborative teaching. In M. Wilkin (Ed.) *Mentoring in Schools.* London: Kogan Page, pp. 133–44.

Calderhead, J. (1981) Stimulated recall: A method for research on teaching, *British Journal of Educational Psychology,* **51,** 211–17.

Calderhead, J. (Ed.) (1987) *Exploring Teacher Thinking.* London: Cassell.

Calderhead, J. (1988) The contribution of field experiences to student primary teachers' professional learning, *Research in Education,* **40,** 33–49.

Calderhead, J. (1989) Reflective teaching and teacher education, *Teaching and Teacher Education,* **5,** 43–51.

Calderhead, J. (1990) Conceptualising and evaluating teachers' professional learning, *European Journal of Teacher Education,* **13,** 153–60.

Calderhead, J. and Gates, P. (Eds) (1993) *Conceptualizing Reflection in Teacher Development.* London: Falmer Press.

Calderhead, J. and Robson, M. (1991) Images of teaching: Students' early conceptions of classroom practice, *Teaching and Teacher Education,* **7** (1), 1–8.

Carr, D. (1993) Questions of competence, *British Journal of Educational Studies,* **41** (3), 253–71.

CATE (1992) *The Accreditation of Initial Teacher Training under Circulars 9/92 (Department for Education) and 35/92 (Welsh Office).* London: Council for the Accreditation of Teacher Education.

CATE (1993) *The Initial Training of Primary School Teachers: Circular 14/93 (England).* London: Council for the Accreditation of Teacher Education.

Chi, M., Glaser, R. and Farr, M. (1988) *The Nature of Expertise.* Hillsdale, NJ: Lawrence Erlbaum Associates.

Clark, C. and Peterson, P. (1986) Teachers' thought processes. In M.C. Wittrock (Ed.) *Handbook of Research on Teaching.* 3rd edn. New York: Macmillan Publishing Company, pp. 255–96.

Claxton, G. (1989) *Being a Teacher: A Positive Approach to Change and Stress.* London: Cassell.

Claxton, G. (1990) *Teaching to Learn: A Direction for Education.* London: Cassell.

Colley, A.M. and Beech, J.R. (Eds) (1989) *Acquisition and Performance of Cognitive Skills.* Chichester: Wiley.

DENI (1993) *Review of Initial Teacher Training in Northern Ireland: Report of Working Group on Competences.* Bangor, County Down: Department of Education for Northern Ireland.

DFE (1992) *Initial Teacher Training (Secondary Phase).* Circular number 9/92. London: Department for Education.

DFE (1993a) *The Initial Training of Primary School Teachers: New Criteria for Courses.* Circular number 14/93. London: Department for Education.

DFE (1993b) *The Goverment's Propsoals for the Reform of Initial Teacher Training.* London: Department for Education.

DFE (1993c) Second round of the School-Centred Initial Teacher Training scheme (SCITT). Letter of 29 September. London: Department for Education.

Doyle, W. (1986) Content representation in teachers' definitions of academic work, *Journal of Curriculum Studies,* **18,** 4, 365–79.

Dreyfus, H.L. and Dreyfus, S.E. (1986) *Mind over Machine: The Power of Human Intuition and Expertise in the Era of the Computer.* New York: Macmillan.

Edwards, A. and Galloway, D. (1991) *Primary Teaching and Educational Psychology.* London: Longman.

Edwards, D. and Mercer, N. (1987) *Common Knowledge: The Development of Understanding in the Classroom.* London: Routledge.

Egan, G. (1990) *The Skilled Helper: A Systematic Approach to Effective Helping.* 4th edn. Pacific Grove, CA: Brooks/Cole.

Elbaz, F. (1983) *Teacher Thinking: A Study of Practical Knowledge.* London: Croom Helm.

Elliott, B. and Calderhead, J. (1993) Mentoring for teacher development: Possibilities and caveats. In D. McIntyre, H. Hagger and M. Wilkin (Eds) *Mentoring: Perspectives on School-based Teacher Education.* London: Kogan Page, pp. 166–90.

Elliott, J. (1991) *Action Research for Educational Change.* Milton Keynes: Open University Press.

Elliott, J. (1993) *Reconstructing Teacher Education: Teacher Development.* London: Falmer Press.

Eraut, M. (1992) Developing the knowledge base: A process perspective on professional education. In R. Barnett (Ed.) *Learning to Effect.* London: SRHE/Open University Press, pp. 98–118.

Fenstermacher, G.D. (1986) Philosophy of research on teaching: Three aspects. In M.C. Wittrock (Ed.) *Handbook of Research on Teaching.* 3rd edn. New York: Macmillan, pp. 37–49.

Fontana, D. (1985) *Classroom Control.* London: Methuen.

Forguson, L. (1989) *Common Sense.* London: Routledge.

Gagné, R.M. (1985) *The Conditions of Learning and the Theory of Instruction.* New York: CBS College Publishing.

Gellatly, A. (Ed.) (1986) *The Skilful Mind: An Introduction to Cognitive Psychology.* Milton Keynes: Open University Press.

Gilroy, P. (1993) Reflections on Schön: An epistemological critique and a practical alternative. In P. Gilroy and M. Smith (Eds) *International Analyses of Teacher Education.* JET Papers One. Oxford: Carfax Publishing Company, pp. 125–42.

Griffiths, M. (1987) The teaching of skills and the skills of teaching: A reply to Robin Barrow, *Journal of Philosophy of Education,* **21**, 203–214.

Hagger, H., Burn, K. and McIntyre, D. (1993) *The School Mentor Handbook: Essential Skills and Strategies for Working with Student Teachers.* London: Kogan Page.

Handal, G. and Lauvås, P. (1987) *Promoting Reflective Teaching: Supervision in Action.* Milton Keynes: Open University Press.

Hargreaves, D. (1980) Common-sense Models of Action. In A.J. Chapman and D.M. Jones (Eds) *Models of Man.* Leicester: British Psychological Society, pp. 215–25.

Hartley, D. (1993) Confusion in teacher education: A postmodern condition? in P. Gilroy and M. Smith (Eds) *International Analyses of Teacher Education.* JET Papers One. Oxford: Carfax Publishing Company, pp. 83–93.

Hirst, P.H. (1971) What is teaching? *Journal of Curriculum Studies,* **3**, 1.

Hirst, P.H. (1974) *Knowledge and the Curriculum: A Collection of Philosophical Papers.* London: Routledge & Kegan Paul.

Holding, D.H. (Ed.) (1989) *Human Skills.* 2nd edn. Chichester: Wiley.

Hollingsworth, S. (1989) Prior beliefs and cognitive change in learning to teach, *American Educational Research Journal,* **26**, 260–89.

Houston, W.R., Haberman, M. and Sikula, J. (Eds) (1990) *Handbook of Research on Teacher Education.* New York: Macmillan Publishing Company.

Howard, R.W. (1987) *Concepts and Schemata: An Introduction.* London: Cassell.

Hunt, D.E. (1987) *Beginning with Ourselves.* Toronto: OISE Press.

Hyland, T. (1993) Professional development and competence-based education, *Educational Studies*, **19**, 1, 123–32.

Jessup, G. (1991) *Outcomes: NVQs and the Emerging Model of Education and Training.* London: Falmer Press.

Joyce, B. and Showers, B. (1988) *Student Achievement through Staff Development.* New York & London: Longman.

Kagan, D.M. (1992) Professional growth among preservice and beginning teachers. *Review of Educational Research*, **62**, 2, 129–69.

Kelchtermans, G. (1993) Teachers and their career story: A biographical perspective on professional development. In C. Day, J. Calderhead and P. Denicolo (Eds) *Research on Teacher Thinking: Understanding Professional Development.* London: Falmer Press, pp. 198–220.

Klausmaier, H.J., Ghatala, E.S. and Frayer, D.A. (1974) *Concept Learning and Development: A Cognitive View.* New York: Academic Press.

Kelly, G.A. (1955) *The Psychology of Personal Constructs.* 2 Vols. New York: Norton.

Knowles, M.S. (1980) *The Modern Practice of Adult Education: From Pedagogy to Andragogy.* 2nd edn. New York: Cambridge University Press.

Kolb, D.A. (1984) *Experiential Learning: Experience as the Source of Learning and Development.* Englewood Cliffs, NJ: Prentice-Hall.

Kounin, J. (1970) *Discipline and Group Management in Classrooms.* New York: Holt, Rinehart & Winston.

Laslett, R. and Smith, C. (1993) *Effective Classroom Management.* 2nd edn. London: Hodder.

Lortie, D. (1975) *Schoolteacher.* Chicago: University of Chicago Press.

McIntyre, D., Hagger, H. and Wilkin, M. (Eds) (1993) *Mentoring: Perspectives on School-Based Teacher Education.* London: Kogan Page.

McManus, M. (1989) *Troublesome Behaviour in the Classroom.* London: Routledge.

Marton, F. and Salijo, R. (1984) Approaches to Learning, in F. Marton, D.J. Hounsell and N.J. Entwistle (Eds) *The Experience of Learning.* Edinburgh: Scottish Academic Press.

Maynard, T. and Furlong, J. (1993) Learning to teach and models of mentoring. In D. McIntyre, H. Hagger and M. Wilkin (Eds) *Mentoring: Perspectives on School-based Teacher Education.* London: Kogan Page, pp. 69–85.

Meadows, S. (1993) *The Child as Thinker: The Development and Acquisition of Cognition in Childhood.* London: Routledge.

Medcof, J. and Roth, J. (1979) *Approaches to Psychology.* Milton Keynes: Open University Press.

Modgil, S. and Modgil, C. (Eds) (1987) *B.F. Skinner: Consensus and Controversy.* London: Falmer Press.

Montgomery, D. (1989) *Managing Behaviour Problems.* London: Hodder & Stoughton.

Nelson-Jones, R. (1982) *The Theory and Practice of Counselling Psychology.* London: Holt, Rinehart & Winston.

Nelson-Jones, R. (1988) *Practical Counselling and Helping Skills: Helping Clients to Help Themselves.* 2nd edn. London: Cassell.

Norman, D.A. (1978) Notes towards a complex theory of learning. In A.M. Lesgold *et al.* (Eds) *Cognitive Psychology and Instruction.* New York: Plenum.

230   *Understanding mentoring*

Norris, N. (1991) The trouble with competence, *Cambridge Journal of Education*, **21**, pp. 331–41.

Olson, J. (1992) *Understanding Teaching: Beyond Expertise*. Buckingham: Open University Press.

Patrick, J. (1991) Types of analysis for training. In Morrison, J.E. (Ed.) *Training for Performance: Principles of Applied Human Learning*. Chichester: Wiley, pp. 127–66.

Pollard, A. and Tann, S. (1987) *Reflective Teaching in the Primary School: A Handbook for the Classroom*. London: Cassell.

Poulton, E.C. (1957) On prediction in skilled movements. *Psychological Bulletin*, **54**, pp. 457–78.

Reason, J. (1990) *Human Error*. Cambridge: Cambridge University Press.

Robertson, J. (1989) *Effective Classroom Control*. 2nd edn. London: Hodder & Stoughton.

Russell, T. and Munby, H. (Eds) (1992) *Teachers and Teaching: From Classroom to Reflection*. London: Falmer Press.

Ryle, G. (1949) *The Concept of Mind*. London: Hutchinson.

Saunders, S., Pettinger, K. and Tomlinson, P.D. (1995) Prospective mentors' views of school-based initial teacher education, *British Educational Research Journal*, **21**, 2.

Schmidt, R.A. (1991) *Motor Learning and Performance: From Principles to Practice*. Champaign, IL: Human Kinetics Books.

Schön, D.A. (1983) *The Reflective Practitioner: How Professionals Think in Action*. New York: Basic Books.

Schön, D.A. (1987) *Educating the Reflective Practitioner: Toward a New Design for Teaching and Learning in the Professions*. San Francisco: Jossey-Bass.

Shaw, R. (1992) *Teacher Training in Secondary Schools*. London: Kogan Page.

Shipman, M.D. (1985) *The Management of Learning in the Classroom*. London: Hodder & Stoughton.

Shulman, L.S. (1986) Those who understand: knowledge growth in education, *Educational Researcher*, **15**, 4–14.

Simon, B. (1988) Why no pedagogy in England? In R. Dale, R. Ferguson and A. Robinson (Eds) *Frameworks for Teaching: Readings for the Intending Secondary Teacher* London: Hodder & Stoughton/The Open University.

Smith, R.N. and Tomlinson, P.D. (1984) RAP: Radio-assisted Practice; Preliminary investigations of a new technique in teacher education, *Journal of Education for Teaching*, **10**, 119–34.

Smithers, A. (1993) *All Our Futures*. London: Channel Four Publications.

SOED (1993) *The Secretary of State's Guidelines for Initial Teacher Training Courses*. Edinburgh: Scottish Office Education Department.

Stones, E. (1984) *Supervision in Teacher Education: A Counselling and Pedagogical Approach*. London: Methuen.

Stones, E. (1992) *Quality Teaching: A Sample of Cases*. London: Routledge.

Tattum, D.P. (Ed.) (1986) *Management of Disruptive Behaviour in Schools*. Chichester: Wiley.

Tharp, R.G. and Gallimore, R. (1988) *Rousing Minds to Life: Teaching, Learning, and Schooling in Social Context*. Cambridge: Cambridge University Press.

Tomlinson, P.D. (1989a) The teaching of skills: Modern cognitive perspectives. In D. Sugden (Ed.) *Cognitive Approaches in Special Education*. London: Falmer Press, pp. 28–51.

Tomlinson, P.D. (1989b) Having it both ways: Hierarchical focusing as research interview method, *British Educational Research Journal*, **15**, 155–76.

Tomlinson, P.D. (1991) *How to RAP: Introductory Guide-lines for Radio-assisted Practice.* (revised) Leeds: University of Leeds School of Education.

Tomlinson, P.D. (1992) Psychology and education: What went wrong – or did it? *The Psychologist: Bulletin of the British Psychological Society*, **5**, pp. 105–109.

Tomlinson, P.D. (1994) Can competence profiling work for effective teacher education? University of Leeds School of Education: Unpublished paper.

Tomlinson, P. and Hodgson, J. (1992) Teaching methods and good practice: Grounds for debate, *Education 3–13*, **20** (3), 19–25.

Tomlinson, P.D. and Kilner, S. (1990) *Flexible Learning, Flexible Teaching: The Flexible Learning Framework and Current Educational Theory.* Sheffield: Training Agency, pp. 42.

Tomlinson, P.D. and Swift, D.J. (1992) Teacher-educator thinking in the context of radio-assisted practice: More patchwork pedagogy? *Teaching and Teacher Education*, **8** (2), 159–70.

Tuxworth, E. (1989) Competence based education and training: Background and origins. In J. Burke (Ed.) *Competency Based Education and Training*. London: Falmer Press.

Verloop, N. (1989) *Interactive cognitions of student–teachers: An intervention study.* Arnhem: National Institute for Educational Measurement.

Warham, S. (1993) Reflections on hegemony: Towards a model of teacher competence, *Educational Studies*, **19**, 2, 205–17.

Watkins, C. and Whalley, C. (1993) *Mentoring: Resources for School-Based Development.* London: Longman.

Wheldall, K. and Merrett, F. (1984) *Positive Teaching: The Behavioural Approach.* London: Allen & Unwin.

Wilkin, M. (Ed.) (1992) *Mentoring in Schools.* London: Kogan Page.

Wilkin, M. (1993) Initial training as a case of postmodern development: Some implications for mentoring. In D. McIntyre, H. Hagger and M. Wilkin (Eds) *Mentoring: Perspectives on School-based Teacher Education.* London: Kogan Page, pp. 37–53.

Wittrock, M.C. (Ed.) (1986) *Handbook of Research on Teaching.* 3rd edn. New York: Macmillan.

Wolf, A. (1995) *Competence-based Assessment.* Buckingham: Open University Press.

Wragg, E. (Ed.) (1984) *Classroom Teaching Skills: The Findings of the Teacher Education Project.* London: Croom Helm.

Wubbels, T. (1992) Taking account of student teachers' preconceptions, *Teaching and Teacher Education*, **8**, 47–58.

Yinger, R. (1986) Examining thought in action: A theoretical and methodological critique of research on interactive teaching, *Teaching and Teacher Education*, **2** (3), 263–82.

Name index

Subject index/glossary

nature of skill, **14**, 15–16, 92, 96,
open skills, 14, **15**, 16, 24, 28, 121,
  149, 184
paradoxes of skill, 16, 91, 216
phases in acquisition, 19, 24, 44, 52,
  95–9
skill cycle, 17–18, **22–4**, 39–40, 47,
  64, 75, 95, 97
  see also PAMR
specificity, 16, 71, 92
strategies multifunctional, 29, 90
teachability, 16
traditional view, 12, 16
  see also dualism
stress
  and mentors, 70–4
  and stressors, 67–74
  and student-teachers, 67–70, 73–4
student entitlement, 204–5
subject pedagogical knowledge, 105
student-teachers' learning
  from others teaching, 46–9, 175–84
  motivation and feelings, 51, 53, 57,
    65–70
  through exploring ideas and issues,
    46, 53–6, 201–2
  through own attempts, 46, 49–50,
    185–96
  through PCT, 46, 51–3, 196–201

task analysis, 97
  see also functional analysis
teacher preparation
  mechanistic view, 204
  traditional models, 2, 11–13, 27, 35,
    37, 43, 46–7, 50, 52, 68, 189

teachers
  professional development, 41, 52,
    54
  thinking, 31–3, 37, 56
teaching
  basic concept, 9–11
  functional analysis, 89–90, 91
    see also DAL, DAM
  guided observation, 48, 51, 179–80
  interactive nature, 9–11, 88
  mechanistic view, 11, 120, 179, 212
  as skill, **14**, 91–2
  strategies, 90, 93–4, 101–11, 119–22,
    133–8, 140–1, 158, 207
  multifunctional, 29
  supporting ongoing teaching,
    189–92
  typical characteristics, 28–30
theory
  and practice, 5, 37, 93, 104, 213
    see also dualism
  theory-in-action, 18, 35
    see also knowing-in-action
tips, 42, 175
training, 11, **12**, 14, 24, 41
trial and error, 23

unconditional positive regard, **60**
  see also counselling core conditions

values
  and skill, 15, 19, 24, 28, 65
  and teaching competence, 154
    see also motives
video recording, 47, 179, 180, 192–3,
  194

MANAGING CHANGE IN SCHOOLS

Patrick Whitaker

Schools are currently undergoing a period of upheaval and change as they adapt to new requirements and altered circumstances. This phase of rapid and accelerating change is a characteristic of organizational life as we move towards the twenty-first century and it presents novel and unprecedented challenges to those charged with the management of schools.

The book sets out to explore the world of change in which education is now set. It explores the changed and changing environment to which teachers are having constantly to respond and adapt, and examines the personal, professional and organizational implications involved. The book proposes that a major shift in our management thinking is necessary if the emerging challenges to education are to be met successfully. The book will offer frameworks for considering the management of change, outline the professional learning necessary and provide practical strategies for management development.

Contents

176pp   0 335 09381 7 (paperback)   0 335 09382 5 (hardback)

PROFESSIONAL DEVELOPMENT IN SCHOOL

Joan Dean

Increasingly, each of our schools is directly responsible for the professional development of its staff; and this book is intended to help schools (primary, secondary and
special) to plan and implement their professional development programme. Joan
Dean provides detailed practical guidelines for promoting professional development within a positive school culture, focusing particularly upon planning for processes of needs identification, school review, design of in-service events, teacher
records, school evaluation, teacher appraisal, and the role of management in professional development. She provides opportunities for all who are serious about professional development to reflect upon its purposes, processes and outcomes and to
plan sensitively, practically and intelligently for the continuing committed and skilled
support of teachers and teaching.

Contents

*Series editor's introduction – Preface – What is professional development? – Teachers learn-
ing – The school and professional development – The individual teacher and professional
development – The professional development programme – Professional development activities – The role of management in professional development – Teacher appraisal – Appraisal:
observing teachers at work – Appraisal: the interview – Teachers records – In-service pro-
viders – Evaluation – Appendix 1: Self-evaluation forms – Appendix 2: Classroom checklists
– Appendix 3: Appraisal record form – References – Further reading – Index.*

232pp   0 335 09590 9 (paperback)   0 335 09591 7 (hardback)

TOTAL QUALITY MANAGEMENT AND THE SCHOOL

Stephen Murgatroyd and Colin Morgan

The management team within the school are currently faced with a great deal of pressure to achieve a range of 'performance' expectations in a climate of increasing uncertainty, financial stringency and competition. Total Quality Management is a framework and set of practical resources for managing organizations in the 1990s. Based on sound principles and a strong body of experience, Total Quality Management provides a school based management team with the tools they need to become highly effective in meeting the goals of their stakeholders, and in creating a place that teachers want to work in.

This book is the first to fully examine the practice of Total Quality Management in the context of schooling. It looks, for instance, at the nature of a school's strategic management in the context of growing competition and expectations for performance; and at the positioning of the school in terms of vision and mission. It considers the setting of 'outrageous' or exceptional goals to create momentum and alignment and explores the nature of high performing teams within the school. It discusses commitment-building as part of the new quality culture and involving stakeholders in the daily management of the school.

It is practical and well-illustrated with case vignettes and examples of Total Quality Management in action. It is based on the experience of two senior academic practitioners who have both carried out extensive work in school management and development.

Contents
Making sense of schooling in the 1990s – Choosing a generic strategy – Definitions of quality and their implications for TQM in schools – A model for TQM in the school – Vision, ownership and commitment – Customers and processes as the basis for schooling – Outrageous goals and the task of continuous improvement – Teams, team performance and TQM – Daily management tools for effective TQM – Implementing TQM in the school – Postscript – References – Index.

240pp   0 335 15722 X (paperback)   0 335 15723 8 (hardback)